ACHILLE MBEMBE

Achille Mbembe is a key thinker in contemporary African philosophy who has been influential in literary and cultural theory, African literature, and postcolonial studies. Oliver Coates introduces key concepts within Mbembe's thought in relation to African history, literature, and philosophy.

This accessible guide:

- Considers examples from African literature in Arabic, English, French, and Yoruba, and shows the relevance of Mbembe's thought beyond Anglophone writing;
- Explores how Mbembe's work relates to contemporary global events and charts Mbembe's intellectual development between Cameroon, France, and the USA;
- Discusses core concepts from across Mbembe's career, including the positioning of Africa within Western and Afrodiasporic thought, the colony, postcolony, necropolitics, decolonization, Afropolitanism, technology, and the environment;
- Reveals Mbembe's engagement with key global events, including the #RhodesMustFall and #BlackLivesMatter movements, and the call for the restitution of African objects in Western museums.

Offering a clear and accessible route into what can be a complex area, this book shows the significance of Mbembe's thought across literature, history, postcolonial studies, gender studies, and critical theory.

Oliver Coates is Director of Studies in History and Politics at St. Edmund's College, University of Cambridge, UK, and Associate Researcher of the Institut des mondes africaines, CNRS, Paris. His recent research has been published in the *International Journal of African Historical Studies*, the *Journal of Asian and African Studies*, and the *Oxford Research Encyclopedia of African History*.

ROUTLEDGE CRITICAL THINKERS

Series Editor: Robert Eaglestone, Royal Holloway, University of London, UK

Routledge Critical Thinkers is a series of accessible introductions to key figures in contemporary critical thought.

With a unique focus on historical and intellectual contexts, the volumes in this series examine important theorists':

- significance
- motivation
- key ideas and their sources
- impact on other thinkers

Concluding with extensively annotated guides to further reading, *Routledge Critical Thinkers* are the student's passport to today's most exciting critical thought.

Also available in the series:

Martin Heidegger
Timothy Clarke
Giorgio Agamben
Alex Murray
Frantz Fanon
Pramod K. Nayar
Paul Gilroy
Paul Williams
Mikhail Bakhtin
Alastair Renfrew
Hans-Georg Gadamer
Karl Simms
Karl Marx
Andrew Rowcroft
Kwame Anthony Appiah
Christopher J. Lee
Achille Mbembe
Oliver Coates

For more information about this series, please visit: www.routledge.com/Routledge-Critical-Thinkers/book-series/SE0370

ACHILLE MBEMBE

Oliver Coates

LONDON AND NEW YORK

First published 2025
by Routledge
4 Park Square, Milton Park, Abingdon, Oxon OX14 4RN

and by Routledge
605 Third Avenue, New York, NY 10158

Routledge is an imprint of the Taylor & Francis Group, an informa business

© 2025 Oliver Coates

The right of Oliver Coates to be identified as author of this work has been asserted in accordance with sections 77 and 78 of the Copyright, Designs and Patents Act 1988.

All rights reserved. No part of this book may be reprinted or reproduced or utilised in any form or by any electronic, mechanical, or other means, now known or hereafter invented, including photocopying and recording, or in any information storage or retrieval system, without permission in writing from the publishers.

Trademark notice: Product or corporate names may be trademarks or registered trademarks, and are used only for identification and explanation without intent to infringe.

British Library Cataloguing-in-Publication Data
A catalogue record for this book is available from the British Library

Library of Congress Cataloging-in-Publication Data
Names: Coates, Oliver, 1984– author.
Title: Achille Mbembe / Oliver Coates.
Description: Abingdon, Oxon; New York, NY: Routledge, 2025. |
Series: Routledge critical thinkers |
Includes bibliographical references and index. |
Identifiers: LCCN 2024034144 (print) | LCCN 2024034145 (ebook) |
ISBN 9780367192693 (hardback) | ISBN 9780367193003 (paperback) |
ISBN 9780429201646 (ebook)
Subjects: LCSH: Mbembe, Achille, 1957– | Philosophers—Africa—Biography. |
Historians—Africa—Biography. | Philosophy, African. | Postcolonialism.
Classification: LCC B5419.M34 C53 2025 (print) | LCC B5419.M34 (ebook) |
DDC 199/.6711 [B]—dc23/eng/20240924
LC record available at https://lccn.loc.gov/2024034144
LC ebook record available at https://lccn.loc.gov/2024034145

ISBN: 978-0-367-19269-3 (hbk)
ISBN: 978-0-367-19300-3 (pbk)
ISBN: 978-0-429-20164-6 (ebk)

DOI: 10.4324/9780429201646

Typeset in Sabon
by codeMantra

To my parents Richard and Jennifer, for their support and encouragement.

CONTENTS

Series editor's preface	xi
Acknowledgements	xv
Why Mbembe?	1
KEY IDEAS	**11**
1 Race, Africa, and questions of knowledge	13
2 The colony	33
3 The postcolony	43
4 The nocturnal sphere and necropolitics	59
5 Out of the dark night: Decolonization and the new human	75
6 Afropolitanism	93
7 Technology	115
8 The planetary and the common	133
After Mbembe	143
Further reading	151
Works cited	162
Index	201

SERIES EDITOR'S PREFACE

The books in this series offer introductions to major critical thinkers who have influenced literary studies and the humanities. The *Routledge Critical Thinkers* series provides the books you can turn to first when a new name or concept appears in your studies.

Each book will equip you to approach a key thinker's original texts by explaining their key ideas, putting them into context, and, perhaps most importantly, showing you why this thinker is considered to be significant. The emphasis is on concise, clearly written guides that do not presuppose specialist knowledge. Although the focus is on particular figures, the series stresses that no critical thinker ever existed in a vacuum, but instead emerged from a broader intellectual, cultural, and social history. Finally, these books will act as a bridge between you and the thinkers' original texts: not replacing them but rather complementing what they wrote. In some cases, volumes consider small clusters of thinkers working in the same area, developing similar ideas, or influencing each other.

These books are necessary for a number of reasons. In his 1997 autobiography, *Not Entitled*, the literary critic Frank Kermode wrote of a time in the 1960s:

> On beautiful summer lawns, young people lay together all night, recovering from their daytime exertions and listening to a troupe of Balinese musicians. Under their blankets or their sleeping bags, they would chat drowsily about the gurus of the time... What they repeated was largely hearsay; hence my lunchtime suggestion, quite impromptu, for a series of short, very cheap books offering authoritative but intelligible introductions to such figures.

There is still a need for 'authoritative and intelligible introductions.' But this series reflects a different world from the 1960s. New thinkers have emerged, and the reputations of others have risen and fallen as new research has developed. New methodologies and challenging ideas have spread through the arts and humanities. The study of literature is no longer – if it ever was – simply the study and evaluation of poems, novels, and plays. It is also the study of ideas, issues, and difficulties that arise in any literary text and in its interpretation. Other arts and humanities subjects have changed in analogous ways.

With these changes, new problems have emerged. The ideas and issues behind these radical changes in the humanities are often presented without reference to wider contexts, or as theories which you can simply 'add on' to the texts you read. Certainly, there's nothing wrong with picking out selected ideas or using what comes to hand – indeed, some thinkers have argued that this is, in fact, all we can do. However, it is sometimes forgotten that each new idea comes from the pattern and development of somebody's thought, and it is important to study the range and context of their ideas. Against theories 'floating in space,' the *Routledge Critical Thinkers* series places key thinkers and their ideas firmly back in their context.

More than this, these books reflect the need to go back to the thinkers' own texts and ideas. Every interpretation of an idea, even the seemingly most innocent one, offers you its own 'spin,' implicitly or explicitly. To read only books about a thinker, rather than texts by that thinker, is to deny yourself the chance of making up your own mind. Sometimes, what makes a significant figure's work difficult to approach is not so much its style or content, as the feeling of not knowing where to start. The purpose of these books is to give you a 'way in' by offering an accessible overview of these thinkers' ideas and works and by guiding your further reading, starting with each thinker's own texts. To use a metaphor from the philosopher Ludwig Wittgenstein (1889–1951), these books are ladders, to be thrown away after you have climbed to the next level. Not only do they equip you to approach new ideas, but they also empower you, by leading you back to the theorist's own texts and encouraging you to develop your own informed opinions.

Finally, these books are necessary because, just as intellectual needs have changed, education systems around the world – the contexts in which introductory books are usually read – have changed radically, too. What was suitable for the minority higher education systems of the 1960s is not suitable for the larger, wider, more diverse, high-technology education systems of the twenty-first century. These changes call not just for new, up-to-date introductions but for new methods of presentation. The presentational aspects of *Routledge Critical Thinkers* have been developed with today's students in mind.

Each book in the series has a similar structure. It begins with a section offering an overview of the life and ideas of the featured thinker or thinkers and explaining why they are important. The central section of each book discusses the thinkers' key ideas, their context, evolution, and reception; for books that deal with more than one thinker, they also explain and explore the influence of each on each. Each volume concludes with a survey of the impact of the thinker or thinkers, outlining how their ideas have been taken up and developed by others. In addition, there is a detailed final section suggesting and describing books for further reading. This section forms an integral part of each volume, offering brief descriptions of the thinkers' key works followed by information on the most useful critical works and, in some cases, on relevant websites. This section will guide you in your reading, enabling you to follow your interests and develop your own projects. Throughout each book, references are given in what is known as the Harvard system (the author and date of a work cited are given in the text, and you can look up the full details in the References at the back). This offers a lot of information in very little space. The books also explain technical terms and use boxes to describe events or ideas in more detail, away from the main emphasis of the discussion. Boxes are also used to highlight definitions of terms frequently used or coined by a thinker. In this way, the boxes serve as a kind of glossary, easily identified when flicking through the book.

The thinkers in the series are 'critical' for three reasons. First, they are examined in the light of subjects that involve criticism: principally literary studies or English and cultural studies but also other disciplines that rely on the criticism of books, ideas, theories, and unquestioned assumptions. Second, they are critical because studying their work will provide you with a 'toolkit' for your own informed critical reading and thought, which will make you critical. Third, these thinkers are critical because they are crucially important: they deal with ideas and questions that can overturn conventional understandings of the world, of texts, of everything we take for granted, leaving us with a deeper understanding of what we already knew, and with new ideas. No introduction can tell you everything. However, by offering a way into critical thinking, this series hopes to begin to engage you in an activity which is productive, constructive, and potentially life-changing.

ACKNOWLEDGEMENTS

I am grateful to the librarians of the British Library, and the School of Oriental and African Studies, University of London. The African Studies Centre Library and Faculty of Asian and Middle Eastern Studies Library at Cambridge have both been a continual and invaluable source of help, thanks particularly to Jennifer Skinner, Miki Jacobs, and Elmi Elmi. Sections of this book were presented at conferences and workshops at the University Sultan Moulay Slimane in Beni Mellal, Morocco, and Chukwuemeka Odumegwu Ojukwu University in Igbariam, Nigeria. The members of the Lagos Studies Association and Professor Saheed Aderinto provided intellectual support and encouragement. I would like to thank Guy Bud, Hannah Grayson and Amatoritsero Ede for kindly reading individual chapters. Professor Rob Eaglestone has been a persistent and insightful editor. The Master and Fellows of St. Edmund's College, Cambridge, provided a congenial environment for the final editing of this book. I am grateful to Dr. Geoff Dumbreck, Dr. Alex Ugwuja, and Mr. José Lluis Jiménez Pina for their hospitality in London, New York, and Cambridge, respectively, during various stages of writing. Finally, I would like to thank my parents Richard and Jennifer for their support. All mistakes remain my own.

WHY MBEMBE?

'Europe is no longer the centre of gravity of the world. This is the significant event, the fundamental experience, of our era.' In a changing world, old geopolitical certainties are breaking down, and, in the emerging order, Africa will likely play a more central role. Achille Mbembe – Cameroonian historian, political scientist, and philosopher – cautions that this 'demotion of Europe' offers 'dangers and possibilities' (Mbembe 2017b, 1): while he is hopeful for a future world emerging from decolonization, Mbembe warns that our planet is also 'combusting' in environmental and humanitarian catastrophe.

Culturally, it is not hard to discern the shift Mbembe identifies; a Netflix viewer can just as easily watch a Nollywood movie produced in Lagos as a Hollywood film created in Los Angeles (Ayeni 2022; Dayo 2020). At a political level, Mbembe warns that the conditions apparent in postcolonial African states a couple of decades ago are gradually becoming common in Europe and North America. Insecurity, unpaid and low-paid work, and the erosion of social security and healthcare provision are all now increasingly common in these latter countries. More pointedly still, Mbembe emphasises that people across the world are now experiencing a level of opprobrium, stigmatization, and

DOI: 10.4324/9780429201646-1

violence, in some ways comparable to those historically reserved for black people, particularly under Western imperialism and slavery. A wider 'becoming African of the world' is taking place, he contends (Mbembe 2020a, 13).

Long consigned to the periphery of Western forms of academic knowledge, Africa occupies a central position in Mbembe's thought. He returns repeatedly to its history, politics, religion, and aesthetics. This is not only a way to think about Africa's past and future, but also that of the wider world. Africa is a location from which the future of Europe, the Americas, and Asia can be conceptualized.

In the past two decades, Mbembe has come to global prominence as a public intellectual and cultural theorist. He is arguably the most cited African scholar in the world, with writings translated into 14 languages (Juompan-Yakam 2021b). One example of his prominence came in October 2021, when French President Emmanuel Macron invited Mbembe to participate in the Africa-France summit at Montpellier (Juompan-Yakam 2021a; 2021b).

Although global in its implication, Mbembe's thought is closely rooted in the historical experience of French-speaking Africa since colonialism. This relationship is more than a simple context to his thought and cannot be ignored. Above all, Mbembe's home country of Cameroon permeates his thinking, such as in his study of France's bloody war against Cameroonian nationalists during the 1950s, and the career of independence guerrilla fighter Ruben Um Nyobè (Mbembe 1990b; Mbembe 1993). Francophone African literature also serves as a key reference point for Mbembe, even shaping the stylistic dimensions of his prose; the dystopian postcolonial novels of the Congolese novelist Sony Labou Tansi recur in Mbembe's descriptions of postcolonial life. Ultimately, however, Mbembe shows how these African texts speak to global challenges.

'THERE'S A REASON THEY CALL IT NECROPOLITICS. IT'S VICIOUS...': MBEMBE'S THOUGHT TODAY

Mbembe's thought has percolated into the media, healthcare, and popular culture. Consider three recent examples:

COVID-19 racial health inequalities, the 2020 controversy relating to accusations of antisemitism levelled against Mbembe in German politics, and Mbembe's involvement in the founding of the Africa-wide *ateliers de la pensée* or 'thought workshops' in Dakar, Senegal. These reveal the way in which Mbembe's thought, as the work of a contemporary thinker, has become global, and forced the wider world to think with and through African philosophy.

Mbembe's idea of 'necropolitics' (whereby states or non-governmental groups consign groups of people to a living death) became prominent in the media debates during the COVID-19 epidemic during 2020 and 2021 (Jagannathan 2021, 1; Mbembe 2003a, 12; Sandset 2021, 1411). The disease also revealed significant inequalities connected to race and racism within healthcare across Western countries. In the USA, concerns about race-based medical injustice combined with wider social protests of the # BlackLivesMatter movement, especially following the killing of George Floyd (Crenshaw 2020). Mbembe's idea of 'necropolitics' became prominent in media debates, with MSNBC host Joy Reid directly referencing it, and explaining that: 'there is a term called necropolitics, which is essentially the politics of who gets to live and who gets to die.' In the southern states of the USA, Reid contended, 'what they have in common is that they have structures which say that black and brown lives matter less.' Ultimately, Reid identified 'necropolitics in states like Texas,' adding 'there's a reason they call it necropolitics. It's vicious…' (Reid 2021).

Mbembe's thought has attracted significant controversy. His allusions to the Holocaust, made in the context of his interventions on the Israel/Palestinian conflict, have provoked considerable offence. This has been especially pronounced in Germany, where Mbembe has faced accusations of antisemitism and Holocaust relativization; accusations that he has fiercely contested (Bayart 2022, 143–146; Böckmann et al. 2022, 9–24; Funke 2021, 9–14). Denying the Holocaust is illegal in Germany, and antisemitic individuals have previously turned to strategies of comparison or 'relativisation' to articulate hatred (Weitzman 2023; Hirsch 2018). Before the controversy, Mbembe's thought won accolades in Germany during the 2010s, with his *Critique of Black Reason* being awarded the Geschwister-Scholl Prize, and Mbembe later receiving the Ernst Bloch Prize from the city of Ludwigshafen in 2018 (Deutsche Welle 2020). However, when Mbembe was invited to give the opening lecture at the *Ruhrtriennale* cultural festival in Bochum, North Rhine-Westphalia, the region's spokesman for the Free Democratic Party objected, citing Mbembe's signature of a petition by the pro-Palestinian Boycott, Divestment, and Sanctions movement, a group subject to a resolution by the German *Bundestag* in 2015 and subsequently declared to be anti-Semitic in May 2019 (Anonymous 2021, 377). Felix Klein, the Federal Commissioner for Jewish Life in Germany and the Fight Against Antisemitism, demanded that Mbembe should be blocked from giving the opening speech over his alleged relativization of the Holocaust (Assmann 2021, 401).

The text of Mbembe's writings themselves became central to the debate, in particular, passages in his 2016 essay 'The Politics of Enmity,' translated into English as *Necropolitics* in 2019, and Mbembe's 'Forward' to the 2015 work entitled *Apartheid Israel: The Politics of Analogy* (Mbembe 2016d 2019b; Soske 2015). Klein highlighted Mbembe's comparison of Israel with apartheid South Africa and the latter's assertion that Israel's treatment of the Palestinians represented the 'biggest moral scandal of our times' (Anonymous 2021, 374). Further passages in *Necropolitics* (2019) that compared the Holocaust to colonial genocides also triggered controversy (Dorestal 2021, 383). Klein and others argued that equating Israel to South Africa was a tactic ultimately motivated by antisemitism, while the comparison of the Holocaust to other historical events represented a form of relativization.

Beyond the immediate controversy, a furious press war erupted between pro- and anti-Mbembe commentators in the German media. Engaging German, American, Israeli, Arab, and African thinkers, the debate rapidly moved to turn on Germany's relationship with its own colonial past (Crétois 2020; Sznaider 2021, 412). Far wider questions emerged about resurgent antisemitism and Islamophobia in Germany, and the memory of the Holocaust and colonialism (Rothberg 2020). Mbembe's emerging status in Africa was itself highlighted when a group of 700 African artists and intellectuals signed a letter condemning the accusations against Mbembe as being unfounded and, more generally, arguing against the 'political instrumentalization' of human catastrophes (Capdepón and Moses 2021, 371; Jegic 2020). Mbembe's thoughts and writings not only became subjects of interest in their own right but also became connected to debates at the heart of German culture. Mbembe's significance in Europe continued to be felt in 2024, when Mbembe's work was acknowledged with the Holberg prize, which was established by the Norwegian Government in 2003 to recognise a world-leading researcher in social, legal or human sciences and theology (Juompan-Yakam, 2024a).

Mbembe has played a key role in intellectual culture within Africa. He has been at the forefront of a major conference series in Dakar, Senegal, co-organized with Senegalese thinker Felwine Sarr. These 'thought workshops' convened intellectuals from across Africa and beyond, attempting to centre the African continent within an intellectual culture that still tended to disproportionately value conferences held in Europe and North America (Tarquini 2020). Mbembe's workshop can be understood as relating to a broader trend for situating new conferences in Africa. The workshops have parallels in Anglophone Africa, such as the *Lagos Studies Association* conference at the University of Lagos, Nigeria (Coetzee 2022, 290). These efforts can be seen as centring Africa within global thought, and defining the continent's potential as a location from which to think about the future of the entire planet (Eboko 2018).

MBEMBE'S LIFE AND INTELLECTUAL INFLUENCES

Mbembe's career connects Cameroon, France, the USA, and South Africa. Born in July 1957 in Otélé, Central Cameroon, Mbembe was educated at a Roman Catholic Dominican boarding school, before attending the University of Yaoundé. In 1982, he left an increasingly repressive political landscape under Cameroonian dictator Ahmadou Ahidjo to study history at

Université Panthéon-Sorbonne, Paris. Mentored by political scientist and Cameroon specialist Jean-François Bayart, Mbembe completed a PhD in history in 1989 and took an advanced master's degree in Political Science from the *Institut d'études politiques* [Institute of Political Studies] in Paris (Kumar 2017). From France, Mbembe continued to academic positions in the USA, Senegal, and South Africa. Mbembe's deep engagement with the history and politics of Cameroon is evident in an early body of research on the country that remains largely untranslated, including his *Les jeunes et l'ordre politique en Afrique noire* (1986) [Youth and political order in black Africa], and *Christianisme, pouvoir et état en société postcoloniale* [Christianity, power, and the state in postcolonial society] (1988), and *La naissance du maquis dans le Sud-Cameroun* [The birth of the maquis in Southern Cameroon] (1996) (Mbembe 1986b; Mbembe 1988; Mbembe 1996b).

Mbembe's writings cross genres and forms, with his style sometimes baffling critics. His academic writing is often understood as 'difficult.' This book seeks to clearly introduce his ideas. Key works such as *Postcolony* interweave literary style with arguments conventionally belonging to the social sciences. References and notes can be sparse, leaving readers struggling to pin down Mbembe's claims (Quayson 2001). Elsewhere, Mbembe uses a long series of lists, and sub-lists, which ultimately become confusing.

Complex relationships exist between various iterations of several of Mbembe's key articles. 'Notes' was originally composed in 1989 in French as a conference paper, before being rewritten and translated into English and appearing in the journal *Africa* in 1992, but a significant extract was also published in *Public Culture* as 'The Banality of Power' in the same year (Bishop 2014, 82; Mbembe 1992b). On the other hand, Mbembe's journalism and interviews are often clear and polemical – qualities which reveal that generalized criticism of his thought as generally 'difficult' are somewhat wide of the mark.

One way to approach Mbembe's stylistic complexity is in terms of his eclectic constellation of intellectual influences. For example, his article *Écrire l'Afrique à partir d'une faille* [Writing Africa from a Rupture] (Mbembe 1993) offers a self-portrait of his intellectual formation in Cameroon, France, and his early years in the USA. It recounts the powerful influence of Cameroonian Christian thought on Mbembe (Syrotinski 2012, 407), who became part of the *Jeunesse étudiante chrétienne* [Christian Student Youth, J.E.C.], then later served on its national secretariat and oversaw the movement's journal. While with the J.E.C., Mbembe travelled to Northern Cameroon, later arguing that his contact with peasants in the Adamawa region helped educate him politically and culturally (Mbembe 1993, 77–78). Mbembe's early interest in liberation theology and his reading of Jesuit thinker Fabien Éboussi Boulaga's (1934–2018) critiques of the Church in *Christianisme sans fétiche* [Christianity without Fetish] were key influences (Boulaga 1981; Boulaga et al. 2006, 106; Mbembe 1993, 76). So too was University of Yaoundé philosopher Marcien Towa (1931–2014) and thinker Jean-Marc Éla (1936–2008), whose work first introduced Mbembe to Frantz Fanon's (1925–1961) thought. Facing a deteriorating academic situation in Cameroon, where the government disapproved of his research on the 1950s anti-French liberation fighter Ruben Um Nyobè (1913-1958), Mbembe left the country in 1982 not knowing when he would come back (Harbi 2013, 15; Mbembe 1984; 1993, 84; 1989b). In fact, he would not return until 1993 (Mbembe and Roitman 1995), although he would make several interventions in the Cameroonian press from abroad (Mbembe 1993, 89).

When Mbembe arrived in France in November 1982, he experienced what he termed as a 'genealogical misfortune,' or a period during which he felt profound conflict about his intellectual identity and relationship with Africa (Mbembe 1993, 88). Based in Paris, his doctoral years established key relationships, such as with his advisor Bayart, who also edited the influential political science journal *Politique Africaine,* that would prove decisive in his later career. As part of the study group 'Popular Modes of Political Action,' under Bayart's direction, Mbembe encountered thinkers that would have a major influence on his later thought, including Michel de Certeau (1925–1986), Michel Foucault (1926–1984), Cornelius Castoriadis (1922–1997), and Mikhail Bakhtin (1895–1975). Mbembe's tutor at Sciences-Po, Jean Leca, also introduced him to the thought of philosopher

Hannah Arendt (1906–1975), whose writings would influence Mbembe's theorization of colonialism. While in Paris, Mbembe met African thinkers such as the Togolese scholar Comi Toulabor (Bayart et al. 1992; Mbembe 1993, 90–91), whose work on the carnivalesque dimension of authoritarian culture constituted a key and rarely recognized influence on Mbembe's own thought on the 'postcolony.'

MBEMBE AND TRANSLATION

Mbembe's writings have now been translated across 14 languages (Juompan-Yakam 2021b). However, significant areas of his work remain untranslated to date, particularly his early scholarship and his journalism concerning Francophone Africa. Important differences exist between the French and English versions of Mbembe's works, particularly between different translations and revisions, such as of 'Notes' in its 1992 English and 1995 French versions (Bishop 2014, 84). These are important because they have implications both for our understanding of Mbembe's ideas and also our appreciation of how he writes.

Issues of translation have the potential to change Mbembe's fundamental meaning. The controversial role of Cameroon as a privileged exemplar in *Postcolony*, for example, varies between English and French. In translation, the country is 'the focus of my analysis,' but in the French original it serves as a *point d'appui* ('starting point'), which could suggest a much looser link, with Cameroon acting as a secondary 'support' to Mbembe's argument (Bishop 2014, 87; Mbembe 2000; 2001b, 103). In Mbembe's key description of a public execution in Cameroon in *Postcolony*, he uses the verb *étouffer* (to stifle) to describe the bullets. Unlike in the English translation, the French text uses this word that carries multiple connotations ('smothering,' 'muffling'), which implies that the bullets are not only stifling the cries of the condemned but also the applause of the crowd itself (Bishop 2014, 86).

Translation is also key to understanding sensitive terms in Mbembe's thought, which often have no direct translation into English. This includes the noun and racial slur *Nègre* which appears in the title of Mbembe's *Critique* (2017b). The term has a history rooted in the French empire's practice of slavery and the development of racial theory (Pierrot 2022, 101). The *Critique's* translator Laurent Dubois has written of the difficulty of rendering the term in English, while accounting for the variety of injuries that it has caused over its history. He uses three terms in his translation of the *Critique*: 'Blacks,' 'Blackness,' and 'the Black Man' (Mbembe 2017b, xiv). While in English, the first two of Dubois's terms are gender neutral, Mbembe's French frequently specifies a male subject. Issues of translation therefore ultimately determine not simply the transfer of meaning, but also the nuance and associative framework which Mbembe's prose evokes. In texts such as *Postcolony*, which have a high degree of literary reference and a significant rhetorical complexity, translation can shift the connotation of words and create substantial ambiguities.

BOOK OUTLINE

This book will explore Mbembe's core ideas and thoughts, largely in relation to colonial and postcolonial Africa. While it has been designed to be read as a whole, it is possible to approach individual chapters in isolation. The book focuses particularly on Mbembe's relationship with African thinkers and writers. It does not devote as much attention to the influence of European philosophers, whose works are described elsewhere in this Routledge series.

The book opens with Mbembe's work on Race (Chapter 1), to colonial (Chapter 2) and postcolonial (Chapter 3) Africa. In doing so, it situates Mbembe's critical thought about African cultures in relation to his historical and political scientific work. Progressing from these earlier historical and representational concerns, it then progresses to explore Mbembe's account of necropolitics (Chapter 4), placing it in relation to the role of death in his earliest work on Cameroon and more recent accounts of contemporary conflicts in Africa. Decolonization and Mbembe's engagement with Frantz Fanon's thought forms the basis of Chapter 5, including the decolonization of universities and Mbembe's engagement with the #RhodesMustFall movement in South Africa. Africa's relationship with the wider world is the subject of Chapter 6, which focuses on Mbembe's idea of 'Afropolitanism.'

The final part of this book examines Mbembe's thought on technology and the environment. His account of digital technology and computation (Chapter 7) relates to Mbembe's more general contention that an era of pervasive 'brutalism' exists in the contemporary world. This is only heightened by the spectre of environmental catastrophe (Chapter 8), which nonetheless, Mbembe contends, also ushers in new ways in which humans can relate to each other and the world around them. Finally, 'After Mbembe' argues that Mbembe's thought epitomizes the significance of African philosophy at a global level and shows how Mbembe has motivated both new intellectual formations and influenced practical political and academic organizing.

KEY IDEAS

1

RACE, AFRICA, AND QUESTIONS OF KNOWLEDGE

How we think about and describe Africa is of prime importance in Mbembe's thought. The act of thinking about Africa has wider social and political implications. In particular, the idea of Africa, Mbembe argues, is closely related to a series of biased stereotypes regarding Africans and the African diaspora. For Europeans, '[s]peaking rationally' about the continent 'is not something that has ever come naturally' (Mbembe 2001b, 1). Mbembe divides knowledge about Africa into two dominant narratives: a 'first' produced in Europe and a 'second' created within the African diaspora in the Americas.

Questions of knowledge and power are key to Mbembe's account of how knowledge about Africa has been produced. He views the question of who gets to create this knowledge as key; inherent biases based on the author's social and cultural location remain unavoidable, no matter how we may try to anticipate these. The present book, for example, is the product of a white, non-African British scholar based at a Western university. Such a position entails particular privilege, and, from Mbembe's perspective, would likely accord this work a relationship with the 'first' narrative of European-authored accounts of Africa and Africans, even as it seeks to address it critically (Mbembe 1999b; 2002c; 2006b).

European accounts of Africa penned by travellers, anthropologists, and colonial officials since the eighteenth century played a key role in spreading prejudicial stereotypes about the continent. Authors drew on such seemingly self-explanatory ideas as 'the African soul,' 'the Bantu world-view,' and 'Dogon wisdom' that treated groups of Africans as static and unchanging (Deacon 2003, 161). This tendency has sometimes been connected to the European philosophical movement known as the Enlightenment. Certain philosophers and natural scientists of the period 'embarked upon the classification of human races according to assumptions about a "naturally" ordered hierarchy' (Eze 1997, 5).

Stereotypical and often negative perceptions of Africa are hardly limited to the past. Celebrity charity volunteers who pose for 'selfies' with Africans experiencing poverty have been accused of elevating their own act of charity above the plight of those whom they claim to help. These charitable activities, although laudable in themselves, often rely on expenditure that only a comparatively wealthy and mobile person might afford. In such an example, the difference in wealth, particularly as it intersects with race, represents a modern parallel to the inequalities that Mbembe identifies in nineteenth-century descriptions of Africa. This modern-day behaviour has been critiqued as representing a 'white saviour' complex (Wainaina 2005, 2012).

We explore Mbembe's account of the construct of blackness and then consider two separate narratives about Africa: one emerging in Europe and particularly associated with colonialism, and a second narrative that Mbembe identifies as emerging in the African diaspora. Finally, we look at the autobiography of Omar ibn Said, a West African enslaved in America. Said's life and writings described a trans-Atlantic world, joining his memory of Islamic societies in Africa with life in the slave-holding USA.

AFRICA, BLACKNESS, AND RACIAL CAPITALISM: INTERCONNECTED HISTORIES

First, we look at Mbembe's account of the emergence of a distinct black subject (or person): for him, it is closely related to the historical development of the Atlantic slave trade. We then consider Mbembe's account of racial labels including, what he terms, *le Nègre* or a racial slur meaning 'the Black man,' and his account of an aggressive idea of whiteness.

A historical narrative of blackness

'Black,' Mbembe argues, 'has its own weight, its own density' (Mbembe 2017b, 151). Any account of how Africa has been described must reckon with common ideas about African people. This notion of the African person (and individuals of African descent origin resident in the Americas) is referred to by Mbembe using the term '*le Nègre*,' a French slur which might be translated as 'the Black,' 'the Black Man,' 'the Negro,' or 'Black.' Many of these English terms continue to cause considerable offence. The term *Nègre* is not static and, Mbembe reminds us, had different usages over time, being the product of 'a long historical process.' While its origins were in the Spanish empire of the sixteenth century and the epithet was commonly used by slavers in the eighteenth century, it became a positive term used by black intellectuals and writers in the nineteenth and twentieth centuries to assert their own identity (Mbembe 2017b, 38). Mbembe's idea of '*le Nègre*' is very often understood to be male, a point that potentially excludes female experience, although how far this is intentional is not always clear.

For much of its history, the term 'Black,' Mbembe contends, was not used to *include*, but rather *exclude*. It functioned like a weapon against the people it claimed to describe. It was used in contexts like slavery and imperial occupation where those people being described as 'Black' often had less power than those making the labels. Despite this asymmetry, Mbembe argues that such attempts at labelling 'others' as different are bound to fail. This is because the term 'Black,' when used by Europeans to describe Africans, lacked recognition of their humanity. Mbembe argues that humans possess an 'uneliminable surplus' that escapes simplistic and prejudicial efforts to contain them within any externally imposed status. Even though they may sometimes be vague and imposed from outside, such terms do considerable damage. Attempting to communicate both the slipperiness and the coercive quality of the label 'Black,' Mbembe writes that it 'is [...] a nickname, a tunic that someone else has dressed me in, seeking to trap me within it' (Mbembe 2017b, 46).

Blackness, Mbembe argues, is dynamic and shifts meaning over time. He maps this changing use against 'three moments': attribution, return/internalization, and reversal/overthrow (Mbembe 2017b, 47). During the era of 'attribution,' Europeans imposed racial labels (particularly connected to the 'first narrative' we examine below), while the next era of 'return' represented an appropriation of these labels by black people themselves (the 'second narrative' discussed below). Finally, Mbembe's era of 'overthrow' has not yet occurred, but is marked by the rejection of racial labels, and the 'full and unconditional recuperation of the status of the human...' (explored in Chapters 5 and 8) (Mbembe 2017b, 47).

Slavery, racial capitalism, and the 'Black Man'

Mbembe's understanding of the 'Black Man' is closely linked to the Atlantic slave trade and its economy. Slavery played a crucial role in the development of capitalism in Europe and North America. Mbembe argues that this relationship between the slave trade and capitalism gave rise to a system of 'racial capitalism,' which he sees as operating both in the slave plantation and the colony (Mbembe; 2013a; 2013b; 2017b, 136–137). Within the formation of 'modern capitalism,' the 'Black Man' was to play a key and often ignored role. Serving as the bedrock of the edifice of capitalism due to his forced labour and abjection, he was 'an essential mechanism in a process of [capitalist] accumulation' (Mbembe 2017b, 47). Mbembe uses several portmanteau terms to describe this predicament including 'man-of-metal,' 'man-merchandise,' and 'man-of-money.' Although as a slave 'the Black Man' was exploited, abused, and denigrated, he was at the same time situated at the very heart of industrial capitalism: his unremunerated labour allowed the making of merchandise, and metal. The label 'Black' may have been used to articulate racist contempt, but it came to be at the heart of the modern world economy (Mbembe 2017b, 180).

The fantasy of whiteness

Mbembe sees the label of 'the Black man' as emerging in tandem with new and pernicious European understandings of what it meant to be white. He is not making objective claims about race, but rather describing constructed social labels (Orkin and Joubin 2019). Whiteness took on a newly central and supposedly normal status in the minds of Europeans during the eighteenth and nineteenth centuries. It became the oxygen that enabled European conquest, and represented 'the mark of a certain mode of Western presence in the world.' Whiteness, when drawn on by colonists and explorers, was far from neutral. It became increasingly defined in relation to comparisons and hierarchies: Europeans had greater confidence than before in the supposed achievements of their societies and economies. The term is still used to exclude others. Whiteness thus becomes a 'figure of brutality and cruelty,' and a 'form of predation,' and one with 'an unequalled capacity for the subjection and exploitation of foreign peoples' (Mbembe 2017b, 45–46). It is therefore linked to a 'structural' or systemic violence because it enables Europeans to seize assets from those deemed non-white and allows the destruction of their cultures. Nor is the damage caused by this cultural understanding of whiteness limited to the past. Rather, as Mbembe reminds us, it extends into the present day.

TWO NARRATIVES OF AFRICA: FROM EUROPE AND THE AFRICAN DIASPORA

Mbembe explores the representation of Africa in terms of two narratives. These he sees as both superficially very different, but actually co-dependent. Both, he argues, constitute narratives of 'Black Reason,' although only the second was written by persons of African descent. A 'first narrative' of European commentary on Africa culminated in 'colonial discourse.' It represented nothing less than a pernicious web of language carefully 'woven around these distant lands...' (Mbembe 2001b, 175). By contrast, a 'second narrative' was crafted in the African diaspora and offered the possibility for people of African origin to use a 'language all of their own' to record their experience (Mbembe 2017b, 3).

A 'first narrative' of Africa: European representations and colonial discourse

European knowledge about Africa constitutes a 'first narrative.' As we have seen, creating knowledge about Africa was not a purely academic exercise. It not only contained 'narratives and discourses' but also concerned the practical and everyday work of justifying 'racial domination' (Mbembe 2017b, 27). Western knowledge about Africa therefore had direct and violent real-world consequences. But to understand how this came to pass, Mbembe suggests, we must grasp the outlines of colonial discourse. This latter body of discourse (or power-inflected language) forms the essence of Mbembe's 'first narrative.' In practical terms, it manifested itself in the everyday interactions of the officials and colonial subjects. Ultimately, colonial discourse allowed for the appearance of a prejudicial understanding of 'the Black Man' in explicitly racialized terms. Already subject to 'moral disqualification,' he was systematically derided as allegedly inextricably different from Europeans (Mbembe 2017b, 28).

What was colonial discourse?

Colonial discourse was above all a 'web of words.' Yet it was a sticky, treacherous web. Adopted in order to dehumanize Africans, this 'web of words' was nothing if not mad. 'What would the colony be,' Mbembe asks, 'if not a place where all sorts of mythical fabrications could be unleashed [?]' Mbembe summarizes some of these fears: 'do the natives not steal freshly buried bodies from the cemetery,' and 'are the dead not [...] thrown to the birds of prey [?]' (Mbembe 2001b, 185). These imaginary anxieties do not *actually* describe Africa but instead belong to the flotsam and jetsam of European lore about the continent. In lieu of fact, they articulate a mix of hearsay, conjecture, and prejudice. All of this formed the bedrock of colonial discourse. Such discourse did not simply reside on the page; it had to be actively performed. Entailing a 'daily work' of repetition and invention, it proved, quite literally, contagious for colonial officials.

As 'crazy' as colonial discourse might seem, Mbembe reminds us that its stereotypes can be found in the works of major European philosophers. He reads a passage from German philosopher Friedrich Hegel (1770–1831) in his *Lectures on the Philosophy of World History* to explore these parallels (Hegel 1975, 218–224, 117–182; Mccarney 2000, 142–145). Hegel writes:

> They [Africans] do not invoke God in their ceremonies; they do not turn to any higher power, for they believe that they can accomplish their aims by their own efforts…If they do not succeed after prolonged efforts, they decree that some of the onlookers… should be slaughtered, and these are then devoured by their fellows…. The priest will often spend several days in this frenzied condition, slaughtering human beings, drinking their blood, and giving it to the onlookers to drink….
>
> (Hegel 1975, 180)

This passage is from a longer excerpt that Mbembe analyses in *Postcolony* (Mbembe 2001b, 176–177). He identifies a 'verbal economy' at work in Hegel's text that has several characteristics including using anecdotes, removing references to time, erasing local reference points, and using dramatic images with little specificity (Mbembe 2001b, 177). Hegel's evocation of 'the priest' thus has little specific cultural context, his use of the third person plural is generalizing, and we do not know when the alleged events are occurring. All of these vagaries play an insidious role in colonial discourse. Hegel's attitude towards Africa was more complex than Mbembe's discussion suggests (Mccarney 2000, 142–145), and his own relationship with Hegelian thought is contradictory (McCaskie 2019, 189). For our purposes, Mbembe argues that Hegel's understanding of Africa relied on 'second-hand' accounts from missionaries and travellers. Mbembe sees Hegel's account of the continent, which went as far as denying Africa's historicity, as anticipating elements later present in 'colonial discourse.'

Colonial discourse I: Time

Colonial discourse, Mbembe contends, reveals two distinct accounts of time: stasis and circularity. While time might appear to be a straightforward dimension of human experience, historians and literary critics have shown how human perceptions of time changes according to social context, and that ways of marking time can be used to amplify or contest political power. In the context of European imperialism, time was sometimes represented as a 'forward vector of progress,' and, in domains such as colonial education and administration, the day became increasingly organized according to the clock, with institutions seeking increasing control over how time was divided (West-Pavlov 2013, 159). Assertions that time does not change in a particular location, or that it goes in circles, both communicate assumptions about the societies and cultures that reside there.

Under 'stasis,' time is frozen or suspended. Mbembe points to recurrent expressions of time in descriptions of Africa including 'since time immemorial,' and 'it was always there' that stress the way that time supposedly behaved differently there (Mbembe 2001b, 4). 'In the Tropics,' Mbembe contends, life is believed to consist of 'weariness.' It is as though time has completely evaporated. Elsewhere 'vast horizons' are 'enveloped in a sort of silence,' or 'calm, deceptive peace,' where the continent is assumed to be completely different to any other area of the world (Mbembe 2017b, 179). Stasis possessed a moral dimension. In Africa, so colonial discourse claimed, the very will to live and to act evaporated. Instead, the continent became associated with moral decay and an inactivity that was emphasized in comparison to alleged European industriousness. 'The idea of progress,' Mbembe observers, 'is said to disintegrate in such societies' (Mbembe 2001b, 4).

Understanding time as 'circular' denied the possibility of historical change in African societies. Anthropologists and travellers obsessed about 'the alleged central place of witchcraft and divination procedures' on the continent. They ignored the degree to which these practices could also readily be found in nineteenth-century Europe. As a consequence, Africans themselves were reduced to being treated as less than human. They were perceived as occupying to occupy 'an enchanted and mysterious universe' motivated not by 'the power of production' [as in European capitalist economies] but by 'the power of [superstitious] invocation and evocation' (Mbembe 2001b, 4).

Colonial discourse II: Hyperbole

A second dimension of colonial discourse focused on its stylistic habits of generalization and exaggeration. This insight invites us to turn to consider the linguistic *quality* of colonial discourse. Mbembe argued that colonial discourse represented a 'language' belonging to 'the order of useless expenditure' (Mbembe 2001b, 178). Part of the 'useless' nature of this discourse was that it did not produce specific representations of actual places and peoples, but instead evinced a willingness to generalize. It had a clumsy and circular nature. This did not puncture its violent power, but instead added to it. Within this grasping, impulsive body of language, a veritable raft of second-hand knowledge was picked up and recycled effortlessly incorporating 'rumour and gossip,' while time and again asserting grand ideas (Mbembe 2001b, 178).

The impact of 'colonial discourse' on the colonized

What impact did 'colonial discourse' have on those who faced it? It could be frightening and intimidating. Despite its inconsistencies, such discourse could lead people to see 'the colonizer' in spiritual and supernatural terms. The colony could therefore become a place of fear and superstition, peopled 'with maleficent spirits that intervene every time one steps out of line.' A net of 'prohibitions and inhibitions' was thus tied around the colonized, which became 'far more terrifying than any world of the colonizer' (Mbembe 2001b, 181). Mbembe's account of the terror of the colonized has intellectual and linguistic parallels with psychiatrist Fanon's argument regarding the role of superstition and the supernatural. Fanon sees such beliefs as blunting the possibility for colonized people to challenge colonial rule. In the colony, he writes, the 'zombies of ancestors' held sway over the living, as well as the 'djinns [spirits] who rush into your body while you yawn' (Fanon 1967, 45). Fanon regarded these beliefs not simply as elements of culture, but as a major aid to the power of colonial officials and local elites alike. He viewed them as antithetical to resistance, liberation, and 'national culture' (Mbembe 2001b, 181). For Mbembe, 'colonial discourse' seemed very impressive to those who were disempowered or oppressed. They lacked the tools to challenge and overturn its damaging claims.

Colonial discourse: Critiques

Mbembe's idea of colonial discourse has been critiqued on several grounds. Firstly, it lacks specific and sustained reference to any individual colonial context. Secondly, it risks overemphasizing the power of the colonizers, while minimizing the ability of Africans to contest colonial oppression. Finally, Mbembe's own prose itself sometimes comes close to the very terms of the discourse he is critiquing, particularly in his account of how the colonized viewed the colonizer in superstitious and magical terms. Ultimately, for Mbembe, 'colonial discourse' is a tenacious force, whose 'corpse... obstinately persists in getting up again every time it is buried.'

A SECOND VISION OF AFRICA: DIASPORA, COMMUNITY, AND SELF-EXPRESSION

The 'second narrative' of Africa emerges in the African diaspora from the nineteenth century onwards. This narrative represents, Mbembe contends, 'the Black consciousness of Blackness' (Mbembe 2017b, 28, 30). Thinkers of African descent refined their own accounts of their relationship to Africa and defined a black community within diaspora. This second narrative was concerned with defining Africa, as well as the efforts of individuals in the diaspora to work through their own relationship to the continent in writing. It mobilized around questions such as '[who] am I?' 'Am I, in truth, what people say I am?' 'Is it true that I am nothing more than ... [than] what people [see] me as and say of me?' and 'What is my real social status, my real history?' (Mbembe 2017b, 28). We will explore some answers below, including co-identification and the formation of communities shaped by mutual concern.

The formation of an African Atlantic diaspora

Mbembe argues that the Atlantic slave trade created a 'transnationalization of the Black condition' (Mbembe 2017b, 15). 'Between 1630 and 1780,' he observes, 'far more Africans than Europeans disembarked in Great Britain's Atlantic colonies' (Mbembe 2017b, 14). The Atlantic slave trade also acted as a 'constitutive moment for modernity,' leading ultimately to movements of emancipation and self-expression, such as the 1791 Haitian revolution and subsequent independence in 1804 (DuBois 2004, 1–2; Gonzalez 2019, 29; Mbembe 2017b, 15). Mbembe identifies the late eighteenth century as the 'height of Black presence' in the British empire and a key point in the emergence of black writing and self-expression (Mbembe 2017b, 14). In arguing for the importance of an African community spread across both sides of the Atlantic Ocean, Mbembe draws on critic Paul Gilroy's (1956–) argument that a distinct 'Black Atlantic' connected the African diaspora in the Caribbean, North America, and Europe, especially during the eighteenth and nineteenth centuries. Gilroy examines historical figures whose lives and careers spanned this 'Black Atlantic' and that were closely engaged in revolutionary politics, such as former slave and abolitionist Olaudah Equiano (1745–1797), Jacobin and sailor Robert Wedderburn (1762–c.1835/1836), and the son of Jamaica attorney general William Davidson (1781–1820) (Gilroy 1993, 12; Somerville 2007). This transatlantic culture gave rise to a subculture that Mbembe terms 'lumpen-Atlantic' and which shared common dimensions with other African groups in diaspora, for example, in the Caribbean or Europe. African Americans, he argues, were 'at once fundamentally American and *lumpen*-Atlantic' (Mbembe 2017b, 25).

Diasporic visions of Africa: Strangeness and mutual concern

The second narrative of Africa led to dramatic changes in self-expression. It engaged in two activities that proved foundational to an emerging black intellectual community: strangeness and 'mutual concern' (Mbembe 2017b, 26). Both elements reflect an experience that had to reckon with a diaspora experience that was 'fragmented' by enslavement and distance from Africa (Mbembe 2017b, 28–29). Both also had to grapple with the fact that 'the historical experience of Blacks did not necessarily leave traces,' and, if it did, they 'were not always preserved' (Mbembe 2017b, 28). Ultimately, the 'second narrative' of Africa had a direct, practical goal: it 'sought... to create community... out of the ... four corners of the world' (Mbembe 2017b, 29).

To build this community, diasporic thinkers had to overcome a sense of estrangement from Africa. Many had been separated from the continent for generations, and Africa remained 'unknowable' for them. Unlike Europeans, Afrodiasporic peoples had close cultural and family links with Africa, but they were nonetheless assailed by 'the continent's strangeness' when they visited it. Within this uneasy relationship, returning diasporic thinkers found that their perceptions of Africa were also influenced by European stereotypes not only of the continent but of black people in general. Returnees' 'encounters with the blacks of Africa,' Mbembe points out, '... constituted an encounter with *another's other*' (Mbembe 2017b, 25).

But this 'strangeness' of Africa was countered by diaspora thinkers' building of a 'mutual concern' and identification with the continent, which became an essential quality of this second narrative. They defined the 'principle of a community of kinship' that bound African American and Caribbean writers to

Africa (Mbembe 2017b, 26). Mbembe discerns such a priority in the writing of nineteenth-century black nationalist Alexander Crummell (1819–1898), whose letter on 'The Relations and Duties of Free Colored Men in America to Africa' is viewed by Mbembe as reflecting an attempt to forge such a community (Mbembe 2017b, 26). Crummell was among a group of diasporic intellectuals writing about Africa during the mid-nineteenth century, including Edward Wilmot Blyden (1832–1912) and Martin Delany (1812–1885) (Gilroy 1993, 22–23). Gilroy shows how Delany's writings, such as his novel *Blake* (1859–1861), examine contradictory responses towards Africa, moving beyond recognition of an 'ancient, ancestral home,' and containing an 'aware[ness] that… [Africa] needed to be remade wholesale' (Adeleke 2003, 1–2; Delany 2017; Gilroy 1993, 24).

Within the intellectual culture of the diaspora, Africa possessed powerful political potential. It signified 'a time before' enslavement (Mbembe 2017b, 26). During the era of Reconstruction, which followed the end of the American Civil War (1865–1877), African American subjugation and impoverishment persisted, even though slavery had ended (Scott 2005, 1). To write about Africa in this enduring context of inequality, Mbembe observes, represented 'an act of moral imagination': 'writing' history 'for the descendants of slaves' meant that this vision of Africa was 'reopen[ing] the possibility for them to become agents of history itself' (Mbembe 2017b, 29). The very act of writing about Africa in the diaspora had moral and political consequences: it showed how Afrodiasporic thinkers could be agents in their own destinies.

THE *AUTOBIOGRAPHY OF OMAR IBN SAID*: WRITING ABOUT AFRICA AND ISLAM FROM AMERICAN ENSLAVEMENT

We turn to one African's memories of life on the continent as written under slavery in the USA. Omar ibn Said's 1831 Arabic language *Autobiography of Omar ibn Said, Slave in North Carolina* represents the earliest Islamic manuscript found in America. Ibn Said's choice of Arabic, and his account of how his life related to a wider Islamic context, differs significantly from Mbembe's chosen examples (Osman and Forbes 2004, 333–334). To this extent, it challenges Mbembe's claim that Afrodiasporic accounts of Africa were necessarily influenced by European discourses. But ibn Said's trans-Atlantic life story also has many other parallels with the 'second narrative's' Atlantic world: it reveals an African in the Americas writing about Africa.

Ibn Said described his early life in Futa Toro, on the middle Senegal River, as well as his Muslim faith. Before enslavement, he was already an experienced traveller within Islamic Africa and beyond. Before being enslaved in 1807, ibn Said had travelled to Cairo and Timbuktu, as well as performing the *hajj* or pilgrimage to Mecca (Gomez 2005, 168). An experienced author, ibn Said wrote several Qur'anic translations, three Lord's Prayers, two lists of his masters' family's names, a commentary on Christian prayer, as well as a dedication to Allah in his Bible, and a copy of Qur'anic surat 110, the *Surat An-Nasr* (Hunwick 2003–2004).

> My name is Omar ibn Seid. My birthplace was Fut Tûr, between the two rivers. I sought knowledge under the instruction of a Sheikh called Mohammed Seid, my own brother, and Sheikh Soleiman Kembeh, and Sheikh Gabriel Abdal. I continued my studies twenty-five years, and then returned to my home where I remained six years. Then there came to our place a large army, who killed many men, and took me, and brought me to the great sea, and sold me into the hands of the Christians, who bound me and sent me on board a great ship and we sailed upon the great sea a month and a half, when we came to a place called Charleston in the Christian language... Before I came to the Christian country, my religion was the religion of 'Mohammed, the Apostle of God – may God have mercy upon him and give him peace.' I walked to the mosque before day-break, washed my face and head and hands and feet. I prayed at noon, prayed in the afternoon, prayed at sunset, prayed in the evening ... I went every year to the holy war against the infidels. I went on pilgrimage to Mecca, as all did who were able. My father had six sons and five daughters, and my mother had three sons and one daughter. When I left my country I was thirty-seven

years old; I have been in the country of the Christians twenty-four years. Written AD 1831.

(Said 2014, 144–146)

From his life in Carolina, ibn Said describes his memories of Africa and Arabia, including waging jihad or holy war and performing the *hajj*. He reveals an imaginative world of recollection straddling the Atlantic.

Ibn Said's introduction to his manuscript demonstrates a series of cultural priorities which pay scant regard to European nineteenth-century understandings of Africa. It consists of a single page in English, communicating information about his relationships to Africa, including his Fulbe ethnic background, and a reference to a 'Lamine Kebby,' a freed slave with whom ibn Said corresponded (Osmanand Forbes 2004, 335). Ibn Said mainly chose to write in Arabic, a language with few American readers before Arab migrants arrived in great numbers in the mid-nineteenth century. He associated Arabic with freedom of expression, and it offered an escape from European and slave-holding languages, such as English. His use of language includes stylistic choices that would have been familiar to those educated in classical Arabic, such as vocative addresses ('O You who have attained to faith') to define a specific audience, while also mirroring the iterative style of the Qur'an, using repetition ('O people of North Carolina…') (Ayalon 1984, 5). For our purposes, ibn Said's narrative reflects an African writing from the Americas about his homeland. It offers both an example of identification with Africa from the Americas as described in Mbembe's 'second narrative,' but it also reveals a form of African writing from diaspora that differs from Mbembe's examples, revealing direct personal experience of the continent and choosing to use the Arabic language and Islamic cultural reference points.

CONCLUSION

Mbembe argues that European accounts of Africa were necessarily partial and enjoyed a close relationship with imperial power. These biases become especially apparent in the case of 'colonial discourse,' a hyperbolic vehicle for speculative and inaccurate claims about African peoples and cultures. Despite its want of factual accuracy, this account of Africa had destructive consequences, including the imposition of colonial rule, and the dissemination of racial capitalism across the Atlantic.

Mbembe's 'second narrative' of diaspora knowledge about Africa was rooted in a 'polyglot internationalism,' and a 'modern Black imaginary' (Mbembe 2017b, 30). It played a key role in forging community and solidarities between diasporic groups in the Americas and established a new writing on Africa. The memory and idea of Africa was delineated and debated by slaves, former slaves, and African American intellectuals during the nineteenth century. As we have seen in the case of Omar ibn Said, some slaves could recall Africa within their own lifetime and chose African languages to articulate their experiences. In ibn Said's case, Arabic offered a cultural resource outside the constraints of European representations of Africa that so preoccupy Mbembe in his 'first narrative' of Africa.

NINETEENTH-CENTURY BLACK NATIONALISM BETWEEN THE AMERICAS, EUROPE, AND AFRICA

Mbembe's account in his 'second narrative' of nineteenth-century intellectual culture across the Black Atlantic connects with the lives of several key African American intellectuals. These figures all played key roles in developing relations across the 'Black Atlantic' between Europe, North America, and West Africa.

ALEXANDER CRUMMELL (1819–1898)

Crummell was a passionate supporter of Pan-Africanism (the belief in shared political, cultural, or social bonds between disparate African peoples), arguing during the 1895 Atlanta Exposition that indigenous Africans should be trained to promote Christianity. His views remain controversial due to his belief that Africans should be encouraged to adopt Western civilization and Christianity, which has been understood as failing to fully respect African cultures, for example, in Liberia. Despite this, Crummell's brand of Pan-Africanist thought was not uncommon among African American intellectuals of the mid-nineteenth century and should be understood in terms of his experiences of slavery and racism (Bevan 2010; Miller 1975). Crummell's experiences of racism in the USA informed his commitment to Pan-Africanism and Black Nationalism. He travelled to Liberia but left in 1873 for the USA following disputes at Liberia College in Monrovia. From his return to North America, Crummell worked at St. Mary's Church in Washington DC and then St. Luke's Church until his retirement in 1894. A year before his death, Crummell founded the American Negro Academy.

EDWARD WILMOT BLYDEN (1832–1912)

Blyden perhaps embodies Mbembe's notion of 'mutual concern' between the diaspora and Africa. Philosopher, educationalist, diplomat, and journalist, Blyden had considerable experience of living and working in West Africa and popularized the region's histories and cultures in the Americas and Europe. Born on St. Thomas Island in the Danish Virgin Islands, Blyden would later turn down the chance to pursue university studies in England. Studying Greek, Latin, and Hebrew, he was ordained to the Presbyterian ministry in 1858. Blyden was particularly interested in the role of Africans in the classical Mediterranean world, and, following encounters with the Mandinke peoples in inner Liberia, he studied Islam and Arabic, undertaking a study tour of Egypt, Lebanon, and Syria to develop his knowledge of these subjects, while also promoting the existence of Liberia. He later introduced the study of Arabic to Liberia College. Blyden published several influential works including *Christianity, Islam, and the Negro Race* (1887) and *African Life and Customs* (1908) (Barrows 2010; July 1967).

JOHN E. BRUCE (1856–1924)

Essayist, journalist, and historian who cultivated a readership across the African diaspora and in Africa itself, Bruce wrote for African newspapers and activist Duse Mohammed Ali's (1866–1945) *African Times and Orient Review*. He grew up in Washington DC having been born a slave in Maryland, and helped in the Washington offices of the *New York Times*, before using the pen name 'Rising Sun' in a series of columns and starting his own newspaper in 1879. He became famous as 'Bruce Grit,' writing columns in the *Cleveland Gazette* and the *New York Age*. In 1911, he founded the Negro Society for Historical Research with Arthur Schomburg (Crowder 1978, 47; Gruesser 2001).

MARTIN R. DELANY (1812–1885)

Journalist and Pan-Africanist Delany's novel *Blake* is explicitly referenced by Mbembe as an example of diaspora understandings of Africa and the Atlantic. Born in Charles Town, Virginia, Delany later studied Classics, Latin, and Greek at Jefferson College. In the 1840s, he founded the early abolitionist paper *The Mystery* (later *Christian Recorder*) and later launched *The North Star* with Frederick Douglass and William Lloyd Garrison. In 1858, Delany was named a commissioner to explore Africa, and sailed to Liberia in 1859, travelling on to Lagos, Nigeria. In 1861, Delany had amassed funding and passengers for a plan to settle African Americans in Abeokuta, Nigeria, but the scheme collapsed with the outbreak of the Civil War. Delany published the first novel by an African American in 1859 *Blake; Or the Huts of America*, which was serialized in the *Anglo-African* magazine, among other works (Adeleke 2020; Gates et al., 2012).

CHEIKH ANTA DIOP (1923–1986)

Mbembe's critique of European knowledge about Africa can be compared to Diop's call for Africa-focused knowledge or 'Afrocentrism,' even though this been critiqued by Mbembe (see

Chapter 6). Diop emphasised Africa-centred interpretations of the continent's history and culture, arguing for the sub-Saharan African origins of ancient Egyptian civilization, and suggesting that sub-Saharan civilizations had been persistently neglected in world history. Diop's arguments caused widespread controversy among Egyptologists. He became widely known for his *Nations nègres et cultures* [Black Nations and Cultures]. Born in Caytou village in the Diourbel region of Senegal, Diop received Western and Qur'anic education, before leaving Senegal in 1946 to undertake studies at the Sorbonne. His doctoral dissertation on the Egyptian origins of African civilization was initially rejected by the Sorbonne, although later published as *Nations nègres* in 1955. Diop founded the first radiocarbon dating laboratory in Africa and served on the committee for the eight-volume UNESCO *General History of Africa* (Adi 2003, 40–43; Coquery-Vidrovitch 2018; MacDonald 2007, 93).

VALENTIN-YVES MUDIMBE (1941–)

Congolese philosopher and linguist Mudimbe's thought forms a key companion to Mbembe's account of European knowledge about Africa. Mudimbe remains best known for his major study *The Invention of Africa* (1988), in which he explored European ideas about Africa. Born in Jadotville (Likasi) in the Haut-Katanga province of the Democratic Republic of the Congo, Mudimbe was educated in Kakanda and Mwera, and studied Romance philology at the Lovanium University in Kinshasa. Returning to Zaire (now D.R. Congo) from a period in France, Mudimbe held chairs and other positions at the National University of Zaire, as well as undertaking pedagogical missions for the Zairean government. He later moved to the USA, after becoming disillusioned with Zairean politics (Desai 1991, 931–943; Fraiture and Orrells 2016, xi–xlv).

2

THE COLONY

Mbembe's concept of the 'colony' is central to his thinking on politics, agency, and culture. 'Colony' primarily refers to historically existing colonies, such as those in Africa colonized by European powers in the nineteenth century. But Mbembe also uses the term in a much looser way, discerning 'colonial discourse' across a broader period of European contact with Africa. The 'colony' forms the backdrop to his theorization of *commandement* or colonial governmentality.

In writing about the 'colony,' Mbembe is not only describing a period in Africa's history, but he is also making a more abstract and theoretical argument concerning the scope of the colonists' control. Although he varies in his account of just how dominant the colonizers were, Mbembe generally paints a picture of extreme, asymmetrical rule that was hard for Africans to challenge. This vision is shaped by his reading of French philosopher Michel Foucault's (1926–1984) understanding of power and governance (Jewisewicki 2002, 595). Foucault argued that, contrary to popular perceptions, power did not reside within entities like the state or institutions. Rather, he saw it as being articulated through relationships that continually had to be made and remade (Mbembe 1991b, 7–24; Smart 2002, 122). Accordingly, it is not the university literature department that is itself powerful as an institution, but rather power resides in the human relationships between its members, such as lecturers and students. Foucault saw a wide variety of social institutions as being channels of power, including ones we might not think of as political, such as psychiatric units, schools, or prisons. Consequentially power can flow through almost any institution, no matter how benign or socially useful it might appear. This model of power as being based in relationships and diffused through many different areas of society is key to understanding Mbembe's account of colonial power (Foucault 2020b, 201–222). Mbembe's earlier work had explicitly engaged with Foucault to understand key aspects of life in the colony, including violence and economic extraction (Mbembe 1991b, 21).

THE COLONY AND THE IDEA OF THE 'NATIVE'

Mbembe's account of colonial Africa revolves around three key concepts: the location of the colony, the category of the 'native,' and the power relation of 'commandement' (literally a 'command' or 'order,' but used by Mbembe to indicate a broader relationship between colonizer and colonized). Cumulatively these ideas coalesce into a bleak and impressive account of a starkly asymmetrical world where the colonized have little power and the colonizer wields authority at whim.

The colony

Despite being a historian of colonial Cameroon, Mbembe's writing on 'the colony' is often general and abstract. The colony is defined by inequality and represents 'a territory seized' by the colonizers for the purposes of enrichment and plunder. It was a location where 'sovereignty' and 'extraction' went hand in hand with a process of domination (Mbembe 2001b, 183). We shall see that this account of the colony is broadly related to elements of the French empire in Africa.

Within the colony, Mbembe argues, a state of 'occupation' existed. This could be divided into three essential properties. Firstly, it represented a way of 'acquiring sovereignty' for the colonizing power; secondly, it was militaristic and relied on warfare undertaken by the colonizers; and thirdly, it dispossessed the colonized of their land. The colonial power becomes the ultimate owner of the territory (Mbembe 2001b, 183). This grim reality was obscured by colonizers who claimed to be conquering 'uninhabited and masterless' land.

The native

But the colony was not empty, Mbembe reminds us. Many colonized territories had been inhabited for thousands of years, and those who resided there were forced into a 'colonial relationship.' In this relationship, the colonized were defined as 'natives.' This term condensed a number of dehumanizing assumptions. The creation of the 'native' as a category within colonial governance consisted of three elements, which closely mirrored Western relationships with the animal world: the 'native' was appropriated by the colonist, a process of familiarization then occurred between both parties, and, finally, the 'native' was put to use by the colonist for the purposes of extracting profit from the colony. In the eyes of the colonist, Mbembe contends, the 'native' was really 'an instrument' for this purpose (Mbembe 2001b, 183).

Mbembe's term 'native' has considerable parallels to the historical administrative term *indigène* (native person), which was used in Francophone Africa to distinguish between those Africans who were 'citizens,' theoretically with the same rights as their metropolitan French counterparts, and the majority of 'subjects' ('natives') who enjoyed lesser rights. 'Indigènes' were subject to a special legal code and lacked political representation until the Lamine-Guèye law of May 7, 1946 (Genova 2004, 56). The category of 'native' was not only a tool of the colonizer, but it also had a significant influence on the way that Africans thought about themselves, shutting down potential avenues for self-expression and thought long into the postcolonial period.

COMMANDEMENT

Within the colony, a relation of power bound 'native' to 'colonist.' This relation is identified by Mbembe as the *commandement*.

Mbembe sees the *commandement* as an unchallengeable power relationship, in which the colonizer dominates the colonized using cruelty and caprice. *Commandement* itself was not located within a single institution or specific policy (recalling Foucault's account of power as being based in relations and not institutions), rather it was located in the *relation* of authority between colonizer and colonized.

Commandement, Mbembe argues, is really an expression of political power or 'colonial sovereignty.' In Europe, states exercised power or 'sovereignty' through some sense of legitimacy or 'right,' and, Mbembe argues, developed a model of 'liberal... debate and discussion.' The colonial state (and hence 'colonial sovereignty' or power) lacked this legitimacy. In the colony, the very idea of the functioning of government became debased. Justice became a 'right of conquest' for the colonizer, and there was no legal recourse for colonized peoples who had been the victim of abuses. In the colony, the law did not function in the same way as in European states, and colonizers acted with a certain impunity (Mbembe 2001b, 24–25).

Violence was key to the way that *commandement* worked. This was closely related to its lack of legitimacy or 'right.' Mbembe argues that colonizers relied on violence at every stage in the process of colonial conquest and rule. He distinguishes between violence used in founding colonial states, such as in wars of conquest, and the violence needed just to continue the daily work of ruling, including shoring up the legitimacy of the colonial state, and making sure that colonial rule survived (Mbembe 2001b, 25). Critically, this violence became diffused throughout every aspect of life in the colony. It did not just involve acts of war or plunder; it also contained manifold ordinary instances of what today we might call 'microaggressions (Mbembe 2017c).' Violence in the colony had therefore become 'miniaturiz[ed]' into daily life. The merest act could bring punishment from colonial officials or their agents.

Mbembe's use of *commandement* is often generalized, but it is related to the history of the French empire in Africa. He draws the term from a colonial source, albeit one that used it in a far less dramatic fashion: a French district commander's account of his career in Niger (Delavignette 2018). Sweeping and discriminatory law codes existed across colonial Africa, creating a situation where there was one law for the colonizers and another for the colonized. France's overbearing 'native' (law) code or *code de l'indigénat* was introduced in Senegal in 1887, and later elsewhere in French West, and Equatorial Africa (AOF/AEF). It had severe provisions including imposing collective penalties on whole villages, as well as corporal punishment, and forced unpaid work (Aldrich 1996, 213; Mann 2009, 331).

Critically, there was also the element of caprice identified by Mbembe in *commandement* as individual colonial officials often had the final say regarding its application, and there was little oversight to ensure that they acted fairly. Among over 20 offences, according to an 1888 law in Algeria, were those designed explicitly to force submission to colonial officials, including penalizing disrespectful or offensive conduct towards a representative of the colonial authorities, and refusal to give food, water, fuel, or transport to administrators (Aldrich 1996, 213). Local rulers who opposed the French were exiled: Algerian leader Abd al-Qadir (1808–1883) was sent to Syria, while Senegalese cleric Amadou Bamba (1853–1927) was exiled to Gabon and Mauritania (Launay and Soares 1999, 509; Mcdougall 2017, 49–85). Critically, however, colonized peoples repeatedly challenged colonial rule, and there is little indication that historical laws, no matter how discriminatory, were quite as overbearing as Mbembe's theoretical construct of *commandement*.

The properties of commandement

Despite his reluctance to locate the colonial power relation of *commandement* in actual institutions or individuals, Mbembe argues that it has four recognizable properties. Mbembe is sometimes prone to using lists, but this one helps us to get a clearer picture of his slippery concept of *commandement*. First, Mbembe argues, *commandement* (and also colonial rule, more generally) was based on a regime of exception. Within this regime of exception, there were no rights and no law, and a classic Mbembian example of this were the wars of colonial conquest at the turn of the nineteenth and twentieth centuries in Africa. Second, *commandement* entailed a system of privileges and immunities for those in power. It paid to preside over the brutal system of colonial rule, and back-handers flowed for those who succeeded in doing so. Third, *commmandement* claimed a moral mission (despite being brutal). It alleged that it was 'civilizing' colonial subjects and helping them attain European social norms. Fourth and finally, *commandement* displayed a faulty or circular logic. It made use of all manner of 'procedures,' 'techniques,' and forms of knowledge. But these did not focus on public good, as colonists often claimed, and frequently encouraged submission. One might think of endless and pointless form-filling, or lengthy protocol and ceremony that serves no real purpose. Ultimately, *commandement*, Mbembe reminds us, was about securing compliance.

LIFE IN THE COLONY: FORMS OF 'COLONIAL CIVILITY' AND 'PUBLIC RATIONALITY'

We have seen how Mbembe stresses the one-sidedness and force of colonial power, but we have so far heard little about Africans' abilities to navigate this unequal landscape. Mbembe is far clearer on the repressive dimensions of life in the colony than he is on African abilities to resist colonial rule (Mbembe 1989a; 1989b). Despite racist injustice, African culture and social relations continued to develop within the colony. If we ignore this fact, we risk assuming that Africans were somehow passive victims of colonial power. Elements in Mbembe's earlier work open a pathway for understanding everyday life in the colony.

Mbembe uses two important terms to describe colonial life: 'colonial civility' and 'public forms of rationality.' 'Colonial civility' indicates new forms of urban behaviour, culture, and emotion that emerged under colonialism. These included new social manners and cultural activities. Not simply material, these developments had underestimated psychological and emotional implications, Mbembe argues, mobilizing desire, and envy. Colonial subjects experienced a new 'psychic economy,' and forged a 'type of 'urbanity' that Mbembe identifies as 'colonial civility' (Mbembe 1996b, 9). Although urbane and refined, this African 'colonial civility' was nonetheless formed against a background of violence and racial discrimination.

'Colonial civility' formed a backdrop to the exercise of a 'public rationality.' This latter term describes the new forms of agency and action open to Africans navigating colonial rule. Mbembe draws on Foucault's understanding of 'rationality,' which the latter sees as the distinct ways in which different institutions seek to control the social and physical world. This 'public rationality' simultaneously challenged the hierarchies of colonial life and at the same time revealed the depth of colonial subjects' subjugation to colonial rule. Colonial subjects were thus caught in a double bind of simultaneously 'submitting to power relations' and acting 'as the moral agents of their actions…' (Mbembe 1990a; 1996b, 10–11). Even though this predicament was constrained by colonialism, colonial subjects nonetheless both expressed themselves and created new identities (Mbembe 1996b, 10).

Colonial domination was therefore only ever contingent, and colonial influences could be selectively drawn upon by Africans (Cooper and Stoler 1997, 6; Lawrence et al. 2006, 4–10). Mbembe's early work on Christianity in Africa had itself suggested that African responses to Roman Catholicism could selectively draw on aspects of the religion, without submitting to every aspect of its theology, which Cameroonians associated with colonialism (Mbembe 1988; 1989a; 1996b, 10). Elsewhere on the continent, examples of cultural innovation during colonial rule can be seen in the flourishing newspapers of 1920s and 1930s Nigeria (Jones 2019, 57). Yoruba journalist Isaac Babalola Thomas (1896–1961) pioneered a serialized narrative 'Life Story of Me, Segilola' for his newspaper *Akede Eko* (Lagos Herald) in which a jaded and now disgraced courtesan shares with the reader tales of the good times and her urban adventures in Lagos (Barber 2012).

CONCLUSION

Mbembe identifies the colony as a core site of unequal power relations in Africa that continued into the 'postcolony,' as we will see in the next chapter. *Commandement* or an unequal imposition of power by the colonizer over 'the native' typifies the asymmetry of life in the colony. Colonial subjects, Mbembe contends, were relegated to the status of 'natives.' They were subject to the arbitrary and circular whim of colonial power, with no real protection in law. Against this bleak situation, Mbembe nonetheless admits that possibilities existed for African subjects to control their situations. His accounts of civility and rationality illustrate two ways in which individuals navigated life in the colony. Not merely coping strategies, these activities represented creative and even subversive responses to colonial occupation. Critically, they ranged widely in scope, including matters of emotional life, psychology, religious belief, and cultural production.

LE CODE DE L'INDIGÉNAT

Most colonized peoples in the French empire had a distinct legal status from French 'citizens' and were instead deemed 'subjects' who lacked political representation. Indigenous men were made to pay the *capitation* or head-tax, with French officials arguing that such taxation was necessary to pay for public works projects. In general, a high degree of power was placed in the hands of European administrators on the ground and their African representatives, such as soldiers and judges, who could sometimes act with impunity (Aldrich 1996, 213; Mann 2009, 331).

ISAAC BABALOLA THOMAS (1888–1963)

Mbembe describes a 'public rationality' in the colony, where Africans began to make their own cultural forms despite the backdrop of European occupation. Yoruba newspaperman Thomas obtained the financial support of Nigerian nationalist Herbert Macaulay (1864–1946) to edit the *Akede Eko* (Lagos Herald), which pioneered a number of forms, including the serialized novel *Segilola Eleyinju Ege* (The Life Story of Me, Segilola) which explored the life of faded courtesan Segilola, who recounts her life as a prostitute in Lagos (Babilola 1985, 187; Barber 2012). Other Yoruba writers soon created their own novels, such as *Igbehin A Dun tabi Omo Orukun* (The sweet shall succeed the bitter, or the orphan) by editor of *Eleti Ofe* (News-monger) Awobo Akinitan (1890–1953) (Babilola 1985, 167).

3

THE POSTCOLONY

The 'postcolony' might superficially be understood as referring to the 'actually exiting' nations that succeeded the 'colony' at independence. There were ample examples of authoritarianism in postcolonial African states (Adesanmi 2004, 227; Nugent 2004, 204). But Mbembe's term 'postcolony' is much wider than this common-sense reference point. It also designates a generalized situation of corruption and misrule. Mbembe refers to only a few specific postcolonial states, chiefly Cameroon, the Republic of Congo, and Togo, leading some critics to discern a vagueness in Mbembe's term (Quayson 2001). Presiding over the 'postcolony' is the abstract but powerful figure of the 'potentate' or dictator (Mbembe 1992c; 1996a). Like the colonial rulers before him, he (and Mbembe repeatedly genders him as male) dominates his subjects, possesses the power to kill them, and allegedly wields supernatural power. In this dystopian and unequal society, spectacle is all important. Those who are ruled must continually be impressed by lavish and violent public displays orchestrated by the autocrat.

Mbembe provides us with a gruesome example of power in the postcolony from the Cameroonian newspaper *La Gazette*'s report on a Douala execution during the 1980s:

> The priest and the pastor who were there came up and called on [the condemned] to pray. To no avail. The soldiers who were to carry out the execution—there were twenty-four of them, twelve for each man—advanced in line, marching in step, under the command of a captain and came to a halt at thirty metres range: twelve kneeling, twelve standing. At the command of the captain, "Ready!" the soldiers cocked their rifles and took aim. "Fire!": a short, terrible burst drowned the cries of the condemned. Twelve bullets moving at 800 metres per second. Then the coup de grace. And, incredible but true, the crowd broke into frenzied applause, as if it was the end of a good show.
>
> (Mbembe 2001b, 112)

In this execution, which takes place before assembled dignitaries and passers-by, the bodies of the condemned are quite literally broken by the will of the postcolonial dictator. Spectators gain an impression of the power of the Cameroonian authoritarian state by attending the scene. They enthusiastically participate in events, even though many of them might be counted among those oppressed by the dictator Paul Biya (1933–).

POLITICAL LIFE IN THE POSTCOLONY

How can people live from day to day in the postcolony? The *clando* is a clandestine 'taxi man who doesn't get stopped at road-blocks and doesn't have papers – he just mentions his name.' He is one inhabitant of a dystopian world where everything can be negotiated and bought for a price (Mbembe 2001b, 125). Checkpoints on urban roads, where public officials sought bribes from motorists, became a commonplace symbol of social and economic problems in Cameroon and other countries. In Jean-Marie Téno's 1996 film *Clando*, Anatole Sobgui, an IT worker from Douala, Cameroon, turns to driving taxis after his career collapses when he is exposed as sympathetic to the regime's opponents. Weathering the hard life of driving clandestine cabs,

Sobgui still finds himself targeted by the government and decides to move to Cologne, only to ultimately return to Cameroon and connect with local dissidents (Videau 1997, 144). The world in which Sobgui finds himself in the informal taxi trade is one which typifies Mbembe's postcolony. Sobgui's fall from his professional career as a result of government persecution reflects the long arm of the postcolonial dictator.

In the postcolony, Mbembe explains, salaried employees often haven't been paid for months. Some have found that it is more profitable to take bribes and kick-backs than to wait for a salary cheque to arrive. This is a generalized predicament of political and economic collapse that Mbembe terms 'indirect private government.' This form of politics feeds on 'off the books' and informal relations, including graft and corruption. The State, which one might expect to be at the centre of an authoritarian regime, in fact, plays a minor role in most areas of the postcolony. It remains a hollow shell bypassed by opportunistic coercion (Mbembe 1999a, 103, 2001b, 83). These bleak conditions occurred in a number of African states during the 1980s as governments tried to implement spending cuts recommended by the International Monetary Fund to become eligible for foreign loans (Cooper 2004, 74).

Commandement in the postcolony

We have met *commandement* in the colony, but Mbembe sees this power relation as continuing into the postcolony. He identifies several aspects as key to the functioning of power in the postcolony, including the existence of states of exception, a system of privileges and immunities for those able to get close to senior officials or the dictator, a blurring between the political project of ruling and the moral project of civilizing, circularity, which in the postcolony is usually seen as the use of jargon and pomp, and, finally, widespread banditry and violence. These qualities are essentially similar to the functioning of *commandement* in the colony (Mbembe 2001b, 84).

Above all, these characteristics of power in the postcolony are linked to a *privatization* of power. Going about things by the book gets people nowhere, and instead, power is thought of in terms of the personal relationships one can establish, ideally with the dictator or his henchmen (Mbembe 1999a). Not only are the relationships that create political power privatized but so too are public assets (Smith 2007, 5–7). Mines, oil refineries, and airports largely stop working, and instead are sold off to the highest bidder, often for the profit of the respective government minister. All of this is to say that the power of the state has been 'socialized': it does not exist in government but has spilled out into external society. Government resources can be redirected into private pockets (Mbembe 1999a).

In the postcolony, violence is essential. Mbembe uses the examples of checkpoints, random security checks where police, soldiers, or militia seek bribes, as a key example of this generalized, everyday violence. The *clando* taxi drivers like the protagonist of Téno's film frequently have to negotiate these, and those drivers in the know have special passes to get through the checkpoints with minimum financial loss. Mbembe uses the term *tonton-macoutism* to describe this violence, drawing on the Haitian Creole term *Tonton-macoute*, which described the armed militia formed under the François Duvalier (1907–1971) regime in that country, and tasked with violent activities on behalf of power (Mbembe 1999a, 109). Checkpoints are just the most visible form of pervasive violence that also includes military attacks on business and seizures of private property.

Life in the postcolony I: Conviviality

Given the brutal reality of life in the postcolony, we might be surprised that Mbembe uses the term 'conviviality' to describe a major dimension of relations between the dictator and his subjects. Conviviality seems to describe a cheery and joyful state of affairs. What can it mean to have a 'convivial' relationship with the postcolonial dictator?

For Mbembe the relationship of conviviality is one that is characterized neither by 'resistance' nor 'collaboration.' Instead, it bursts out in ludic moments of humour and comedy that do little to overthrow the dictator and stop his abuses

(Mbembe 2001b, 84). More surprisingly, this relationship between the dictator and his subjects is an intimate one where both parties 'share the same living space' (Mbembe 2001b, 104).

All roads lead back to the power of the potentate, and under 'convivial' relations in the postcolony jokes and humour only underline the dictator's power. Citizens are not simply oppressed in any straightforward sense. They can mock the dictator (as we see in the next section), but this poking fun only makes the potentate more powerful. They can even pick apart the jargon of the dictator, but this too does little to erase his power. Mbembe allows subjects to go as far as 'tear[ing] apart the gods that African autocrats aspire to be' (Mbembe 2001b, 112). Yet his account of this picking apart of the taboos of power stops far short of a more generalized account of resistance. It appears that the citizens of the postcolony are trapped in their own 'convivial' relationship with the autocrat.

Life in the postcolony II: The grotesque and the obscene

The convivial relation between the dictator and his subjects relies on humour. It might not seem like a funny situation, but life in the postcolony gives both oppressor and oppressed the occasion to have a laugh (Mbembe 1992c; 1992d). Mbembe here is thinking back to Foucault's account of power (examined in Chapter 2), and his argument that power exists in relations, not institutions, and that it must be actively maintained or it will be lost. Humour, especially in its grotesque and obscene forms, plays a key role in maintaining the power of the dictator.

Both the grotesque and the obscene violate the aura of authority surrounding the dictator. Mbembe is particularly interested in cultural and symbolic representations of power, including the sexual and digestive functions of the dictator. 'An image such as that of the presidential anus,' Mbembe explains, once demystified in the subversive humour of the governed, 'is brought down to earth' and 'it becomes nothing more than a common garden-variety arse that defecates like any other' (Mbembe 2001b, 112). Mbembe sees popular humour as puncturing the 'taboo' that protects 'the totem' of presidential power. In using terms like 'totem,' 'fetish,' and 'taboo,' Mbembe is deliberately using highly controversial terminology with considerable colonial baggage in European ethnographic writing about African beliefs (Roca 2015, 105–111).

The significance of Mbembe's account of the grotesque is that he sees it as subverting political power, but only to a certain point. By joking about the dictator's phallus or anus, people are bringing him down to earth, and seeing him as being like anyone else. In placing such social importance on the grotesque, Mbembe is drawing on the analysis of Russian critic Mikhail Bakhtin (1895–1975), who argued that humour had socially subversive consequences, particularly in the carnivals of medieval Europe. On this special occasion, boundaries could be crossed, and powerful people could be questioned – at least as long as these activities fell within the boundaries of humour (Renfrew 2015, 130–137). Bakhtin saw evidence for this in the work of Renaissance poet François Rabelais (1483/1494–1553), and especially how Rabelais used imagery connected to 'food, defecation, and sexual life.' Bakhtin regarded this earthy humour as reflecting a widely existing and suppressed 'folk humour' (Bakhtin 1984, 18). All of this meant that laughing about earthy subjects was a form of popular criticism of power only permitted in certain environments, like carnival. In a colonial and postcolonial context, the grotesque retained carnival's potential to 'transgress' colonial boundaries (Edwards and Graulund 2013, 124). Critically, the subversive potential of this type of humour only lasts as long as it is sanctioned by the powers that be. When carnival ends, so too does the joke, and oppression's heavy fist returns.

Mbembe's focus on the grotesque in the postcolony allows us to take seriously areas of life that might otherwise be ignored or seen as coarse and vulgar. This includes the violent execution explored earlier in this chapter, which from this perspective can be seen as a display serving to prop up political power. It comprises the vulgar and sexual rumours and jokes that swirl around the autocrat and his henchmen. Focusing on such material enables a 'shift [in] our perspective.' We can understand how the dictator 'dramatize[s] [his] own magnificence,' and amplifies his power in practical terms. More generally we must also appreciate how much of the dictator's daily activities are performances. The potentate offers ceremonies 'as spectacles' for the governed (Mbembe 2001b, 84). At the same time we can see how at the very moment the dictator tries to display and perform his power, elements of subversion still creep in. A story of sexual conquest, for example, might simply collapse into popular mockery of the autocrat's sexual capacity. As theorist Judith Butler (1956–) has argued, the very process of the 'ratification' (or authorization) of state power simultaneously becomes 'the site for the subtle *de*-authorization' of this same power (Butler 1992, 68). In this way, the potentate's power is slowly eaten away, even as it builds itself up. Whether or not this process of eating away actually comes close to toppling the dictator is far from clear.

Life in the postcolony III: Hallucinatory power

Power in the postcolony is 'hallucinatory.' This is to say that it goes beyond everyday experience, and, in its excesses, seems unreal. Language plays a key role in creating this 'hallucinatory' or excessive quality of power. Jargon or *langue de bois* with its tedium, pointlessness, and circularity is an ideal candidate for provoking hallucinations. Mbembe gives some examples of the tedium including 'rhetorical devices,' such as 'repetition,' 'lists,' 'superlatives,' 'hyperbole,' and bizarre expressions. While jargon might just seem plain boring, this language works to move the subject 'beyond reality.' The vaguer the language, the more one feels unmoored and lost on a sea of equivocation (Mbembe 2001b, 118).

Titles and honorifics form a classic area for 'hallucinatory' protocol. The potentate receives title after title, each bolder than before. Ahidjo's titles included 'Father of the Nation,' 'Great Comrade,' 'Apostle of Peace,' 'Providential Guide,' 'Indefatigable Builder of the Nation,' and even 'The Great Peasant' (Mbembe 2001b, 120). The haemorrhaging of these titles creates a 'verbal trance,' that relies on the sonic aspects of oral repetition, where 'the particular arrangement of sound... brings on a state of "possession"' (Mbembe 2001b, 118).

Cumulatively 'hallucinatory power' produces 'fables and unreal images.' Along with its ceremony, the effect of this giddying linguistic trip is to 'zombify' or stupefy subjects into their 'convivial' relation with the potentate (Mbembe 2001b, 104, 118).

Boring language is accompanied by banal protocol, including the endless waiting, lining up and processing around the dictator. In the execution described earlier in this chapter, an entire array of civic functionaries and priests were required to turn up at a roundabout to witness the deaths. It is as though the Cameroonian state itself were on show. Ultimately, the dead weight of protocol slowly eats away at one's sanity (Mbembe 2001b, 118).

THE BODY OF THE POSTCOLONIAL POTENTATE

We have described the conditions of life in the postcolony, but we have not fully considered the body of the potentate himself. This, after all, forms the staple of popular humour and subversive jokes.

Popular perceptions of the postcolonial dictator: Sexuality and the occult

In the postcolony, the body of the dictator is everywhere and unavoidable; his photograph adorns schools and torture chambers alike. He is present within the very fabric of everyday experience (Mbembe 2001b, 155–156). This omnipresence of the dictator is not simply some Mbembian whimsy; actual dictators behaved in this manner. Ugandan dictator Idi Amin (c. 1925–2003), for instance, 'would regularly demonstrate his sexual voracity' as well as being 'famously gluttonous' (Karlström 2003, 71). The autocrat's power was sometimes believed to have occult dimensions (Mbembe 2001b, 160). Central African dictator Jean-Bedel Bokassa (1921–1996) 'encouraged the notion that he was a formidable sorcerer' and that 'secret rituals, perhaps involving cannibalism, had given him extraordinary powers,' including reading people's minds and being in several places at once (Titley 1997, 49–50). The dictator is seen in monstrous and animal terms, particularly when these are linked to supernatural meaning. He is 'not only [a] vampire. He also appears as a reptile. He is a boa' (Mbembe 2001b, 162). Mobutu Sese Seko's (1930–1997) *authenticité* campaign in Zaire included his use of a carved cane 'embodying symbols connoting power and courage,' as well as his name change from Joseph-Désiré Mobutu to Mobutu Sese Seko or the 'all-conquering warrior who triumphs over all obstacles' (Nugent 2004, 235).

The dictator's ability to eat

The dictator is a paragon of excessive appetite, whether for food, sex, or the devouring of his enemies through execution or liquidation (Mbembe 1991c, 170; 2001b, 160). The arrogance of power extends beyond the potentate to his henchmen. Mbembe draws on Congolese novelist Sony Labou Tansi's novel *Life and a Half* to illustrate the behaviour of these henchmen, who act as 'kings of the bush,' enjoying 'practically unlimited rights over those in their charge' (Labou Tansi 2011; Mbembe 2001b, 160). These prerogatives include widespread sexual and physical abuse; Mbembe invokes the feudal *droit de cuissage* or the seigneurial sexual rights supposedly exercised in medieval Europe by a lord over young women under his jurisdiction as a parallel to the entitlement of the potentate and his henchmen (Boureau 1998).

Digestion and scatological imagery also play a key role in popular fascination with the dictator's authority. 'The obesity of men in power,' or, 'more crudely, the flow of shit from such a physique' was a particular source of interest (Mbembe 2001b, 107). Mbembe equates the ability to eat, including metaphorically to consume people, money, and luxury goods, with the dictator's display of power. Although this may appear strange, it is a comparison that is well supported in the anthropology of Cameroon. Bayart uses the phrase the 'politics of the belly' to describe a model of political authority where 'big [or powerful] men' have the capacity to 'eat' endless resources and, critically, to defecate them out or redistribute them to their poorer followers (Bayart 1993, 233).

Cumulatively, the body of the potentate, including his ubiquitous use of the obscene and grotesque weaves together a mix of 'of fascination and dread' that 'enclos[es]' the governed. All of this creates 'a sort of consciousness whose peculiar feature is to be hallucinated' (Mbembe 2001b, 165). In the final assessment, Mbembe is clear that relations in the postcolony are profoundly unequal. 'Hallucinated' postcolonial subjects are reduced to 'beast[s] of burden' of the Potentate, who 'sits on his subject's back, harnesses him, and rides him' (Mbembe 2001b, 167).

CRITIQUES OF THE POSTCOLONY

Mbembe's vision of the postcolony has had enormous influence on the study of African and postcolonial cultures. Yet scholars have repeatedly expressed reservations about Mbembe's account. If his idea of the postcolony serves as a 'powerful heuristic [exploratory] term,' it has nonetheless proved 'difficult' to 'build upon' and assimilate into subsequent research (Adebanwi and Orock 2022, 47; Karlström 2003, 57). Memorable elements of Mbembe's account, including the Douala execution examined above (previously discussed by Mbembe in a 1991 article (Mbembe 1991c)), remain hard to tie down: Mbembe does not tell us what crimes the accused had been convicted of, why the audience celebrated, or whether such spectacles were unusual or not (Coronil 1992, 92).

More generally, Mbembe's understanding of the postcolony is often treated in isolation. In fact, he was just one of a number of African scholars working on parallel lines in Paris during the 1980s. For example, Mbembe himself acknowledges Comi Toulabor's research on the carnivalesque in African politics (Toulabor 1981, 55; 1986, 1994, 59) in his 'Provisional Notes.' We consider four key critiques of Mbembe's account of the postcolony below.

Critique I: The postcolony as unreflective of African politics

Considering Mbembe's discussion of 'private indirect governance,' critic Ato Quayson points out how his discussion 'sweeps across Africa without situating... finer points of distinction' between different examples of state collapse. Still, more significantly, Mbembe gives little account here of how African governments attempted to organize transitions of power (Quayson 2001, 160). This risks minimizing the agency of African states. It says little about the potential checks and balances on personal power that exist within such political cultures. More generally, Mbembe does not articulate the promises of an earlier era of independence and nationalism and, as Quayson pointedly asks, if the dictatorships were 'failed dreams of transition,' then 'what were the dreams?'

Critique II: The grotesque makes value judgements about the postcolony

Mbembe's concept of the 'vulgarity' of power, including the grotesque and the obscene, has been criticized for not openly stating its assumptions. To label something grotesque implies a moral judgement. Against what value systems are the 'grotesque' and the 'obscene' defined in different societies, and how does the role they play differ between cultures? Although Mbembe has critiqued scholars who treat Africa as different to the rest of the world, he himself comes close to doing precisely this (Trouillot 1992, 98). Some of Mbembe's descriptions of the postcolonial dictator read almost as though they were taken from his critique of the 'first narrative' of colonial discourse on Africa, particularly regarding the occult and violence.

Critique III: The postcolony doesn't allow for popular resistance to authoritarianism

Above all, the prospects for resisting and overthrowing the dictator are unclear in Mbembe's account. Humour and risqué jokes only go so far and do not lead to full-scale revolution. From this perspective, Mbembe reflects a 'radical pessimism' about widespread opposition or 'popular political subjectivity' more generally (Karlström 2003, 61). Granted, Mbembe allows that resistance of a kind is possible, but this is limited to individual and inconclusive interventions. Mbembe has little to say about groups and how people can organize to contest political oppression (Coronil 1992, 105). All of this could be seen as forming a kind of 'Afro-pessimism' or belief that African politics and affairs must necessarily end badly. Ultimately, as one critic puts it, Mbembe's postcolony says little about 'how to save the African continent...' (Mudimbe 1992, 62).

Critique IV: Does the postcolony make sense beyond Cameroon?

All of this raises the question of how accurate Mbembe's account of the postcolony really is. Quayson has asked how Cameroon 'come[s] to occupy' the position of 'articulating in and of itself the whole reality' of misrule in Africa (Quayson 2001, 161). Can Cameroon encompass all of Africa and the entire postcolonial period? It is true that Mbembe draws on a relatively dense body of quotes from Republic of Congo/Congo-Brazzaville novelist Labou Tansi, but the distinction between the experience of Cameroon under dictators Ahidjo and Biya, and that of Congo-Brazzaville under Denis Sassou-Nguesso (r. 1979–1992, 1997–) is not made clear.

CONCLUSION

Towering above Mbembe's account of postcolonial autocracy and decline is the figure of the postcolonial potentate, whose bodily needs are writ large across society. His portrait adorns the walls of torture chambers and classrooms alike. In the postcolony, power has been privatized. The dictator and his officials turn the state to their benefit, as do functionaries at all levels. Ultimately, the dictator is all powerful and he can literally smash the bodies of his opponents. This often occurs in the form of public spectacles, like the executions in Douala, which also serve to re-enforce the power of the dictator.

If this seems like a bleak prognosis, we must remember that within the postcolony a convivial relation also exists. The subjects of the potentate acquiesce in their own oppression and eagerly help craft jokes and 'take-downs' that unwittingly perpetuate the powerful myth of the dictator. The bizarreness and violence of life in the postcolony, including boring elements like protocol, procedure and ceremony help to numb the brain, distract from reality, and produce a sense of hallucinogenic power. No matter what they have suffered, the inhabitants of the postcolony are doomed to a progressive 'zombification.'

THE POSTCOLONY AND FRANCOPHONE NOVELISTS

A small number of Francophone African writers play a major role in Mbembe's thought. Their writings often appear as cited and uncited reference points in Mbembe's prose, including his description of the autocrat's henchmen we saw above. They also influence Mbembe's own concepts, particularly in relation to his account of the African postcolony.

SONY LABOU TANSI (1947–1995)

Sony Labou Tansi was a Congolese novelist and serves as a key reference point in Mbembe's writing on the postcolony. Labou Tansi's dystopian novels reveal misrule and repression in a postcolonial African state closely paralleling Congo-Brazzaville. Novels such as *L'état honteux* [The Shameful State] and *La vie et demie* [Life and a Half] depict fictitious states riven by cruel and dictatorial regimes (Labou Tansi 1995, 2011, 2015). In both novels, the body, sex, and death play a key role, as well as the lingering cruelty of the dictator (Riesz and Allen 2000, 117). *L'état honteux* recounts the 40-year reign of Colonel Martillimi Lopez in a fictional African state. In *La vie et demie*, a fictional republic of Katamalanasia suffers under the misrule of successive dictatorial regimes (Ndiaye 2000, 113). Born in the Belgian Congo in 1947 as Marcel Ntsoni, Labou Tansi moved to Congo-Brazzaville aged 12. He was educated at the *École Normale supérieure d'afrique*, before teaching French and English, and a career in several government ministries, eventually being elected to parliament in 1992 and dying at age 48 (Nzabatsinda 2009). Labou Tansi wrote novels in French, published by the prestigious French publishing house Seuil, as well as poetry in Kikongo, and his plays were performed in both France and Congo-Brazzaville (Clark and Ricard 2000, 37).

YAMBO OUOLOGUEM (1940–)

Yambo Ouologuem's fiction connects the precolonial, colonial, and postcolonial periods of Africa's history. Ouologuem never lets us forget that postcolonial African politics is no utopia. Poet and novelist born in Bandiagara, Mali in 1940, Ouologuem won the *Prix Renaudot* for his 1968 novel Bound to Violence (*Le Devoir de violence*). *Devoir* trenchantly criticizes colonialism, as well as romantic notions of precolonial Africa, and offers an account of the tyrannical rule of postcolonial despotism. These themes align with Mbembe's thought on knowledge about Africa's past, as well as his critique of authoritarianism in the postcolony. Ouologuem later published '*Letter to Black France*' (1969), '*The Thousand and One Bibles of Sex*' under the pseudonym Utto Rodolph, and a school textbook '*Lands of Sun*' (Hawkins 2002, 195; Ouédrago 2003a; Ouologuem 1971, 2003; 2015; Wise 1999).

AHMADOU KOUROUMA (1927–2003)

Kourouma's fiction also frequently appears as a reference point in Mbembe's writings. Exiled from Ivory Coast as an alleged coup conspirator in 1963, Kourouma lived in Algeria where he wrote *Les Soleils des Indépendances* (*The Suns of Independence* (1968)) (Corcoran 2007, 92). Kourouma's novel *En attendant le vote des bêtes sauvages* (Waiting for the Vote of Wild Animals (1998)) examines a favourite Mbembian theme of postcolonial dictatorships, eschewing a recognizable authorial voice in favour of a framing narrative based on the ritual *donsomana* or Malinké hunting brotherhood. Kourouma also experimented linguistically, adopting an innovative form of French that he attempted to fit to the syntax and rhythms of Malinké, his mother tongue (Corcoran 2007, 94–95; Julien 2006, 678). Born in 1927, Kourouma spent part of his childhood in Guinea as well as his native country, before studying at the École primaire supérieure in Bamako. *Monnew (Monné, outrages et défis)* (Monnew (Monné, insults and challenges)) his second novel did not appear until 1990, and *Allah n'est pas obligé* (Allah is Not Obliged) in 2000 (Ouédraogo 2003b).

4
THE NOCTURNAL SPHERE AND NECROPOLITICS

Death and the dead play a key social role in Mbembe's thought. From his early work on Cameroon to his well-known elaboration of 'necropolitics,' Mbembe sees death as playing an important role in the world of the living. Death creeps among the living and targets certain groups of people who are then judged to lack the rights and social status usually accorded to human beings: they are consigned to the status of the living dead (De Boeck 1998, 50).

This idea of a 'living death' mapped out by neglect, casual labour, or the denial of basic rights, is also increasingly familiar in the contemporary world. Perhaps unsurprisingly, Mbembe's term 'necropolitics' is drawn on extensively in both mainstream media and academic discourse (Estévez 2021; Haritaworn, and Kunstman 2014; Ringer 2021). COVID-19 health inequalities, police brutality, and prison reform have all been understood in relation to the abandonment of certain groups such as low-income patients, ethnic minorities, or stigmatized prisoners to a form of 'living death' shorn of the basic rights that the rest of society enjoys (Grunawalt 2021; Robertson and Travaglia 2020; Sandset 2021, 1411).

Mbembe's early thought about death in colonial Cameroon provides an important context to 'necropolitics' and remains rarely explored. It maps out the way in which the dead in southern Cameroonian cultures had pivotal social and political roles. In the context of France's violent war of decolonization in Cameroon (1955–1964) and the subsequent authoritarian regime of Ahidjo, Mbembe shows how it was the dead rather than the living that provided the authority to challenge political oppression.

'THOSE WHO MOVE BY NIGHT': THE POLITICAL LIFE OF THE DEAD IN SOUTHERN CAMEROON AND RUBEN UM NOYBÈ'S DREAM DIARIES

The realm of the dead was termed 'the nocturnal sphere' (and the world of the living the 'daytime' or 'diurnal' sphere) in a number of southern Cameroonian cultures (Delaney and Mbuh 2010, 63–64; Laburthe-Tolra 1985). Um Nyobè's own ethnic group, the Bassa-Bakoko (known as the Bassa) shared this worldview. While the daytime world was seen as 'visible,' the 'nocturnal sphere' remained 'invisible' (Mbembe 1996b, 384). Both realms were implicated in each other, but symbolic power was accorded to the world of the night. Only those proficient in occult arts, including witches and dream diviners, were adept at navigating this night-time world, whether for good or ill (Argenti 2007, 2; Atangana 2010, 167–168). These people could also leave their bodies by night and undergo physical transformations. The 'double' of a person could undertake a nocturnal journey for diverse purposes, including devouring their enemies, or protecting themselves from such 'invisible' attacks by others (Mbembe 1996b, 385).

The important role of the dead in the world of the living, including through warnings or insights into the future, differed from European colonists' perceptions of life and death. During the colonial period, this sphere represented a cultural space where colonial rule could be challenged, and alternative ideas of power and authority were advanced. In the independence war,

Mbembe argues, there was a revitalization of traditions linked to the nocturnal world, including secret societies, divination, dream interpretation, and measures to protect against bullets (Mbembe 1996b, 381, 390; Nkwi 2019, 390). These were not only practical responses to war and political uncertainty, they also harnessed the power of the dead.

Mbembe views the dreams of the nationalist leader Ruben Um Nyobè as showing how the world of the dead was intimately involved with the fight against the French (Mbembe 1985, 459, 1991a, 90–91). Um Nyobè and the Union of Cameroonian Peoples (UPC) had turned to armed conflict following the July 13, 1955 French banning of the UPC, with the situation being exacerbated by a July 1957 British ban (Terretta 2010, 195; 2013). Um Nyobè was hunted by the French army in the rainforests of the southern *Sanaga Maritime* region of Cameroon until his September 13, 1958 death at the hands of a French military patrol (Deltombe and Domergue 2011; Deltombe, Domergue, and Tatsitsa 2016; Mbembe 1986c; 2016f; Terretta 2005, 79).

The nocturnal sphere: The public 'rationality' of dreams and dreaming

In our discussion of the 'colony,' we have seen how Mbembe described the ways that Africans navigated colonial society as a 'public rationality.' He makes a parallel argument about dreams. While it might seem unrelated to the world of the dead, dreaming was a nocturnal activity perceived in southern Cameroon to have direct links to the world of the deceased. The Bassa described sleep as the 'spouse of death' (Mbembe 1996b, 384). Dreams also form an important source for historians, Mbembe argues, because they provide unique insights into individuals' lives that are otherwise undocumented.

Dreams are understood by Mbembe as ways of understanding political power and organizing resistance. In this sense, they represent strategies, or a form of 'rationality,' for surviving colonial occupation. It is therefore of great interest to Mbembe that Um Nyobè was practicing dream divination in his final weeks of life and left notebooks recording his dreams in some detail.

The notebooks were recovered by the French military from Um Nyobè's body after his death. These are understood by Mbembe not only to reveal information about the fighter's own private subjective world but also to show Cameroonian responses to colonial occupation.

Um Nyobè's dream notebooks: The nocturnal world and the colony

Um Nyobè's dream notebooks are unique sources on his life and allow us to follow the leader during his final days. He attempted dream divination and worked with a spiritual advisor, Mayi Matip, to achieve his goal, recording his dreams as he went. Um Nyobè's decision to turn to the dead and dreams had far-reaching political and social implications (Mbembe 1996b, 391). Those who interacted with the dead were particularly well-placed to challenge colonization, because they had insights and spiritual powers unavailable to others. 'The act of colonisation' needed to be 'denounced by men supposed already to "see in the dark" and be capable of deciphering the invisible' (Mbembe 1996b, 391).

Um Nyobè's written accounts of his dreams do not present a clear narrative, but they incorporate many elements from the independence fighter's world of the 1950s. These wider contextual elements, Mbembe suggests, enable historians to recover the worldview or subjectivity of figures like Um Nyobè. Mbembe quotes extensively from the notebook. On January 4th 1958, Um Nyobè wrote:

> Misfortune. I dreamt of a tomb. Then, I got into a wagon. It had brought a person at death's door; he smelt like a corpse. I left the wagon saying that I wouldn't come back.
>
> (Mbembe 1996b, 391)

In another example, Um Nyobè records:

> We were seated around a record player which was singing and people listened. Someone had brought meat and we ate. Walk at the confluence

> of two rivers. I was on the airfield where people were speaking Arabic, but there were also numerous Bassas who were looking at me.
>
> (Mbembe 1996b, 391)

Mbembe analyses these narratives in a way that deliberately focuses on the local and practical implications of these dreams. He warns against imposing Western theoretical perspectives on the texts, such as psychoanalysis. Mbembe stresses that we cannot reduce dreams to symbolism. Such an interpretation, he cautions, ignores the way that the colonial state was already deploying its own symbols and myths to build power (Mbembe 1996b, 399). In other words, symbols carried inherent political biases because of the degree that colonial officials had interfered in local cultures. We might, for example, note practical elements of the dreams, such as the reference to Arabic speakers at the airfield, a potential gesture towards Egyptian support for Cameroonian independence fighters, or the location of the airfield itself, which reveals mobility and the connections between the local guerrillas and the wider world.

Everyday experiences like visiting the airfield were significant because of the dreamer's proximity to the dead during sleep. Dream activity illustrates public and social understandings of colonial power that were only available because they were encountered in dreams. No simple archive of fantasy, these dreams belong to a southern Cameroonian public understanding of colonial rule. They can be considered as 'schemes of thought' or forms of 'rationality' used to navigate colonial rule (Mbembe 1996b, 399, 403). They ultimately take their legitimacy and importance from their status as nocturnal experiences believed to have privileged proximity to the dead.

NECROPOLITICS

What does it mean, Mbembe asks, to be given up for dead? This is the predicament faced every day by certain groups of people who are condemned to a state of 'living death.' They are very much still alive but have been discarded from the living. More specifically, they have been denied the basic rights accorded to other living beings, including human rights, access to medical care, and freedom from sudden, violent death. In other words, even if they live beyond tomorrow, certain people's lives are treated as though they are worth less than the lives of others.

Mbembe's conceptualization of 'necropolitics' is often understood in relation to the very recent past. He himself firmly roots part of his idea in relation to the twenty-first century 'new wars' in Africa and the Middle East, and their associated practices like extraordinary rendition, torture, offshoring suspects, and drone warfare. But Mbembe is also very clear about the historical background to his term. He sees a broader history of necropolitics that reaches backwards to include the slave plantation and the colony (Mbembe 2020a, 2023).

Necropolitics I: Racism and the right to consign to death

'Necropolitics' can be used to explore the marginalization of human beings from any background, but Mbembe's account of the term is closely linked to a specific engagement with race. Most fundamentally, 'necropolitics' involves consigning a chosen group of people to death (even if this won't occur for years). This act of determining who must die belongs to the 'sovereign power,' typically a nation-state or, in historical periods, a personal sovereign, such as a monarch, colonial official, or slave-owner. To understand this right to put to death, we need to turn to Mbembe's engagement with Foucault's account of racism. This is chiefly located in Lecture 11 of Foucault's *Society Must Be Defended*. In this lecture, Foucault understood racism as key to the functioning of a biopolitical state (a state that used life as a form of power since c. 1800 in the West) (Foucault, 2020b; Taylor 2011, 754). Foucault focuses here on how sovereign power (the power of the state) possesses the ability to decide 'what must live and what must die' (Foucault 2020b, 254).

The 'biopolitical state' gave particular importance to the management of life and death. 'Biopolitics' and 'biopower' were terms used by Foucault to describe the way in which human life is harnessed in a state's attempt to exercise power (Cisney and

Morar 2016, 4). For Foucault, 'biopolitics,' and the 'biopolitical state,' emerged as an attempt by governments to regulate questions such as 'health, sanitation, birth-rate, longevity, [and] race' (Foucault 1997, 57). 'Biopower' was used by Foucault to describe the power to manage life. The very fact of having been born thus took on a profound political significance, because biological life itself became a key terrain of government power. States in the nineteenth century increasingly became concerned with managing different 'populations.' Those who *threatened* this biological model of society were therefore endangering the very survival of life itself. They became the targets of 'racial warfare' or repression, including warfare, judicial killing, or psychiatric interventions. The politics of life or biopower thus contained within it a sanctioned space for death: racism formed the ultimate expression of this.

Foucault understood racism in extremely broad terms and believed that it entailed the mobilization of the state against all minorities (including groups not defined by ethnicity, such as the mentally ill). Key to racism was an 'acceptability of putting to death,' which meant those who threatened the biological survival of society could be killed (Foucault 2020b, 214, 228). This meant that the state itself wielded a 'sovereign right to kill' or *droit de glaive* (right of the sword). This right is essential to Mbembe's formulation of 'necropolitics.' According to it, those defined as Other by a given society can be consigned to death in a manner that is nevertheless deemed compatible with that society's core beliefs.

The relation of enmity

Mbembe believes that state power is centrally concerned with this ability to assign people to death. Drawing on Foucault, he sees racism as intimately concerned with the right to put others to death who seem different from oneself. This in turn involves a relation of hate or enmity that is central to Mbembe's thought about contemporary society, warfare, and immigration. Enmity revolves around the belief that 'the existence of the Other' represents 'an attempt on my life.' Enmity targets societies' supposed enemies, including those perceived as foreign and racially 'Other.' Ultimately, this enmity leads down a bleak road: it results in the decision to consign other people to death (Mbembe 2016e).

Necropolitics II: Sovereign power

But who exactly enjoys the power to consign to death? A sovereign who exercises supreme power within a given state or society holds this capability (Mbembe 2003a, 11; Mbembe 2006e). In Foucault's nineteenth century-focused discussion, that sovereign is the nation-state. But in Mbembe this link is not as clear. While Mbembe stresses that 'sovereign power' is central to the functioning of necropolitics, he includes numerous examples of necropower that do not involve the direct action of governments, including the plantation, colony, and forms of modern warfare relying on mercenaries or warlords. While it could be argued that these examples involve individuals acting on behalf of monarchs or nation-states, they do not suppose the same direct role for the state that Foucault suggests. In contemporary African wars, Mbembe contends, a key logic can be found in 'giving death.' This involves the 'spectacular manifestation of absolute and sovereign power,' and many of these wars involve mercenary groups or warlords that do not have clear links to any one state (Mbembe 2006c, 299–300).

Mbembe sees sovereign power as being 'excessive,' meaning that it goes beyond everyday boundaries and values that we accept in daily life. Death is one important domain where the sovereign exceeds common experience. Here, Mbembe draws on French thinker Georges Bataille (1897–1962) (Bataille 1990, 9–28; Mbembe 2003a, 15). Bataille understood sovereignty as closely linked to death; indeed, he defined it as a 'refusal to accept the limits that the fear of death would have the subject respect.' According to Bataille's perspective, the sovereign is one who does not fear death as others do (Mbembe 2003a, 16). Mbembe connects this to the political sphere to argue that it is not the abstract human subject that achieves this sovereignty and defies the fear of death, but rather political power (Mbembe 2003a, 16). Power becomes free from all the limits that we might think of as characterizing human experience, including the fear of death: it can impose power where it wishes (Mbembe 2003a, 15). We now have an account of death that sees it as intrinsically political. For those who can defy the fear of death, exceptional power awaits.

Necropolitics III: The living dead

We have considered power and the sovereign in Mbembe's formulation of necropolitics, but what of those condemned to 'living death'? What are their conditions of 'life'? Necropolitics after all does not describe actual death, but rather 'conditions of life' that 'confer... [upon other people] the status of [the] living dead.' 'Politics' in this situation, Mbembe contends, 'is therefore death that lives a human life' (Mbembe 2019b, 40). It is this existence that is 'living death' outside of the protective umbrella of sovereign power, including basic rights. From this perspective, necropolitics epitomizes a form of living alienation experienced by those shorn of human dignity.

This state of 'living death' may sound like a borrowing from a zombie film, but Mbembe's thought here is closely informed by philosopher Giorgio Agamben's own account of 'biopolitics,' which differs from that of Foucault. Agamben describes a type of life devoid of all protections. He differentiates between two forms of life: *zoë* or the fact of biological life, and *bios* or political life. Between these two, he argues, is located a *bare life* 'bare life' which serves as a limit for all political activity (Murray 2010, 56). Agamben argues that *zoë*, as the basic form of life, existed before political institutions and language, as well as later classical politics (*bios*). Significantly, Agamben defines two exceptions which he sees as removed from the sphere of politics: the sovereign, and *homo sacer* or the 'sacred man.' *Homo sacer* was the citizen who had been excluded from the city by the sovereign. Shorn of his rights, it was now legal to kill *homo sacer* (Agamben 1998, 9). This idea is extremely close to Mbembe's characterization of the victims of necropolitics. Not only are these people outside the law but they can be killed at any time. Like *homo sacer*, Mbembe's notion of necropolitical power focuses on those utterly excluded from human society, yet condemned to live on until the day that death is visited upon them.

Necropolitics IV: Death-worlds

Where do the 'living dead' of necropolitics live? Even though they are rejected by society, they must live somewhere. Mbembe argues that they inhabit 'death-worlds' (Mbembe 2019b, 40). Creations *par excellence* of necropolitics, some 'death-worlds' include areas under military occupation, police surveillance, prisons, and refugee camps. These social worlds, Mbembe argues, are defined by their attempts to contain groups of people who have been consigned to a status less than that of the 'living.' They are spaces that are proximate to death. These are very much living worlds and are often subject to active policing and enforcement by state or private security and law enforcement companies. In these 'death-worlds,' there is no recourse to legal rights, and death could come at any time.

A VERY SHORT HISTORY OF NECROPOLITICS

Mbembe argues that 'necropolitics' is not solely a contemporary phenomenon and has a lengthy history. Its past makes clear the intimate relation between necropolitics and racism. Mbembe charts the history of necropolitics around Europe's expansion across the globe, via the slave plantation, colonies, and postcolonial forms of war and occupation.

The plantation and the state of exception

Atlantic slavery plays a key role in the history of necropolitics. Mbembe sees it as 'one of the first instances of biopolitical experimentation.' He discerns two critical aspects of the slave plantation as a necropolitical space: the 'state of exception,' and the figure of the slave as 'a shadow' (Mbembe 2003a, 21).

The plantation was a 'space where the slave belongs to a master' (Mbembe 2003a, 21). On the plantation, the operation of law was suspended, and a sense of impunity surrounded the actions of the owner. No legal redress was possible within its walls, and the slaves lacked all rights. This, Mbembe claims, ensured that the slave's horizon of actions was limited to 'rebellion and suicide, flight and silent mourning.' Violence eroded the potential for communication and broke down the possibility for language (Gilroy 1993, 57). Ultimately, Mbembe argues that the plantation was in no sense a community, a term that 'implies the exercise of the power of speech and thought,' but instead existed in a permanent 'state of exception,' outside of the law, and at the mercy of the overseer's whim (Mbembe 2003a, 21).

Denied rights and dignity, Mbembe points out that the slave was rarely allowed to actually die. This was because although mistreated by the slave-owner, an enslaved person was valued 'as property and an instrument of labour.' Mbembe sees the slave as consigned to death, but not actually permitted to die. Instead, they were 'kept alive but in a *state of injury*,' so that their labour could be of value to the slaveholder. This condemns the slave to endure 'in a phantom-like world of horrors,' which often stops short of death itself (Mbembe 2003a, 21).

Mbembe's account of the slave plantation echoes many aspects of the 'social death' hypothesis, a critical analysis in the history of Caribbean plantations. Some historians of slavery have used the term 'social death' to describe the status of slaves, in which immediate isolation from family was accompanied by divorce 'from the social heritage of [their] ancestors' (Patterson 1982, 5). This has been disputed by subsequent scholarship, which has argued that slaves formed their own social and cultural networks (Brown 2010; Klein 2010, 132–161; Miller 2008).

The colony

The colonial world constitutes Mbembe's second historical example of necropolitics in action. Like the plantation, Mbembe sees the colony as being characterized by a 'state of exception,' but also by the workings of 'biopower' (the treatment of humans as biological assets), and a 'state of siege' (Mbembe 2003a, 22). Mbembe discerns these qualities in the case of colonial armies. These, he argues, were unlike their European counterparts, because they 'do not form a distinct entity,' and did not fight other 'regular armies' (Black 2016, 51–76; Mbembe 2003a, 24; Stapleton 2018, 11–35). Mbembe sees the colony as a zone of 'war and disorder,' in which politics and violence were bound together. Colonial wars reveal several necropolitical qualities: the belief that war is fought not against human opponents, but rather 'savage life,' the mobilization of a sovereign 'right to kill,' and a relation of hatred or enmity that pitted colonial power against an 'absolute [allegedly savage] enemy.' The sovereign was free to kill 'at any time or in any manner' (Mbembe 2003a, 24–25).

Colonial wars, Mbembe argues, were particularly insidious because they were fought against an enemy viewed not as human, but as an abstract category of 'savage life.' This latter idea drew on long-held stereotypes of Africa (discussed in Chapter 1), to treat Africans as 'just another form of *animal life*,' and something 'alien beyond imagination or comprehension' (Mbembe 2003a, 24–25). Because there was no law in the colony, 'the sovereign right to kill' was exercised with impunity. It was 'not subject to any rule' because colonial warfare itself evaded the law and institutional rules that constrained European armies. 'Absolute hostility,' or enmity, 'sets the conqueror against' a vague, general and 'absolute enemy.' There was a 'denial of [the] common bond between conqueror and the native' (Mbembe 2003a, 24–25).

Contemporary wars

Conflict in Africa since 1990 constitutes a final example of necropolitics. For Mbembe, there are four characteristics of this contemporary warfare, each revealing its necropolitical properties: the 'state of siege,' global mobility, 'war machines,' and the 'management of multitudes.'

First, the 'state of siege' enables 'a modality of killing that does not distinguish between the external and the internal enemy.' Paranoia means that opponents could even be found within one's own ranks. In this siege-like situation, war progresses technically, but regresses strategically. While 'killing becomes precisely targeted,' conflict itself grows diffuse, embracing all areas of existence. Even the skies become a key domain of security, policing, and surveillance. Drones enable an 'occupation of the skies' (Chamayou 2015; Mbembe 2003a, 29–31). Second, 'global mobility' ensures that state and non-state actors can move internationally with ease, while the widespread use of mercenaries and child soldiers challenges the very boundaries of 'regular armies.'

Third, 'war machines' play a key role in these developments; Mbembe uses the term to describe the link between military groups and the economics of the neoliberal security sector. Warfare has, Mbembe reminds us, become a 'market commodity' in modern Africa, in which urban militias, the personal forces of individual warlords, and private military and security companies (P.M.S.C.s) all compete with the formal armies of nation-states (Reno 2011, 166, 242–256). The armed groups that Mbembe terms 'war machines' have important political functions: they can take on the features of a state, while also acting like a business. They can create special areas focused on extracting natural resources, or trap adversaries into debt. All of this has made conflict a profitable economic sector in multiple African nations, while warfare has been linked to the economy in new ways (Mbembe 2003a, 33–34).

Finally, Mbembe links these developments in contemporary warfare to the 'emergence of an unprecedented form of governmentality that consists in the *management of multitudes*' (Mbembe 2003a, 33–34). This draws on Foucault's account of biopolitics where the state was tasked with controlling groups of people. Wars make populations behave in different ways. Large flows of displaced people can be released, while refugees also concentrate in new border zones. Fugitives from these new wars are often 'confined in camps and zones of exception' by warlords Western states, and their regional allies. This 'management of multitudes' brings 'war machines' closely into the practice of exercising power or 'governmentality.'

THE GHOSTLY REALM AND SPECTRAL WRITING

Literary texts provide a unique insight into necropolitics and its accompanying forms of marginalized life. Mbembe draws on the figure of the ghost to explain forms of existence he sees in necropolitics such as 'living death' and 'savage life': groups of people targeted by sovereign power and marked for death become like 'phantoms,' 'unreal,' and 'ghostlike:' they are relegated to the status of being merely 'part of nature' rather than fully human (Mbembe 2003a, 24).

In many West African societies, ghosts had important uses for the living: they could remind the living of past injustices and wrongs, and narrate socially stigmatic deaths (Parker 2020, 211–213). Amos Tutuola's (1920–1997) *Bush of Ghosts* draws extensively on Yoruba folklore, but its protagonist's experience is conditioned also by slavery, Christian missions, and colonialism (Achebe 1980, 256–257; Fox 1998, 203–206; Tutuola 2014a; 2014b). The novel has been understood as examining historical experiences, and especially slavery, using metaphor and the deployment of spectral terror (Murphy 2012, 49; Tutuola 2014a, 99, 14, 41, 49, 161). It is this dimension of Tutuola's novel that attracts Mbembe, who argues that only such 'figural writing' and its 'scriptural style' can fully evoke the 'nocturnal face' of capitalism apparent in slavery, questions that closely relate to his separate discussions of 'necropolitics.' The role of ghosts in the novel provides insights into the experiences of the enslaved and their erasure from archival and literary representation (Lynn 2016, 54).

In Mbembe's reading of Tutuola, the 'ghost' enjoys an active life with direct political relevance, as well as exhibiting caprice, terror, and ugliness. The spirit world of the bush reflects a 'fractured and mutilated' life, with ghosts possessing a fearsome energy combined with guile to trick the living. Consider the following ghostly dance:

> When he lit the pipe with fire then the whole of the ghosts and hostesses were dancing round me set by set. They were singing, clapping hands, ringing bells and their ancestral drummers were beating the drums in such a way that all the dancers were jumping up with gladness… So at this time I forgot all my sorrow and started to sing the earth the songs which sorrow prevented me from singing about since I entered the bush. But when all these ghosts were hearing the song they were dancing from me to a distance of about five thousand feet and then dancing back to

me again as they were much appreciating the song and also to hear my voice was curious to them.

(Mbembe 2017b, 149–150)

Although Mbembe sees the spectral dance as an example of ghostly energy and caprice, it is closely related to the material past (Mbembe 2003b). Tutuola's spectres can be read as representing the history of those denied social identities or the status of the fully human. Ghosts could be understood as representing the experience of those marginalized by necropolitics. Tutuola sees the spectres as engaged in energetic behaviours that mirror the violence of enslavement. One behaviour includes 'capture,' where ghosts can 'bind… [their human captive] hand and foot' and 'gag… him like a convict.' Even the rhythms of the ghostly dance might be seen as a way of presenting histories not found in conventional archival sources (Spivak 2013, 317–334).

Mbembe's use of Tutuola's fiction as a philosophical resource can be compared with Cameroonian thinker Francis Nyamnjoh (1961–), who reminds us that Tutuola's novels present a way of understanding 'frontierness.' By using this term, Nyamnjoh refers to those Africans who 'collapse dichotomies and build bridges,' including between the 'visible and invisible' worlds; a point graphically illustrated in Tutuola's fantastical bush inhabited by spirits and ghosts. We must, Nyamnjoh suggests, find a way of encompassing its denizens in our conceptualization of the world, including 'gods, spirits, ghosts, animals and kindred creatures of the bushes, and humans' (Nyamnjoh 2017a, 6–7).

CONCLUSION

In 'necropolitics,' the dead return to indict the living. By pushing those still alive to the very frontiers of death, a grotesque form of political power sees the light of day. The objects of necropolitical power are those condemned to 'living death' and deprived of all rights. This victimization has a history, and Mbembe traces it through the plantation, colony, and postcolony.

Foundational to Mbembe's thinking about death, and at work behind necropolitics, is his identification of a 'relation of enmity.' This condemns 'the Other' to the status of 'savage life,' who needs neither be respected nor permitted to live. In postcolonial Cameroon, the state erased the memory of Um Nyobè's resistance, and attempted to suppress even the historical knowledge of his death. He was not accorded the dignity of funerary rituals (Mbembe 1986b, 70). Under necropolitics, the sovereign power treats those consigned to death with enmity. Above all, those condemned to a 'living death' by necropolitical power are frequently the victims of racism, stigmatized as irredeemably 'Other,' and categorically denied rights.

Death plays a key role in Mbembe's thought not for the sake of the departed but for that of the living. Mbembe reveals how in colonial Cameroon the realm of the dead offered a powerful resource for anti-colonial resistance. Dreams were one area of daily life where individuals could gain proximity to the dead. Ghosts also form a bond with an otherwise hidden past in Mbembe's reading of Tutuola.

5

OUT OF THE DARK NIGHT

Decolonization and the new human

Decolonization plays a key role in Mbembe's thought. To understand it, he urges us to read and reread the writings of Martinican psychiatrist and philosopher Frantz Fanon (Mbembe 2007a; 2011a; 2011b; 2012a; 2012b). 'It is practically impossible to read …Fanon and come out unscathed,' Mbembe warns; the reader continuously struggles to avoid being drawn in by Fanon's 'voice…writing … rhythm, … language, … above all, his breath' (Mbembe 2019b, 189). Fanon's intimate proximity pervades Mbembe's thought. But Mbembe is clear that Fanon must be translated 'into the language of our time' and be relevant today (Mbembe 2013c; 2013d; 2017b, 169).

In this chapter, we examine Mbembe's readings of Fanon on violence, focusing particularly on his account of the violence of the colonized and ethics, before turning to consider Mbembe's engagement with Fanon's clinical writings, especially the question of alienation, and the relation of 'care.' We then consider the future dimensions of Mbembe's thoughts on decolonization, including his account of the 'Passerby,' and a new humanism, leading to an 'era of the Earth.' Finally, we examine Sayyid Qutb's (1906–1966) account of a small boy's perception of anticolonial nationalism in a rural southern Egypt in A Child of the Village.

DECOLONIZATION I: FANON'S 'METALLIC' THOUGHT AS A CONCEPTUAL RESOURCE

Mbembe turns to Fanon repeatedly in works like *Necropolitics* and *Critique*, while his 2010 essay collection *Out of the Dark Night* makes a titular reference to the theorist (Mbembe 2021a). Mbembe has contributed to scholarship on Fanon, writing 'Prefaces' to his collected works and a pocket edition of key writings. He sees Fanon's thought as a permanent resource, describing it as 'metallic,' 'metamorphic,' and 'animated by an indestructible will to live.' Cumulatively, Fanon offers a 'pharmakon,' argues Mbembe, borrowing philosopher Jacques Derrida's (1930–2004) term indicating an ethical and conceptual resource. Fanon's thought can be practically used to think through contemporary racism and inequalities (Mbembe 2019b).

Despite the potential of Fanon's thought, Mbembe's approach is nuanced. He reminds us that we cannot inhabit Fanon's world. His thought was necessarily situated in the historical experiences of subjection and racialization during the French occupation of Algeria from 1830 (Mbembe 2012b, 27). The living must focus on today's problems, but Fanon's thought nonetheless still remains disruptive. It has direct consequences for political activism, forming an 'injunction to uprising' (Mbembe 2011a; 2012a, 28; 2012b, 20). Even at a personal level, reading Fanon involves 'uproot[ing] oneself from oneself,' and 'put[ting] one's life in the balance' (Mbembe 2017b, 169). Mbembe raises the very widest questions about the position of intellectuals in our era, and what it means to think critically.

In particular, Mbembe and Fanon understand decolonization (the overthrow of colonial occupation) in the broadest sense. The term entails not only removing the historical traces of colonial rule but also a contemporary effort to challenge present-day inequalities that are rooted in the historical experience of colonialism. This contemporary focus ultimately looks to building a new future standing in contrast to racism, enmity, and environmental despoilation. A significant element within Mbembe's recent thought is concerned with mapping out this utopian future. Mbembe sees Fanon not only as a historical figure, but also as a resource for contemporary issues, and as a guide to an unrealized future.

Less widely known than *Wretched*, Fanon's psychiatric writings form a key influence on Mbembe. His medical work forms an indispensable context to Mbembe's thought on the clinic and care. Trained in France, Fanon's practised in Algeria and Tunisia. At Blida, Algeria, Fanon worked at the Psychiatric Hospital of Blida-Joinville, the largest psychiatric institution in North Africa (Lee 2015, 115). Colonial psychiatry was far from objective and incorporated derogatory ideas about colonized peoples. The 'Algiers School' of psychiatry, which was associated with Fanon's superior at Blida, Antoine Porot, placed Arab people on a developmental continuum between supposedly 'primitive' sub-Saharan Africans and allegedly 'civilized' Europeans (Lee 2015, 115).

Fanon attempted to challenge these assumptions, applying innovative sociotherapeutic methods, and taking local cultures seriously in designing therapeutic care. Critically, he saw local cultures as underscoring the importance of social activities and reintegration into human relationships during the patient's recovery. In providing sociotherapy to Muslim Algerian men, Fanon and his intern Jacques Azoulay argued that cognitive meaning, essential for therapeutic care, could only exist within culturally determined frames of reference (Fanon and Azoulay 2018, 353). This meant that patients' cultural backgrounds had to be respected. At Blida, Fanon had patients build a football pitch, a North African café, and developed storytelling evenings (Khalfa 2019, 190). Along with his assistants, Fanon made a serious attempt to engage with North African cultures, travelling to villages in the Kabylia mountains of North Algeria to research the exorcisms performed by spiritual leaders or *marabouts*, and belief in possession by *djinn* or spirits (Fanon and Sanchez 2018, 421–422; Murand 2008, 31).

DECOLONIZATION II: THE VIOLENCE OF THE COLONIZED BETWEEN POLITICS AND THE CLINIC

Violence has popularly been seen as central to Fanon's thought on decolonization. His alleged call for the colonized to engage in a 'purifying' violence to overthrow colonial rule is understood as a key justification of armed violence on the part of the dispossessed. But Fanon's arguments on violence have often been misunderstood and taken out of context (Lee 2015, 149). In particular, philosopher Jean-Paul Sartre's 'Preface' to *Wretched* de-contextualized and over-exaggerated Fanon's account of violence, while obscuring Algerian the influence of Algerian intellectuals on Fanon's thought, such as assassinated activist Abane Ramdane (1920–1957) (Abane 2011; Cherki 2006, 152). In his teaching, Mbembe has warned South African students against poorly informed readings of Fanon on violence, especially following the 2015 student protests (Mbembe 2015c).

The violence of the colonized

Fanon does not advocate generalized violence. He instead 'proposes a defined set of historical origins and legitimate uses for violence' (Lee 2015, 156). His arguments are laid out in Chapter 1 of the *Wretched* entitled 'Concerning Violence' (Fanon 1967, 46). Grounded in his experience with the National Liberation Front (FLN) in Algeria and Tunisia, Fanon argued that armed struggle potentially led to 'personal transformation.' It could erase the central distinction that undercut colonial society: 'settler' versus 'native' (Lee 2015, 156). In the context of the war in Algeria, the violence of the colonized was a response to the actions of the French army, including torture.

Three forms of violence

Mbembe's reading of Fanon takes violence as its departure point. His chief concern is that the violence of the colonized is in turn bound up with Fanon's notion of the 'struggle' against imperialism. For Mbembe, Fanon's understanding of the 'struggle' was typified by mourners' cries for the fallen Algerian *mujahid* or fighter. Mbembe differentiates three types of violence: violence perpetrated by colonial states, the violence of the colonized, and violence in international relations (warfare between states).

It is the violence of the colonized that is key for Mbembe (Mbembe 2012a, 17). This is because it carries psychological and subjective implications. First, the violence of the colonized involves colonized people's exercise of freedom and their right to name themselves. Second, it necessitates risking one's very existence in the act of standing up to the colonizer. Finally, this violence of the colonized has a wider social consequence: it implies a deep faith in the ability of the collective or the 'masses' to act. It makes the individual part of a collective and leads to the colonized person becoming, in Fanon's words, 'a man among other men' (Mbembe 2012a, 25).

Violence, healing, and a spiritual community of grief

Mbembe argues that Fanon's violence of the colonized possesses a critical ethical dimension. It is closely linked to care and healing. This might seem paradoxical: how could violence be linked to care? Consider Fanon's image of those who cry out in their grief for a fallen warrior. On the one hand, the mourners' agony speaks of suffering and death, but it also testifies to the emergence of a 'new "spiritual community"' (Mbembe 2012a, 21). If violence necessitates grief, Mbembe points out that it also creates new forms of community. Mbembe discerns this in Fanon's account of the FLN hospitals that cared for enemy combatants alongside their own wounded (Mbembe 2012a, 21).

The 'jolt' of violence and the return to social relations

When faced with overwhelming violence, colonized people may well retreat into themselves and away from an unbearable reality. In such a predicament, Mbembe argues that revolutionary violence provides the 'jolt' which challenges this unhealthy but inevitable retreat into the self (Mbembe 2012a, 15). Mbembe sees this 'jolt' as therapeutic. It enables a process of rebuilding and renewing social relations, thus escaping from the alienating impact of illness (as reflected in the isolation of a torture victim). This process of restoring social bonds is fundamentally therapeutic. In Mbembe's reading of Fanon, the violence of the colonized plays a role in helping to rebuild the shattered subject who has faced colonial exploitation.

Mbembe views Fanon's violence of the colonized as having a still wider social role. He sees it as anticipating a more general social rising of the downtrodden, which he terms 'a rising to humanity' (Mbembe 2012a, 25). This ascent away from humiliation and disenfranchisement refers to the ability of the colonized to transcend the place accorded to them by colonial condescension. We will return to this utopian vision later in the chapter.

DECOLONIZATION III: DISALIENATION AND RESTORING THE COMMON

Mbembe focuses especially on the psychological damage of racism and colonialism. Any act of decolonization must be focused on restoring social relations after the damage and alienation caused by racism and colonial stereotypes. In Fanon's work, these issues are addressed especially in *Black Skin, White Masks*, where Fanon focuses specifically on the psychical impact of racism (Fanon 2021; Lee 2015, 172). More recently, awareness of Fanon's clinical work has grown with increased scholarship on his scientific research (Khalfa 2018, 167; Mbembe 2017b, 168).

Mbembe's understanding of the psychical economy of colonialism is centrally influenced by Fanon's account of racism in *Black Skin* (Mbembe 2019b, 130). In that work, Fanon explored the subjective alienation caused by destructive stereotypes and their role in a dualistic colonial society divided on racial lines between white and black. In Chapter 5 of *Black Skin*, entitled 'The Lived Experience of the Black Man' in the 2008 translation, Fanon argued that racial identification was relational, or based on our relationships with others (Fanon 2008). He showed how French claims of non-racism and cultural assimilation in fact coincided with a simultaneous emphasis on racial difference. Other people's ideas about one's skin colour, specifically white notions of black people, generate a destabilizing experience. A black person might find themselves reduced to public judgement and identification based solely on colour. Fanon himself admitted to feeling 'overdetermined from the outside' due to these factors, and therefore alienated from himself, and 'a slave... to my appearance' (Fanon 2008, 95). It is only, Fanon argued, through analysing this dual structure of racial identification that the experience of alienation felt by black people could be overcome, and 'disalienation' achieved. Despite its influential account of the psychological wounds caused by racism, *Black Skin* focused chiefly on prejudice within France and had relatively little to say about the colonial world (Bhabha 1994, 61). Mbembe, by contrast, focuses his account directly on the colonial world.

Internalization and alienation

Mbembe develops two ideas from Fanon's account of alienating colonial stereotypes. These externally imposed labels lead to two results: *internalization* (the process whereby one comes to believe or use someone else's stereotypes about oneself), and, ultimately, *alienation* (a state of being distanced from oneself because the self is only encountered through the hostile images of others). Internalization leads to the individual being 'reduced,' Mbembe argues, to being seen exclusively in terms of race. Seeing themselves through the eyes of the colonizer, the individual faces being 'installed immediately in the position of the Other,' even inside their own heads (Mbembe 2019b, 132). The humanity of the individual has been reduced, along with their self-respect.

This process of 'reduction' created by internalization is one that creates enormous psychological stress. The person who has been labelled as 'Other' must be 'on the alert,' and constantly expects rejection. The desire to sidestep rebuttal comes to motivate every action. One may feel that one must excel to get just as far as everyone else or become hyper-vigilant about conforming to the cultural norms of the majority: self-policing becomes the order of the day (Mbembe 2019b, 132). All this forms an undesirable predicament: the 'tragedy of the Other.'

Unsurprisingly, this troubled psychological landscape leads to greater mental wounds. Chief among these is alienation. Seeing oneself through someone else's highly prejudiced eyes leads to a crisis of identity. One comes to see oneself as an 'object,' and someone else's object at that (Mbembe 2019b, 132). 'For the natives,' Mbembe argues, 'the dilemma... became to know how, in everyday practice, to discern what pertained to the psychic object they had been asked to interiorize' (Mbembe 2019b, 47). Even though they do not own the stereotypes foisted upon them, the victims of such labelling are forced to work out exactly how these alien identities work. 'Psychic life in the colonies' saw colonized people reduced to being the 'object' of others. This process led to the internalization of damaging stereotypes and the alienation that this, in turn, provoked.

If all of this might seem a bleak prognosis, Mbembe offers a clear pathway out of alienation. He regards all illness as ultimately involving alienation from 'the common,' and hence from social relations with others. The psychic alienation of colonial racism presents just such a situation. To combat alienation, one must establish a 'relation of care' ultimately aimed at rehabilitating the patient into inhabiting the 'common' once again. Within this enterprise, Mbembe sees language and a restitution of common or social bonds as central. To do so is a critical labour of decolonization via restoring common bonds. This has the capacity to break the psychological shackles of colonialism.

Language and alienation

We have seen how alienation can be inflicted by colonial stereotyping, but we have yet to examine its social consequences. The alienated patient in the psychiatric clinic has been severed from their daily world. Or perhaps one might say that their world has unravelled. The external routines and identities that make up a person's life have all collapsed; so too have language and its representational powers. Fanon's own psychiatric practice was concerned with remedying this breakdown. It focused specifically on creating the 'special conditions and processes that would... enable the patients to reconstruct their personality.' This is why it placed importance on psychotherapy or group therapy, as well as conventional institutional treatments (Khalfa 2018, 186). This social therapy created the routines and structure that would enable the patient's personality to be reconstructed. Mbembe, like Fanon, stresses the importance of local culture in overcoming alienation. Acts such as 'celebrating Aïd el-Kébir, the sounding of the Angelus, [and] the hearing of Easter bells' have their own clinical importance, depending on the patient's faith and cultural background (Mbembe 2019b, 143). These cultural and social dimensions of therapy aimed to combat the alienation provoked by illness, and also attempted to re-insert the patient into a cultural context which may previously have been devalued or erased by colonialism.

Mbembe stresses the linguistic implications of this attempt to overcome alienation. In the colonial situation, Mbembe argues, language itself breaks down. In the colony 'reference is neutralized,' signifiers are 'destroyed,' and there is a 'degeneration of language' (Mbembe 2019b, 143). This is reproduced by illness, which, like the experience of colonial rule, 'places me in a state' that 'scarcely allows me to encounter my neighbour, my fellow human' As this last quote suggests, language enables social communication. Mbembe recognizes that part of Fanon's clinical practice was aimed at restoring language to the world of mental illness; it helped patients to speak once again. By using language to narrate the hatred that they had experienced, patients were able to defy its power. The patients themselves gave enmity 'a voice and a face, well removed from all miserabilism [and suffering]' (Mbembe 2019b, 143). All of this defies the corrosion of language and of communication caused by colonial occupation and the mental illnesses with which it was associated.

Restoring the common

The 'common' refers to a shared domain of social interactions. When meaningfully interacting with other people and engaging in shared enterprises or experiences, one is part of the 'common' or shared world. This domain of the common is the key end goal of Mbembe's therapeutic interventions aimed at decolonization (Mbembe 2019b, 144). The common involves the work of reconstituting bonds between humans, with the goal of establishing what is 'common to us.' This process can be termed the 'reconstitution of the common,' Mbembe argues. There is a 'breaking of silence' and speech with its social and communicative potential is re-established (Mbembe 2019b, 142–143).

Disalienation

Above all, any restoring of the 'common' entails *disalienation*. This undoing of alienation restores the patient's bond with the 'common' and undoes the isolation of illness. Disalienation is based around communication with the patient. Those who have suffered illness and alienation are able now to speak. This granting of language to the patient restores them to the world and to the possibility of communication with others. Disalienation is essentially an ethical project because it involves accommodating the Other. It offers to 'walk back over the trace of the person who has been defeated' and 're-create' a way of engaging with society (Mbembe 2019b, 145). However, regenerating this social bond is uncomfortable and unpredictable, because interaction with others is inherently uncontrollable. Disalienation forces us to confront society and history, rather than to hide from it (Mbembe 2019b, 147).

DECOLONIZATION IV: THE DECOLONIZATION OF KNOWLEDGE AND THE #RHODESMUSTFALL MOVEMENT IN SOUTH AFRICA

Mbembe has become a key figure in the decolonization of academia in South Africa (Bénit-Gbaffou 2016, 169; Mbembe 2008a; 2015a; 2016a). Fanon, along with Black Consciousness Movement leader Steve Biko (1946–1977), were major inspirations for the 2015 #RhodesMustFall student movements (Wilson 2012); Mbembe has written on both figures (Mbembe 2012b; 2018b). We focus on Mbembe's engagement with the movement, before moving to his thoughts on decolonizing universities.

Mbembe and #RhodesMustFall

Mbembe has described the #RhodesMustFall movement as 'an important and necessary moment.' He acknowledges the way that South African student movements have mobilized Fanon's thought, and identifies the toppling of the statue of English industrialist and Prime Minister of Cape Colony Cecil John Rhodes at Cape Town as a 'Fanonian moment' (Bénit-Gbaffou 2016, 171).

At the time of the 2015 protests, the Library of Johannesburg reported that Fanon's *Wretched* had become frequently borrowed, along with Biko's *I Write What I Like* (Biko 1988; Gibson 2016, 40). Some students made a ready equation between Fanon's endorsement of a call to decolonization and his supposed sanction of purifying violence, although other students made more nuanced uses of Fanon to critique African National Congress corruption (Gibson 2016, 43; Manzini 2016). For his part, Mbembe initiated a seminar focusing on Fanon's library and aimed at encouraging those 'really interested in Fanon' to reflect on his work, while also warning against a romantic idea of violence based on erroneous readings (Bénit-Gbaffou 2016, 171). In particular, Mbembe has argued that Fanon's project of decolonization was more extensive and radical than simply removing colonial oppression. This concern refers to Mbembe's vision of Fanon's 'pharmacy,' with its healing power at a global level. Reading Fanon, Mbembe argues, reminds us that decolonization constituted a 'vast project of the radical destruction of a world order corrupted by racism,' which opened the possibility to a fresh beginning linked to a new subject which had escaped from Western domination. This rebirth is conceived in the most general terms as being 'the unconditional inauguration of a truly planetary era' (Bénit-Gbaffou 2016, 171).

The decolonization of knowledge

Despite Mbembe's sympathy with the student protestors and his support for decolonization as a broad philosophical and political enterprise, he has advanced significant and nuanced criticism of existing calls for epistemic decolonization. These, he argued, compared to movements for 'Africanization,' 'indigenization,' and 'endogenization' from the 1960s to 1980s (Mbembe 2021a, 56). To date, he argues, calls to decolonize have 'consisted of a critique of the colonial knowledge chain' and its impact on African cultures. Mbembe warns that this poses problems. Calls to decolonize, he cautions, risk avoiding a thoroughgoing critique of knowledge and education as concepts (Mbembe 2021a, 56). Mbembe has criticized two key elements of demands for epistemic decolonization in African universities: firstly, the demand for African forms of knowledge to be centred in academic teaching, and, secondly, lobbies for African language teaching to be prioritized.

Mbembe's critique of epistemic decolonization I: 'ethno-knowledge'

In the first case, Mbembe contends that any abstract appeal to African forms of knowledge risks leading to 'ethno-knowledge.' Mbembe is suspicious of these fields, which he regards as having 'connections with the politics of identity and ethnicity' (Bénit-Gbaffou 2016, 176; Mbembe 2021a, 56). Such identifications risk promoting xenophobia, which Mbembe has explicitly critiqued in the case of South Africa (Mbembe 2016c). More generally, too simplistic an account of the relationship between knowledge and power, Mbembe warns, can easily avoid critical analysis of material factors, including political and economic relations (Bénit-Gbaffou 2016, 176).

Mbembe's critique of epistemic decolonization II: African languages

Mbembe critiques the claim that African language education necessarily leads to a decolonization of knowledge. Some African thinkers, such as Kenyan writer Ngugi w'a Thiong'o (1938–), have argued that African language education is key to re-centring Africa within continental universities. Teaching in African languages reduces students' exposure to languages and ideas from outside the continent that are linked to colonialism. Ngugi views education as 'a means of knowledge about ourselves,' and, as such, education in African languages is central to achieving African self-knowledge (Mbembe 2022, 57; Ngugi 1986, 94). The widespread use of European languages in African academia could also lead to cultural alienation (Hountondji 1996).

Mbembe counters these perspectives. He warns against any ready privileging of African languages. Such a position, he contends, assumes a simplistic philosophy of language itself. His critique is twofold. First, Mbembe argues that humans do not control linguistic meaning, which is not stable and predictable. This makes it hard to claim that using any given language will lead to specific social or political outcomes (Mbembe 2021a, 59). Second, calls to use African languages in universities ignore the degree to which languages such as French have become part of African culture and changed through their use on the continent (Mbembe 2021a, 98). Mbembe shares the political and ethical aims of Ngugi and Beninese philosopher Paul Hountondji (1942–2024) in decolonizing African universities, but he sees them as not going far enough down a path of philosophical rigour.

THE ETHICS OF THE PASSERBY

Mbembe is clear that Fanon's thought looks not to the past but to the future of humanity. What shape does this future take? One answer to this can be found in Mbembe's account of the 'passerby.'

The passerby

Who is this 'passerby,' or *passant*? (Mbembe 2019b, 186). They represent an image of mobility (Mbembe 2021a, 225). An ambiguous figure, whose name in French betrays multiple meanings, the 'passerby' is from 'elsewhere.' They 'will not stay here,' but rather move 'toward other skies.' The 'passerby' is also someone who has 'left... his country,' and lived abroad. Forced by necessity into 'tying his fate to those who welcome and recognize their own face in his,' the passerby is therefore thrown upon the hospitality of fellow human beings (Mbembe 2019b, 187). Their presence has more general implications: it reveals 'the fugitive character of life' for all humanity (Mbembe 2019b, 187).

The disenclosure of the world

Mbembe sees decolonization as leading to the breaking down of frontiers and boundaries. It therefore entails a process of 'disenclosure' or 'departitioning' (Mbembe 2021a, 42, 44). To speak of 'disenclosure' is really to think of making a new world, one to which all of humanity is the heir (Mbembe 2021a, 61). The appearance of this 'disenclosed' world is connected to a resurgent humanity, rising up to claim its rights and dignity in a new form of self-consciousness. It is ready to lay claim to a joined-up world beyond the relations of hatred that Mbembe links with all frontiers and borders. Instead, he sees a planetary state hinted at in Martinican writer and philosopher Edouard Glissant's (1928–2011) concept of *Le tout-monde* or 'the all-world,' and understands this as representing a connected sphere of global interaction (Dash 1995: 177; Mbembe 2019, 9). Like those who welcome the 'passerby,' the rising humanity of the 'disenclosed' world is in the process of emergence from the dark night of enmity, colonialism, and racism: they are becoming decolonized.

DECOLONIZATION IN THE COUNTRYSIDE: SAYYID QUTB'S *A CHILD OF THE VILLAGE*

Mbembe highlights the need to think about decolonization beyond the rarefied confines of the university seminar room. Decolonization and anti-colonial nationalism can be understood in terms of popular cultural responses, as much as elite ideas. Although we have focused on contemporary examples of Mbembe's engagement in decolonization activism, we here consider an autobiographical text set in the early twentieth century. Even if of an earlier period, the themes of intellectuals' own relationship to colonized people and of the way that nationalist lobbies play out in rural or non-elite environments are key themes in both Fanon and Mbembe.

Egyptian Islamist thinker Sayyid Qutb's (1906–1966) autobiographical account of rural childhood *A Child of the Village* (1946) raises questions of anti-colonial nationalism and knowledge around 1920, as seen through the eyes of a child in a southern Egyptian village (Gershoni and Jankowski 1995, 11; Qutb 2006). It presents a child's view of Egyptian nationalism that was very different from the terms of intellectual elites, even if Qutb later became a prominent intellectual figure in his own right. *Child* is a 'retrospective autobiography,' recounting life in the village of Musha, around 200 miles south of Cairo, during the British occupation of Egypt (1882–1922) (Calvert 2019, 36; Whidden 2017, 8). The Nationalist Party or *al-Hizb al-Watani* demanded the removal of the British from Egypt, and its founder Mustafa Kamil (1874–1908) also argued for Egypt's place in the wider Islamic world (Qutb 2006, 141).

Qutb's narrator distances himself from the world of Musha, adopting a tone that could be regarded as similar to an anthropologist, sometimes relying on footnotes to detail the village's cultural and spiritual beliefs. He portrays himself as somewhat separated from Musha children by his intellect, as evinced in a passage where he challenges a visiting scholar from Cairo's prestigious Al-Azhar University on grammatical matters.

If nationalist books are foreign to the world of Mushin, their arrival is interpreted in terms of broader Arabic literary and poetic culture. Qutb's 'child' finds these works fascinating not for their content, but due to their material presence. He also sees them as representing a whole world of illicit knowledge:

> The value of this book increased for our friend when he learned that its author was a political prisoner and that the administrative laws that were in effect at that time had banned the collection.
>
> As for the book of history, it meant a great deal to him that its author wrote at the end of its introduction, 'This book will perhaps not be printed again, unless these sections are deleted.' He was referring to the passages immortalizing the Khedive 'Abbas Hilmi II.
>
> ... He then began with admirable patience and perseverance to copy the collection, verse by verse, into his notebook, and he also copied the introduction to the historical work, which would not be reprinted until the offending passages were removed. Today he marvels at how he was able to make such a great effort. But what is even more amazing is that he was able to memorize the collection by heart...
>
> When he rushed out into the village to tell his friends what he had memorized and claimed that it was by a poet who was living at the time, no one believed him. For poetry was a feature of the early inhabitants of the Arabian Peninsula. Since that time no one was thought capable of composing a single verse of poetry. When he supported his case by pointing to other living poets of whom he learned from his great teacher, one of which was Shawqi and the other Hafiz [Ahmad Shawqi

and Ibrahim Hafiz, Egyptian neo-classical poets], every one still denied his claim, which was simply unbelievable.

He desired to prove his case and so they made a wager, waiting patiently for one of the scholars who were studying in Cairo at the Azhar, or the fellow who was studying at Dar al-'Ulum ['House of Sciences' in Cairo], or the one who was studying in the faculty of law, to come by (You can see that the village had made great progress) and decide the serious matter...

(Qutb 2006, 94–95)

Qutb's passage reveals how people used nationalist texts and ideas in ways that went far beyond the formal ideological influence imagined by nationalist elites. It echoes Fanon and Mbembe's separate injunctions that intellectuals must explain questions of colonialism and decolonization in terms that resonate outside elite environments, such as university lecture theatres. It illustrates the ways in which local people drew on different forms to conceptualize nationalism and how these went beyond those used by intellectuals. For example, Qutb describes how nationalist ideas were seen in relation to the mystique of printed book culture or situated in relation to longer-term traditions of literary culture in Egypt, such as copying sections of books by hand, or linking poetry to ancient Arabia (Ostle 1998, 709; Starkey 1998, 386). Elite literary culture, including nationalism, remains something exotic to Musha: the villagers do not see poetry as something in the here and now, but rather as connected to ancient Arabia. Decolonization and anti-colonial nationalism appear in Musha as a remote activity, comparable to Mbembe and Fanon's warnings about how efforts to decolonize risk becoming irrelevant if restricted only to elites.

CONCLUSION

In aiming to break from the relations of colonialism, Mbembe's view of decolonization requires nothing short of a rebuilding of social relations from the ground up. This is true in individual and collective terms. At an individual level, it involves the labour of overcoming alienation and internalization. It points to helping the colonized person or patient to speak once more and form bonds with others. This allows for the possibility of language, but also for the disalienation that returns the individual to the 'common' or social world. At a collective level, decolonization involves questions of knowledge and education, such as the debates surrounding the role of African languages in African universities, or the racial inequalities that persist within higher education. Mbembe's thought reveals how Fanon is still relevant today as a tool in these contemporary debates, but one that must be used with caution. If calls for the decolonization of knowledge are made in terms that are not sufficiently rigorous theoretically, Mbembe warns that they risk falling short of their goal.

Ultimately, decolonization is unfinished and it reaches on into the future. Mbembe's recent engagement with the resurgence of the far-right in France and elsewhere reminds us of the stakes (Juompan-Yakam, 2024b). This world that has yet to come offers humanity the possibility of new social bonds and relations. These move beyond old animosities and enable humans to accept each other and the planet in new terms, which largely remain unelucidated. This is the era of the 'passerby' and of the Earth. Our ability to forge these new relations is uncertain and mirrors Mbembe's account of the patient's journey from alienation to disalienation and a restoration of language and 'common' social bonds.

SAYYID QUTB (1906–1966)

Egyptian Islamist thinker, member of the Muslim Brotherhood, and writer, Qutb is best known for his later career as a political theorist. During the period from 1933 to 1936 he wrote literary criticism, a novel, and a volume of poetry. Qutb spent two years in the USA on an educational mission, before returning to Egypt in 1950. By 1951, Qutb was active in the anti-government Muslim Brotherhood, leaving his post at the Ministry of Education in October 1952. From 1954, Qutb was arrested several times for his involvement in the Brotherhood, and after alleged implication in a plot to assassinate Egyptian president Gamal Abdel Nasser (1918-1970) in Alexandria, he was jailed for 15 years in 1955. Released in 1964, Qutb wrote a series of major works, including 'Milestones' (1964), which alleged that a number of contemporary Muslim regimes, including Nasser's, were not based on truly Islamic values, and were instead mired in pre-Islamic *jahiliyya* or ignorance. Qutb was arrested again in August 1965 and sentenced to death on 21 August that year, before being executed the following week. Aside from *Milestones*, Qutb's writings on Islam including his Qur'an commentary *In the Shadows of the Qur'an*, which ran into 30 volumes, and *Social Justice in Islam* (1949), while his literary critical works included *The Task of the Poet in Life and the Poetry of the Present Generation*, (1933), a poetry volume *The Unknown Shore* (1935), a novel *The Enchanted City* (1946), and the autobiographical *A Child of the Village* (1946) (Bergesen 2008; Calvert 2009; Jansen 2012; Qutb 2006; 2016).

FRANCIS NYAMNJOH (1961–)

Cameroonian anthropologist Nyamnjoh explores important Mbembian themes, including migration, decolonization, and the #RhodesMustFall movement in South Africa, including in his 2015 book, *#RhodesMustFall: nibbling at resilient colonialism in South Africa* (2015b). Nyamnjoh has called for a 'convivial scholarship' in universities, as part of wider efforts to decolonize knowledge. This 'convivial' approach indicates a broad-mindedness that seeks to account for the fact that under still-influential colonial educational systems in many African countries, local forms of knowledge were devalued. Nyamnjoh sees 'conviviality' as enabling the incorporation of hitherto dismissed popular worldviews that have been traditionally marginalized from philosophy and academic research more generally (Nyamnjoh 2020a).

6

AFROPOLITANISM

'The destiny of our planet,' Mbembe argues, 'will be played out, to a large extent, in Africa' (Mbembe 2021a, 222). The continent is a key location for the thinking through of emerging social and global realities (Mbembe and Sarr 2016, 8). Africa's relationship with the wider world has long been obscured, with the continent often being relegated in colonial discourse to the status of separation and exception (Mbembe and Sarr 2016, 8). Now, Mbembe contends, in the twenty-first century, these links are being rethought with urgency.

Thinking about Africa's relation to the world is not merely an intellectual exercise, Mbembe warns, but connects to the opening of all that is frontiers demanded by decolonization (Mbembe and Sarr 2016, 9). It is not simply that 'a part of African history lies somewhere else…,' but rather that the history of Africa is also that of the world as a whole (Mbembe 2020b, 10). Africa is not only firmly within the world, and has always been so, but it forms central location for rethinking the planet's future.

Mbembe's account of 'Afropolitanism,' a term referring to African engagements with the wider world is understood in relation to two key moments: a 'first' and 'second' moment. Afropolitanism's 'second moment,' as a general aesthetic

DOI: 10.4324/9780429201646-8

informed by the global connectedness of African elites, is widely known in the Anglophone world. But the term's 'first moment' is specifically literary and less well-examined. Mbembe charts this 'first moment' of the Afropolitan through an engagement with the fiction of novelists Ouologuem and Labou Tansi. Basing itself around an aesthetic of 'whirlwind' writing, this first moment of Afropolitanism blows away the past-facing concerns of its predecessors: Pan-Africanism, Négritude (a Francophone movement stressing Africa-wide cultural consciousness), and African nationalism.

AFROPOLITANISM: THE HISTORIES OF A TERM

Afropolitanism is a slippery term with a complex history. It crosses between popular culture and media, as well as academic scholarship. In popular media, an *Afropolitan* magazine once covered a compelling consumerist lifestyle within its pages (Coetzee 2016, 101). Although Mbembe is sometimes assumed to be the originator of the term, 'Afropolitanism' actually existed in earlier and distinct usages during the 2000s. This further muddies the waters around what is sometimes seen as an inherently loose concept.

In a 2005 usage by the essayist Taiye Tuakli-Wosornu (later Taiye Selasi), 'Afropolitan' signified the experience of an educated, internationally mobile, second-generation diaspora who had lived in several cities of the Global North, while remaining connected to Africa and having familiarity with urban centres on the continent. In her influential 2005 essay *Bye-Bye Babar*, in the online magazine *Lip* (Coetzee 2016, 101), Selasi explained:

> Like so many African young people working and living in cities around the globe, they belong to no single geography, but feel at home in many. They (read: we) are Afropolitans – the newest generation of African emigrants, coming soon or collected already at a law firm/chem lab/jazz lounge near you.
>
> (Selasi 2013; 2020 [2015], 3–6)

Selasi's usage of the term has sometimes been misunderstood as indicating collaboration between herself and Mbembe, whereas the two usages in fact have distinct meanings. Selasi's term denotes a specifically diasporic experience, whereas Mbembe's, as we shall see, is focused on the continent itself. Criticism of Selasi's term is nonetheless relevant to understanding how Mbembe's distinct notion of 'Afropolitanism' has been received. Selasi's early focus on city-skipping mobility drew sustained criticism for perceived class privilege and consumerism. Dabiri made this point in a 2014 piece that has since become a key text in anti-elitist critiques of the Afropolitan (Dabiri 2014). Similarly, the status of a mobile, elite Afropolitan mobility has been negatively contrasted to previous constructions of African identity by Wainaina, especially Pan-Africanism (Santana 2013). Dabiri specifically engages Selasi's term and represents part of a generalized trend to critique an, often very general, notion of the Afropolitan. Several similar, but distinct, terms exist, particularly the 'Afropean,' designating the experience of diasporic groups in Europe (Hitchott and Thomas 2014, 1).

Mbembe's own use of the term is complex. Before we explore it in detail, we must briefly consider the textual history of 'Afropolitanism' within his thought. Mbembe's first use of the term 'Afropolitanism' appeared in a 2005 essay for the catalogue of the Pompidou Centre exhibition *Africa Remix: Contemporary Art of a Continent*, also published in the Francophone *Africultures* magazine (Njami 2005). However, a more extensive exposition of the term remained untranslated in English until 2021, when his *Out of the Dark Night* was translated, Mbembe additionally reflects on the term in interviews (Santana 2016, 120–121). His account in *Night* expands understandings of the term both in terms of Mbembe's engagement with African fiction and in relation to preceding notions of African and Afrodiasporic identities, such as *Négritude* and Pan-Africanism. Nonetheless, with the *Night* chapter available only in its French original during the 2010s, many accounts of Mbembe's Afropolitan thought relied on the 2005 essay.

'Afropolitanism' suggests a more common term: cosmopolitanism. Understood as mobility and mixing between different cultural traditions, 'cosmopolitanism' plays a key role in our understanding of culture. Philosopher Kwame Anthony Appiah used the term as the foundation for a moral philosophy in his 2006 work

Cosmopolitanism: Ethics in a World of Strangers (Appiah 2006). Appiah identifies several positive strengths of the cosmopolitan, such as curiosity, the ability to hold cross-cultural conversations, and a respect for pluralism (Lee 2021). These ethical values can also be understood as 'an indispensable component' of Mbembe's Afropolitanism (Gehrmann 2016, 63). The matter of quite how cosmopolitan values are distinct from Afropolitanism remains unclear. While cosmopolitanism is a more general and universalist concept, Afropolitanism could be understood as focusing specifically on African historical and cultural experiences.

AFROPOLITANISM IN HISTORY: THE SAHARA AND JOHANNESBURG

A key criticism of Afropolitanism in all its guises has been that it describes global exchanges involving Africa that are nothing new. Mbembe does go to some length to account for the historical examples of Afropolitanism, specifically identifying a 'precolonial African modernity that has not yet been sufficiently accounted for' (Mbembe 2021a, 214). He does not seek to argue that these historical forms represent a direct continuity with twenty-first century Afropolitanism, but rather that these earlier examples offer parallels to contemporary developments.

Although this historical account of Afropolitanism is already present in his 2005 essay, where he defines the Sahara, and the Atlantic and Indian Oceans as key regions for slave trading (Mbembe 2020b, 9), it is more explicit in *Night* where Mbembe argues that precolonial Africa, without artificial borders imposed by colonial powers, witnessed both *networks* of exchange between different regions (like trans-Saharan trade routes) and *institutions* that were themselves transregional (such as Sufi brotherhoods).

Afropolitan histories: The Sahel in the nineteenth century

Mbembe draws on the example of the nineteenth-century Chad basin, connecting the Sahel (the southern shores of the Sahara) and North Africa as one important network. He identifies the *zariba* or villages that grew up along the caravan trade routes as examples of institutions with connections across the wider Sahara (Mbembe 2021a, 182, italics in original). Critically, Mbembe views this nineteenth-century environment as being fundamentally mobile and joining together three key elements: war, mobility, and commerce.

It was in this context that colonial 'pseudostates' emerged against 'what fundamentally was a *federation of networks* and a *multinational space*' consisting of networks rather than nations ((Mbembe 2021a, 183). A 'cycle of predation' co-existed for Mbembe with mobility and cultural mixing. This mobile constellation of networks, commerce, and war cumulatively formed what Mbembe has termed the 'logic of moving sands.' Colonialism was forced to co-opt these 'logics' (commerce, mobility, and predation), because it was unable to modify them to any significant extent. The Sahel reveals the historical existence of the interactions that Mbembe identifies in his contemporary term Afropolitanism.

Afropolitan histories: Johannesburg

Mbembe's most developed account of a 'history' of Afropolitanism can be found in his work on Johannesburg. Although the city grew on the back of European investment in mining, as in many cities of the colonial era, Africans in Johannesburg explored and developed new cultural forms (Akyeampong 2000, 222). Mbembe has identified Johannesburg as 'the centre of Afropolitanism par excellence' and a symbol of the 'African modern' (Mbembe and Nuttall 2004c, 347; Nutall and Mbembe 2007, 1). With its origins bound up with the Witwatersrand gold rush during the latter half of the nineteenth century, Johannesburg, writes Mbembe, 'has always imagined itself to be a modern city':

> It had its own newspapers, its horse-drawn trams, its solid stone buildings, its stock exchange, its banks... and various social clubs.
> (Mbembe 2008b, 40)

One could extend elements of Mbembe's analysis of Johannesburg to other African urban centres of the period, which hosted vibrant social associations, and 'print cultures' connecting growing newspapers to new readerships (Jones 2019).

The significance of Afropolitanism's urban history is material, as well as cultural. African professionals' relative wealth enabled them to escape the daily grind and engage in cultural production. This enterprise took place in an environment structured by racism. In Johannesburg, these factors combined to create a 'contradictory' relationship, whereby the economic centrality of African labour 'in the market sphere' ran up against a racism that led to 'the constant depreciation' of black people, and their exclusion 'by the forces of commercialism and bigotry...' (Mbembe and Nuttall 2008, 43). While colonial elites could be seen as predecessors of contemporary Afropolitan intellectuals, they nonetheless faced concrete forms of discrimination specific to their times.

Superfluity

Johannesburg, Mbembe argues, was 'founded within the sphere of superfluity' (Mbembe 2008b, 41; 2004b, 373). He refers to a paradox between the way that African labour was central to the Johannesburg economy's production of high-value goods but, at the very same time, that this African labour force was actively concealed. There was 'the obfuscation of any use value black labour might have had' (Mbembe 2008b, 42). Mbembe uses the term 'superfluity' to indicate this double bind, drawing on Karl Marx (1818–1883) and historian Fernand Braudel (1902–1985). On the one hand, 'superfluity' indicates 'a mode of relation to objects' often associated with luxury. For instance, Braudel linked the concept with 'luxury, vanity, caprice, spectacle, [and] phantasm' (Braudel 1981, Ch. 3–4; Mbembe 2008b, 41). On the other hand, 'superfluity' indicates the existence of populations and labour beyond the active labour force. Arendt thus relates superfluity to 'misery and destitution,' regarding European immigrants in South Africa as 'a class of superfluous men' (Arendt 1966; Mbembe 2008b, 41). These paradoxical extremes of opulence and destitution, of economic centrality and marginalization, come together to constitute 'superfluity.'

The phenomenon of a superfluous labour force re-emerges in Mbembe's account of a 'vernacular cosmopolitanism' in postcolonial African society during the 1990s and 2000s, found in the early paragraphs of his chapter on 'Afropolitanism' in *Night*. This writing comes closest to establishing a concrete social and economic context for Mbembe's ideas on contemporary Afropolitanism, and, as such, provides an important and largely unrecognized complication of the perception that Mbembe's elaboration of Afropolitanism is elitist. Mbembe opens his chapter by placing Afropolitanism in the context of social transformations in postcolonial African society. These transformations are complex and include warfare, the notion of development as a political metaphor, and economic changes, some of which will be familiar from Mbembe's writing on 'private indirect governance' (Mbembe 2001b, 66–101). However, for our purposes, it is Mbembe's account of a heavily stratified society in which the 'professional' classes benefit from opportunities now unrecognizable to the growing precariat that epitomizes a contemporary form of superfluity.

THE FIRST MOMENT OF AFROPOLITANISM: WHIRLWIND WRITING

Mbembe's lesser-known first moment of Afropolitanism focuses on a literary aesthetic of 'whirlwind writing.' Mbembe argues that this type of 'Afropolitan writing' embodies 'surplus' and 'excess': it breaks down established cultural boundaries, narratives, and preconceptions. Above all, it attacks the 'fetishism of origins,' by seeking to demolish all notions of a pure origin point for any cultural movement, and even questions the very status of reality (Mbembe 2021a, 209). This focus especially refers to attempts to fix African cultural or political movements in terms of one specific origin point, such as 'precolonial Africa.' Mbembe cautions us to be more worldly-wise and resist the appeal of grand narratives of all kinds. Mbembe particularly has Pan-Africanism in his sights, Afrocentrism (the emphasizing of the African roots of African cultures and histories), and Afropessimism (the claim that all aspects of life in Africa are necessarily in decline). He sees such ideas as constraining our understanding of Africa. It is in this context that the 'whirlwind' and excessive qualities of literary Afropolitanism are so important. Excess of all kinds, Mbembe contends, replaces the stability of established narratives.

Mbembe sees literary forms (such as texts or even genres) as 'real, floating and mobile.' He believes that these need to be free from past ideologies (Mbembe 2021a, 212). Despite this, Mbembe is not entirely clear about the outlines of the new literary forms that he identifies. He is content to observe that they proceed by 'cross[ing] out, eras[ing], replac[ing], effac[ing], and recreat[ing],' and 'proceed[ing] by jump cuts…discordances, substitutions, and assemblages' (Mbembe 2021a, 212). A key quality here is the mobility of these forms and their heterogenous composition, drawing on multiple sources and concepts. All of these work against the singular and static nature of the overarching narratives critiqued by Mbembe.

The 'whirlwind' of Afropolitan writing is subversive in that it engages in deliberate 'transgression' (Wolfrey 2008). Mbembe identifies this one quality as key to Afropolitan writing and sees it as epitomizing the crossing of all boundaries. Transgression is a form of creative mobility, which Mbembe problematically describes as 'above all to write in fusion, to write rape and violation' (Mbembe 2021a, 211). This faith in transgression assumes that literature has an essentially social role, a view reflected in Labou Tansi's 'Preface' to *The Shameful State*, which offers a key statement on the latter writer's fiction in relation to Congolese society:

> The novel is, it seems, a work of imagination. However, this imagination must find its place somewhere in reality. I write, or I cry, a bit in order to force the world to come into the world.
>
> (Labou Tansi 2015, xi)

Writing a novel here is not seen as a work of 'pure' imagination, but rather it is a creative act that works in tandem with the outside world. Imaginative writing enlarges the 'real' world, rather than existing at a divide from it.

Mbembe draws on Ouologuem's fiction as an example of this Afropolitan writing. Ouologuem, Mbembe argues, writes not only about existing things, but also explores 'what covers up, surrounds, and exceeds what exists' (Mbembe 2021a, 210). Disruption and excess characterize Ouologuem's prose and do so in ways that irreverently break with the concerns of Négritude and Pan-Africanism.

Labou Tansi's fiction offers similar possibilities. Mbembe argues that in *L'Autre monde*, care for the titular other world predominates over and above everyday practicalities (Labou Tansi 1997). The novel is concerned with the future and reveals how Labou Tansi's writing enables 'a way of scrutinizing the night' or unseen world (see Chapter 4) (Garnier 2015). This attempt to move away from the everyday and into the supernatural has political implications. It 'engag[es] with "the final resting place of [authoritarian] sovereignty," that emerges out of a "[postcolonial] epoch characterized by crudeness and cruelty"' (Mbembe 2021a, 211). Whirlwind writing makes imaginative leaps beyond daily reality, treating such topics as the supernatural or the fantastical. In doing so, it can be viewed as a final resting place of grand projects, in this case, the dictatorship of postcolonial despots. While it overturns preceding paradigms, Afropolitan writing carves out a new future, whose outlines have not yet taken shape.

Critically, while an Afropolitan aesthetic recognizes the past, it is not bound by it. Mbembe attaches the act of literary creation to the future. It has the potential to liberate people from claims about their origins. They are no longer 'a walking spectator of one's own life,' and literature opens the possibility for 'the broken man who slowly gets up again and frees himself of his origins' (Mbembe 2021a, 212). In other words, Afropolitan literature is not only one of radical excess or even shapelessness but also a space of possibility. In this way, 'Africa itself is now imagined as an immense interval' or a fertile gap. It forms an 'inexhaustible citation,' anticipating the future works of literature that might draw on it, while being malleable and 'open to many forms of combination and composition.'

THE SECOND MOMENT OF AFROPOLITANISM: 'A NEW AGE OF DISPERSION AND CIRCULATION'

The second moment of Afropolitanism focuses on Africa's engagement with the wider world. Africa enters 'a new age of dispersion and circulation,' in which migratory flows intensify, and 'new African diasporas' are established (Mbembe 2021a, 211). Africans become connected to the extra-African world in new ways. This reality of 'worlds in movement' forces a reconsideration of who counts as African and who doesn't. To be African, Mbembe urges, cannot be simply synonymous with the black African majority. Significant migrant diasporas exist on the continent, such as the Lebanese, Greek, or Afrikaner communities, and these groups often 'see themselves as full-fledged Africans, even if they also belong somewhere else' (Mbembe 2020b, 8). Acknowledging this ethnic and cultural diversity in Africa, for Mbembe, does not obscure ongoing practices of anti-black racism. He explicitly acknowledges the way in which certain migrants who arrived in Africa absorbed a mentality associated with colonialism, and aspired to racial supremacy (Mbembe 2020b, 10).

Africa also serves as the departure point for journeys into the outside world, especially to those zones connected to slave-trading economies: the Sahara, and the Indian and Atlantic Oceans (Mbembe 2020b, 9). This process has left 'traces of Africa' across 'the face of the capitalist and Islamic worlds…' Cultural 'mixing, blending, and superimposing' took place, in which few cultural forms 'have survived the bulldozer of miscegenation and vernacularisation' (Mbembe 2020b, 9).

Why is the Afropolitan moment distinctive?

Afropolitanism's 'second moment' connotes a specifically contemporary search for *aesthetic forms* (not limited to literature) that reflect forms of mobility that now exist in a globalized, postcolonial Africa. There are two reasons why it is distinct.

Firstly, this moment is shaped by social and cultural changes that Mbembe sees at the turn of the twenty-first century in Africa. These include changes in leisure practices in African societies, but also a wider series of reconfigurations identified by Mbembe, including new family structures, sexual identities, and ideas about the person. These modifications affect the poor as much as the wealthy, although they do so in distinct ways. In African cities, precarity and the evaporation of many older career paths have led to contingent and transitory cultural forms among the expanding ranks of the poor, while among the wealthy, conversely, a new and consumerist culture of leisure is informed by travel, education, and the cultural consumption of products from across the world (Ferguson 2015, 1–6). Although radically distinct, the cultural forms circulating among both rich and poor can both be understood as 'Afropolitan' in their engagement with contemporary transnational cultural flows and products.

Secondly, this contemporary 'second' Afropolitan moment delineates an intellectual impulse to move beyond those theorizations of African identity that remain firmly attached to questions of race and origins. Just as Mbembe saw Afropolitan literature as challenging grand narratives, so he sees contemporary Afropolitan culture as undermining claims to nativism or autochthony (claims about being rooted in a specific region) in African politics, which Mbembe contends, are rising. These divide 'us' from 'them,' according to notions of geographical, ethnic, and linguistic belonging (Geschiere 2009). Faced with this emergence of aggressively localist politics, reflected in community groups or militia organizations, Afropolitanism seeks 'a way of being in the world' that 'refus[es] on principle any form of victim identity...' (Mbembe 2020b, 11). Critically, Mbembe does not regard this emphasis on worldliness as an evasion of historical injustice inflicted upon African societies. Instead, he sees an Afropolitan outlook as acknowledging past abuses (Mbembe 2020b, 11).

Afropolitanism's relation to Pan-Africanism and African nationalism

Afropolitanism resists grand narratives, and two are particularly within Mbembe's sights: Pan-Africanism and African nationalism. These ideals might be considered liberatory and transformational, but Mbembe has reservations about both.

But how is Afropolitanism different from these grand narratives? African nationalism provided political ideologies that challenged colonial occupation. Indeed, Mbembe recognizes that such nationalism 'represented…a powerful utopia, and that it offered a call to resistance.' But, Mbembe warns, these ideals also gave birth to states that became 'predator[s],' like a demon 'who roams at night and flees the light of day' (Mbembe 2020b, 11). The reality of postcolonial states has tarnished historical ideals.

Pan-Africanism differs from Afropolitanism in the former's emphasis on the role of racial solidarity underlining African unity. This, Mbembe argues, obscures 'the forms of multiplicity' including 'racial multiplicity' that serves as a key element of Africa's historical experience (Mbembe 2020b, 12). In other words, Mbembe sees Pan-Africanism as overly simplifying what it means to be African.

Afropolitans are geographically scattered, albeit with a meaningful connection of some kind to the African continent. Some 'have decided of their own accord to live on the continent,' although in countries other than those of their birth, some 'had the opportunity to experience several worlds,' and have 'not stopped coming and going,' while many 'can express themselves in more than one language' (Mbembe 2020b, 12). All of this means that Afropolitans are developing 'a transnational culture' that Mbembe identifies as 'Afropolitan' (Mbembe 2020b, 12).

Practical and elite Afropolitans

In contemporary African societies, Mbembe distinguishes between a 'practical' and an 'elite' cosmopolitanism. Both play an important role in Afropolitanism, showing that Afropolitan cultural creativity can occur among rich and poor in different ways (Mbembe 2021a, 177).

Practical cosmopolitanism is of a resolutely 'vernacular type.' Even though it rests 'on the obligation to belong to a distinct cultural or religious entity,' it nonetheless which intense needs 'commerce with the world' (Mbembe 2005a; 2021a, 177). Mbembe offers concrete examples, such as the way new technological and religious ideas emerge in regions like the Sahel, including 'divine sects.' Another important area is that of illegality and 'shadow' economic activity within the informal (off the books) sector. Although undocumented, the informal economy, including black market and undocumented trading, is an important area, forming 'shadow zones,' in which longstanding community structures are 'shattered, and new bonds are formed' (Mbembe 2021a, 178; Chipkin and Swilling 2018, 1). In the low-income areas of large cities, entire groups of people live 'off-grid' at the margins of governmental record-keeping, paid in cash, and working in the informal economy (Mbembe 2021a, 177). These people are hardly jet-set, but their cultural activities are still influenced by products and ideas from outside of Africa.

Elite cosmopolitanism among the rich is linked to an intellectual project: the attempt to 'reconstruct African identity and public space' in relation to 'the universal demands of reason' (Mbembe 2021a, 178). Social identities are changed in ways that take account of cultural trends outside the continent. This Afropolitanism takes two forms: an effort to 're-enchant' tradition and custom, and the emergence of 'a private sphere' of life. Mbembe sees this reconstruction of a private sphere as being closely linked to social change. Evidence of this included the ability of elites to migrate, and find opportunities to enrich themselves beyond the state. They experienced a psychological tension between the competing claims of locality and transnationalism (Mbembe 2021a, 178). Within the new private sphere emerging from these changes, there is an increased emphasis on leisure, including clothing, sport, cinema, and 'care for the body in general' (Mbembe 2021a, 191). Mbembe draws on the increasing visibility of queer cultures in contemporary Africa, and sees this as part of a more general 'silent sexual revolution'

(Awondo et al. 2012, 145; Mbembe 2021a, 195). As well as 'homosexual practices [becoming]...more widespread than many in Africa want to admit,' Mbembe argues that practices of erotic gratification have changed, including the growing use of aphrodisiacs (Abbas and Ekine 2013; Mbembe 2021a. 196; Nyeck 2019, 1–11).

This elite cosmopolitanism causes social tensions. The poor, especially low-income males, occupy a problematic relationship to this new 'private sphere.' The prevalence of homophobia reveals some of these anxieties (Geschiere 2017, 7). Mbembe sees this prejudice as being adopted by ordinary people 'as a way of disqualifying the ruling classes.' This is only one part of a wider anxiety that surrounds the masculinity of the poor, who 'everywhere, have the impression [that] they have been demasculinized.' More generally, Mbembe regards the changing status of masculinity in elite cosmopolitanism as of particular significance. He argues that while the phallus has hitherto played a key role in the symbolism of political authority in many African societies, its position is now changed or even imperilled as patriarchal authority has been challenged by the growing economic power of women, as well as the emergence of queer cultures (Mbembe 2021a, 195–196).

AFROPOLITANISM IN QUESTION

During the 2010s, Afropolitanism generated intense debate in academic journals and online, with the portmanteau term being accused of serving as a byword for elitism, class privilege, as well as an escape from politics and history (Ede 2016, 88). What about those left behind by Afropolitan elites? What of the 'have nots' excluded by its seeming celebration of transnational mobility and leisure? Didn't Afropolitanism have a much longer history than Mbembe admitted? Almost all of these critiques focus on Mbembe's 'second' form of Afropolitanism, and very little scholarship examines his first, literary manifestation of the term.

Critiques of Afropolitanism begin with the very makeup of the term, which joins together 'African' and 'cosmopolitan' (Gehrmann 2016, 62). 'If [Afropolitanism] is an African way of being cosmopolitan...what do you call a European or Asian way of being cosmopolitan...?' 'Why can an African not just be cosmopolitan?' (Eze 2014, 239).

Critiques of Afropolitanism I: Elitism

Afropolitanism is often taken as a general short-hand for a mobile, consumer-oriented culture of upper middle-class Africans. An immediate and basic problem with Afropolitanism in this sense is the question 'what about the non-affluent African diaspora?' (Tveit 2013) In this sense, too much emphasis on Afropolitans, or the diasporic elite, risks 'obscur[ing] the grittier stories of the African immigrant experience' (Tucker 2013). Afropolitanism could be accused of 'blue sky thinking' in its praising of cultural mobility when 'there is no Western country... that will grant an African a visa merely to visit...museums' (Ogbechie 2008). In short, Afropolitanism might have laudable notions of global mobility and creativity, but it falls far short on the practical, material details that constrain many Africans in the present day. We have seen that Mbembe directly accounts for an Afropolitanism of the poor. Although this fact is rarely discussed by his critics, it is nonetheless true that Mbembe does seem to have less to say about this 'practical cosmopolitanism' than about its elite counterpart. It might be argued that Mbembe sees 'practical cosmopolitanism' as largely describing social phenomena, while he accords 'elite cosmopolitanism' far wider philosophical implications around issues such as gender.

Critiques of Afropolitanism II: Commodification

Afropolitanism has been understood as commodifying African cultures. The term is arguably uncritical in its celebration of a consumerist lifestyle more generally. Its emphasis on transnational mobility could be understood as endorsing neoliberal economic attempts to defend the mobility of labour or capital. In practice, this critique is harder to level specifically at Mbembe's contribution, as compared to Selasi or the *Afropolitan* magazine, a 'premium magazine for the African elite.' But its existence reveals the sheer generality that continues to surround debate about the term (Afropolitan, n.d.; Tutton 2012). One simply needs to Google 'Afropolitan' and find 'aspirational luxury lifestyle magazines' and shopping, Dabiri complains, taking aim at:

> That whole lifestyle of *Sex And The City* feminism, cocktails, designer clothes, handbags and shoes is not particularly liberating in an Anglo-American context, so I see no reason why we should transfer such models to Africa and declare it progress.
>
> (Dabiri 2014)

More troublingly still, 'insights on race, modernity and identity appear to be increasingly sidelined' in a headlong rush to celebrate consumerism. Even if he elsewhere criticizes neoliberal finance (see Chapter 8), Mbembe 'also identifies [consumerism] as part of the Afropolitan assemblage' (Dabiri 2014). Dabiri regards this as risking the commodification of African cultures, a process that she argues parallels Gilroy's warnings about the destructive effect of consumerism on black culture more generally (Gilroy 2001, 164; Williams 2013, 56–57).

Critiques of Afropolitanism III: It is apolitical

These warnings about the Afropolitan reach their height in concerns about the apolitical nature of the term. Afropolitanism in Mbembe's rendering is explicitly concerned with decentring this focus on the continent and, potentially, on race itself (Mbembe and Balakrishnan 2016, 30). It represents a 'radical break with a longer intellectual history of emancipatory politics in African Studies,' and, in doing so, risks playing down the injustice of colonialism and neo-colonialism (Balakrishnan 2017, 2). Mbembe critiques Pan-Africanism and African nationalism, but he suggests only 'excess,' mobility, and fluidity to replace it. Mbembe imagines a future in which 'difference is so superfluous' that it 'breaks down entirely' (Balakrishnan 2017). Any sense of the Other risks being overly aestheticized, and even lost, in 'Afropolitanism.'

Cameroonian writer Calixthe Beyala (1961–) has argued that Mbembe misrepresents Pan-Africanism, and ignores the achievements of politicians in favour of superficial social media commentary (ActuCameroun 2023a). Arguably, Pan-Africanism 'creates a more stable foundation' with a broader applicability beyond the arts (Santana 2013). One might question the utility of Mbembe's notion of fluid and border-crossing Afropolitanism for those working in exploitative conditions on the continent. Consider the traumatizing conditions for Kenyan workers hired to staff offshore content-checking warehouses for American social media giants (Hanspal 2023).

Critiques of Afropolitanism IV: It lacks historical awareness

Critics have perceived Afropolitanism's supposedly apolitical nature in its relationship with the past. Nigerian novelist Chimamanda Ngozi Adichie (1977–) has described herself as being tired of the word 'Afropolitan,' observing that:

> history (sadly not well known) shows that cosmopolitanism doesn't date from yesterday: many African kings from the West coast sent their children to study in Europe...
>
> (Santana 2016, 122)

Such histories have been described by Kenyan writer Binyavanga Wainaina as 'not a shocking thing... it's a thing that is very, very old and enduring' (Santana 2016, 122). As we have seen earlier in this chapter, Mbembe acknowledges longstanding forms of African engagement with the wider world, including the slave trade, trans-Saharan exchanges, and the development of cities such as Johannesburg. He also identifies precolonial 'modernity' as particularly relevant to present-day creativity. But it could nonetheless be argued that he does not make it clear how contemporary mobilities relate to historical Afropolitans.

Critiques of Afropolitanism V: Does Afropolitanism marginalize Africa?

More generally, critics have argued that Mbembe celebrates 'a perceived "immunity" to Africa' among the mobile, upper middle class who travel outside the continent (Santana 2016, 123).

These people have the choice to escape from the economic problems of African states. They have an 'immunity' to socio-economic conditions on the continent, which includes the privilege of not being exposed to the racial and financial discrimination faced by other Africans. 'What immunity is,' Wainaina has argued:

> [is that]... you have a credit rating in America. What immunity is, you have a green card... You become this kind of internationalized class of people...
>
> (Santana 2016, 123)

Although it seems to celebrate Africa's global connections, Afropolitanism can be understood as actually marginalizing the continent. Afropolitans get by because of their financial ties, health plans, and passports located *outside* of the African continent. Why, one might ask, does Africa need its global links? Mbembe clearly situates his account of both 'moments' of Afropolitanism in the economic effects of liberalization and the development of urban precarity. But he does appear to have more to say about the rich than the poor, and most of all about how elites engage with cultural trends beyond the continent.

THE AFROPOLITAN FUTURE: BETWEEN HUMANISTIC REBIRTH AND ONLINE SCAMMERS

'Afropolitanism' describes the future as much as the past. We explore two distinct examples of Afropolitan visions at work in contemporary scholarship (Ede 2019, 35; 2023): one philosophical and one rooted in popular culture.

Afropolitanism has been understood as leading to 'a new ethics of being.' It could be absorbed into a more general humanistic philosophy. This is particularly true if we understand spatial mobility as 'symptomatic of ... interior mobility' and representing changes within the person (Eze 2016, 116). According to this understanding, the geographical basis of Afropolitanism becomes interiorized, with physical distance coming second to 'psychic boundaries' such as 'nativism, autochthony, heritage, and other mythologies of authenticity.' Accordingly, Afropolitans are those who 'possess [a] multiple-consciousness,' and an interest in relating to others. This relation to others is already reflected in African thought such as the Igbo proverb *ife kwulu, ife akwudebe ya*, or 'one things stands, something else stands beside it,' which has in turn been compared to Hegel's dialectical structure of reasoning (Eze 2016, 117–118).[1] The Afropolitan asks, firstly, 'what do I...have in common with [the Other],' secondly, 'what is beautiful or admirable' in them, and finally, 'what can I learn from this person?' These questions, once examined, will serve to reduce any immediate and superficial barriers of difference, and thus enable Afropolitans to engage with those from distinct cultural backgrounds. This is not just a project of self-realization, but rather a 'moral re-examination of the world' (Eze 2014, 244). Afropolitanism has therefore become incorporated into philosophical thought, and compared both to African and European traditions of thinking about how to relate to others.

A less utopian world is offered by the Afropolitan anti-heroes populating the world of online scams. Mbembe has argued that technology and commodities (like smartphones) enable a deceptive 'promise of total liberation,' but that they have positive aspects and can contribute to the development of 'the Afropolitan mindset' (Mbembe and Van der Haak 2015b). Critic Yékú contends that it is possible to discern an 'anti-Afropolitan' ethics and 'Afropolitan anti-hero[s]' in the online world of Nigerian 419 scams. These fraud schemes, popularly known by the section of the Nigerian legal code that theoretically prohibits them, are familiar to email users across the world. They attempt to trick the recipient of the email into transferring funds to the scammer, or at least in surrendering financial details to the fraudsters. 419 scamming is a source of cultural fascination in Nigeria and the diaspora, being the subject of popular songs such as '419 state of mind' (Gray 2006). The scammers, Yékú argues, represent anti-heroes whose 'obverse' are the 'sophisticated heroes and cosmopolitan subjects' articulated in the writings of Selasi and other advocates of the Afropolitan (Yékú 2020, 243). The emphasis on physical travel in Afropolitanism's celebration of mobility is somewhat dated, because, Yékú observes:

> Social media [now] is... particularly central to how the Afropolitan has evolved in the last few years... it has become a major platform for the transnational mobility and circulation of everyday life...
>
> (Yékú 2020, 245)

Digital culture, such as Instagram and X feeds, do not simply 'alter and reconstitute' daily life, but also 'reproduce and enable new expression,' including the forming of new articulations of Afropolitan identity. More generally, social media has the potential to make digital mobility available to those who cannot afford physical travel.

BEFORE AFROPOLITANISM: NANA ASMA'U'S (1793–1865) INTELLECTUAL AND POETIC CONNECTIONS ACROSS THE SAHARA

Mbembe's critics have taken him to task over how far Afropolitanism reckons with history. Transregional and transcontinental connections have a long history in Africa. African travellers described Europe for hundreds of years. In the late 1820s, Egyptian cleric Rifa'ah al-Tahtawi (1801–1873) produced a widely read account of his stay in Paris, while Uganda's Sir Apollo Kagwa (1864–1927), and his personal secretary Ham Mukasa (c. 1870–1956) visited England for the coronation of Edward VII in 1902 (Al-Tahtawi 2004; Kahyana 2018, 36; Mukasa 1998). During the 1940s, Nigerian journalists and clerics wrote detailed accounts of their visits to London (Ochonu 2022).

Focusing on one example of a West African intellectual's links across the wider Saharan region, we consider the example of prominent nineteenth-century West African female writer and thinker Nana Asma'u (1793–1864). In her poem 'Welcome to the Mauritanian Scholar' [*Qasida min Asma'u da Mualim al-Murtanya*], Nana Asma'u welcomes a visitor from Mauritania, some 1,500 km away across the Sahara. The scholar was Alhaji Ahmad bin Muhammad al-Shinqiti, and he was already familiar with Nana Asma'u's reputation and writings. The work points to a network of scholarly connections binding individuals across the Sahara desert. Asma'u chose the *qasida* form, itself stipulating a certain length (over seven lines), and obeying one of the metres established by Arab grammarian al-Khalil in the eighth century C.E. (Hammond 2018). Her poem contains culturally specific imagery, such as using smell to communicate inner grace:

> Honour to the erudite scholar who has left his home
> To journey to Medina
> ...
> His immense knowledge can be likened to a sweet scented load,
> So big, even a bull camel could not carry it...
>
> (Boyd and Mack 1997, 283)

Asma'u also shared poems with her kinsman, Shaikh Sa'ad, on his return from the pilgrimage to Mecca. A scholar from Gwandu in modern-day northern Nigeria, Sa'ad's pilgrimage would most likely have taken him to the Red Sea via Wadai, Darfur, and Khartoum (Boyd and Mack 1997, 284). Asma'u's correspondence offers an insight into a world of scholarly exchange across the Sahara hundreds of years before the jet-setting Afropolitans that grace the pages of contemporary magazines. Her poem to al-Shinqiti reveals an inter-regional relationship stretching across the Sahara, but remaining within Africa. However, several of the scholars with whom Asma'u corresponded and who respected her work had travelled beyond Africa, including making the pilgrimage to Mecca.

CONCLUSION

Afropolitanism constitutes one of Mbembe's most influential ideas. Yet, it has often been partially understood, and sometimes conflated with other contributions. This is partly an outcome of the complicated publication history of Mbembe's work on the subject, at least in terms of its availability in English. As we have seen, there are substantial differences between Mbembe's treatment of the term in his 2005 essay and his 2010 book. In particular, the 2010 account presents a far greater degree of social and historical context than the earlier essay.

Mbembe's 'first moment' of Afropolitanism explores a literary aesthetics that celebrates 'excess' and 'transgression,' while challenging preconceived narratives. Mbembe does not chiefly engage with 'Afropolitan' Anglophone novels in his literary elaboration of Afropolitanism, such as novelist Teju Cole's *Open City*, instead developing close readings of Ouologuem and Labou Tansi (Cole 2012). His 'second moment' of Afropolitanism is far better known and refers to contemporary African cultural engagements with the non-African world. Within this, he includes two different forms of cultural activity: a 'practical cosmopolitanism' among the poor, and an 'elite cosmopolitanism' among the wealthy, which includes the formation of a new private sphere that he links to innovation in gender and sexual identities. Ultimately, far more attention has focused on this latter, elite form of the second moment of Afropolitanism.

NANA ASMA'U (ASMA'U BINT SHEHU USMAN DAN FODIO (1793–1865)

Philosopher, Islamic scholar, and poet Nana Asma'u was daughter of Usman dan Fodio, founder of the Sokoto Caliphate in modern-day Northern Nigeria. She wrote extensively in Arabic, Hausa, and Fulfulde, making a major contribution to West African literature in these languages. Asma'u's contribution to nineteenth-century African philosophy and literature also reminds us of the connections that linked northern Nigeria to the wider Saharan world. Ideas, books, and religious debate crossed the Sahara between different parts of Africa and the wider Islamic world. In centres such as Kano and Timbuktu, prominent literary cultures flourished. In the area of modern-day northern Nigeria, compositions in Arabic, or using the Arabic script ajami in Hausa, Fulfulde, or other languages, were written using ink made from vegetable dye, and kept in specific leather book bags known as *gafaka* in Hausa (Boyd and Mack 1997, xvii; Hutson 2019, 1).

NOTE

1 I am grateful to Dr Alex Ugwuja for his advice on Igbo language.

7

TECHNOLOGY

Digital technology has come to dominate our interactions. Mbembe warns that our obsession with all things technological risks becoming a new religion. This is epitomized in the seductive, image-centred world of social media platforms, with their dopamine-inducing architecture, including the promise of 'likes,' endless scrolling, and incessant notifications. Generative artificial intelligence (AI), epitomized in software like Chat GPT, carries with it the possibility of profiling, bias, and job losses. Mbembe's account of the seductions and perils of technology speaks to this era of ambivalent fascination with technology.

The rise of digital technology raises far more general philosophical questions about what it means to be human and regarding the status of immaterial virtual worlds. It is African philosophies and cultures that provide an essential intellectual support as we navigate our relationship to this increasingly virtualized world.

BRUTALISM AND THE RISE OF DIGITAL LIFE

Our relationship with technology can only be understood in terms of a more general socio-political conjuncture: the era

DOI: 10.4324/9780429201646-9

of 'brutalism.' This is a time, Mbembe argues, of multiple, contending forms of violence. In this world of emerging and new inequalities, Africa is at the forefront of humanity's future. This is an era of what Mbembe terms the 'becoming-black' or *devenir-nègre* of the world (Mbembe 2017b, 5; 2018a; 2019a; 2021d). The social and economic realities seen in the postcolony now can be found in New York, Paris, and London. More and more people are consigned to the lowest rungs of the socio-economic ladder in the world's richest countries. Insecurity and precarity are now all too visible in these societies, such as in the conditions of those who work in the gig economy.

We consider Mbembe's exploration of digital culture and its perils, focusing on his critique of human/machine relations in Western philosophy, before turning to human and technological reason, and his idea of 'technolatry.' Finally, we contextualize Mbembe's thought in terms of the parallel treatment of digital media in the thought of African philosopher Joseph Tonda (1952–), his engagement with the work of Africanist anthropologist Jane Guyer (1943–2024), and in relation to Mbembe's own writing on Afrofuturism.

Brutalism

The term 'brutalism' originally referred chiefly to architecture (Mbembe 2020b, 9–11). It is used by Mbembe to account for the organic impact of multiple forms of violence and marginalization in the contemporary world. It is 'a contemporary process,' wherein 'power is constituted, expressed, and reconfigured,' while also 'act[ing] and reproduc[ing] itself as a geomorphic force' (Mbembe 2021c, 11). It evokes a form of blunt but mobile power (see chapter 2 on Mbembe's models of power) that proceeds like a mechanical or natural force by 'fracturing and fissuring,' or 'emptying…drilling, and expelling organic matter.' And most centrally, its wasteful expenditure can be understood as 'depletion.' Brutalism is central to Mbembe's account of technology, as well as its specialized interactions with financialized capitalism, and the environment. Within all of this, one point is central: speed. Operating at the accelerated speed of the internet, brutalism is hyper-rapid and crosses between national borders, always accentuating inequality and injustice. If Mbembe has written about enmity and hatred in the colony and postcolony, brutalism turbocharges the speed and mobility of these animosities. Above all, the aftermath of the global COVID-19 pandemic, Mbembe argues, may well usher this new era of 'tension and brutality' (Mbembe 2021b, S2, S59). For our purposes, this 'escalation of technology' plays a key role in what Mbembe sees as an 'intensification of brutalism' (Mbembe 2023, 8).

Digital technology: Positives and negatives

Although we have earlier encountered Mbembe's warnings on technology, his attitude is ambivalent. He does acknowledge that the internet and smartphones offer new ways for Africans to access knowledge and contribute to the global economy. But despite its liberating potential, Mbembe starkly warns about the dangers of technology. These warnings are linked to the wider era of brutalism that we have seen above, but they also relate to the sheer scale of our dependency on technology. We are increasingly reliant on algorithms, abstraction, and software in most areas of life, from dating to job hunting. Our personal relationship to technology is expressed by a quasi-religious awe: the 'animism of technology.'

TECHNOLOGY I: MACHINE/HUMAN RELATIONS AND THE AFFORDANCES OF THE DIGITAL

Our adoption of digital technology represents a distinctive transformation in humanity's longstanding relations with machines. Far from being entirely an innovation, this development of digital devices builds on the longer history of how we interact with technology. Mbembe focuses particularly on how Western philosophy has framed this relationship. He identifies two distinct trends within this body of thought: first, 'the regime of signs' (in which language had a key role) and second, 'the kingdom of action' (in which tools and artefacts had a governing role) (Mbembe 2020a, 33). The relationship between these two realms was not equal. The first sphere was long accorded priority, with language being the supreme activity. As mechanical knowledge developed, so automata could undertake basic practical tasks that were once reserved for humans.

However, certain functions remained the sovereign capacity of humanity, or at least so humans themselves thought. Language and symbolic thought were chief among these. Humans therefore developed self-confidence, not only in their capacity for knowledge, but also in their position within the world in relation to both non-human species and inanimate machines. This confidence was neither innocent nor disinterested, but instead tied to more general and ambitious projects, particularly that of expanding the field of knowledge and attempting to control the physical world (Mbembe 2020a, 34). At the most general level, knowledge of all kinds, including technical skills, was linked to wider beliefs about humanity's mastery of the universe.

Offering humanity considerable mastery of the physical world, people began to assign complex cultural meanings to technology. Machines soon became linked to the very notion of 'truth,' as well as to eschatology (the theology of the world's end). This latter, eschatological role of technology (that technology represents the end of history) meant that people believed it to have the power to transcend man's alienation within the universe. Technology posed the ultimate promise of returning humanity to itself and simultaneously revealing humanity's true purpose within the universe (Mbembe 2020a, 35). One illusion remains central to this technological eschatology: that the world beyond our own bodies is controllable. This assumption reveals a Promethean faith in human inventiveness; it sees the power of creation as having no limits. All areas of the world could be measured, recorded, and brought under the grasp of technology. This faith in technology contained an attractive idea of humanity's ultimate role in the world as being master of machines, which were ever-ready to undertake human commands. This growing faith in technology ultimately led to what Mbembe terms the 'demythologization' of the world. As a result, all that is autonomous, mysterious, and unaccountable in nature collapsed. Man 'gave himself... the task of getting nature to submit [to him] and of marking it with his traces and imprints' (Mbembe 2020a, 36).

The animism of technology

To describe our faith in technology, Mbembe draws on the concept of 'animism.' The term describes a belief that inanimate objects have spiritual power, typically in a religious context. It is a term with significant stereotypical baggage in anthropological scholarship, and it was often linked to dismissive accounts of African religions (Mulemi 2010). In short, Mbembe warns, we 'are haunted[...] by[...] technolatry' or the idolization of technology (Mbembe 2020a, 66).

Our attitudes to technology have the outlines of religious thought. We live in a 'relative co-naturalism' with digital devices, which, nonetheless, contribute to a 'drying out of [our] symbolic reserves.' Although we bring our devices into our beds, they are really draining our mental and physical well-being. Mbembe sees this 'animism' as having direct economic implications, and, like all elements of digital technology, it is closely related to neoliberal capitalism (Mbembe 2017b, 4). Digital technology offers us the prospect of love and attention, but it converts all areas of our lives into code and data. It has created a quantitative archive that is rife for commercialization. In the process, human experience has been given a market value (Mbembe 2017b, 4–5; Newell and Pype 2021, 17).

The 'spectacular return of animism' is nonetheless distinct from older forms of animistic belief (Mbembe 2020a, 23). Turning to older instances of 'animism,' Mbembe argues that previous forms of such beliefs were based on 'the model of an ancestor cult.' But in the animism of technology, the self or the ego is squarely at the centre. We see our devices as doubles of ourselves, including smartphones or wearable technology. This toxic relationship is cultivated by the everyday narcissism of curating social media profiles and attracting likes and comments. These cumulatively form 'the sign' (or external trace) of our deepest unconscious lives (Mbembe 2020a, 27).

In this digital era, Mbembe suggests, a far older belief has been reawakened. The compelling possibility of being able to bring something inanimate to life was the dream of novelist Mary Shelley's (1797–1851) Doctor Frankenstein. Today, this desire for 'psycho-prosthetic' power is driven by algorithmic reasoning and allows us to create new inanimate spaces and environments that simulate those that exist in the physical world. These not only have the illusion of being living objects, but we increasingly fail to distinguish the inanimate from the animate, the 'fake' from the 'real.' If this sounds too far-fetched, we might think of 'deep fake' photographs and videos or the routine availability of generative AI tools like Chat GPT (Mystakidis 2022, 486–487; Timol 2023; Vergos 2021, 428).

Unsurprisingly, this new animism of technology is not a purely private affair; it has direct political implications. While Mbembe acknowledges that virtual worlds carry the substantial possibility for empowerment, they also serve darker purposes (Mbembe 2020a, 28). Again, the ability of 'fake news' to undermine the results of a democratic election constitutes a stark example of the risks. At a less direct level, the cult of the self that is fostered by social media could easily break down alliances and the potential of individuals to organize to challenge repressive political systems.

African thought and a critique of the animism of technology

For Mbembe, Africa itself plays a key role in facilitating the critique of this new animism of technology. Mbembe understands a putative critique of technology as needing to address very broad issues. It must, he contends, interrogate the very status of the human subject, as well as of the principles of mechanics and technology. Above all, it must be practical in its focus and aim at 'protecting the living against the forces of desiccation' (Mbembe 2020a, 28). He draws on Jane Guyer's studies of the organization of knowledge in African societies, and her identification of African 'traditions of invention.' Guyer argued that societies in Central Africa displayed 'a constant and volatile engagement' with the 'frontiers' of knowledge and that this innovative and inventive capacity had long been ignored by Western scholars (Guyer 1996, 1). This tradition of inventiveness continues to be relevant, as we critique digital technology.

African objects and the boundary between material and immaterial worlds

If all of this seems a tall task, Mbembe sees one avenue for hope in his conceptualization of 'African objects.' These are physical objects belonging to the material world; they have a complex relationship with human beings. In European museums, they were often labelled as 'artworks' regardless of their social or cultural roles in African societies (Mbembe 2024). Although inanimate and material, they are ultimately human creations. These objects are therefore positioned between the human and the material. Occupying this boundary, they represent 'a strident call' to move beyond the constraints of the human. Indeed, these objects challenge the very boundary between the animate and inanimate. Mbembe sees them as posing 'an unconditional critique' of a society that puts too much value in immaterial, digital worlds (Mbembe 2020a, 28).

Afro-computation

Mbembe admits that digital technology might prove liberatory for Africa, especially in economic terms. In his Abiola lecture to the 2016 General Meeting of the African Studies Association of the USA, Mbembe used the middle part of his address to identify the degree to which decolonization impacted 'new cognitive assemblages' and knowledge formations (Mbembe 2016b). In particular, he identified the possibilities of 'Afro-computation' or the African harnessing of digital technology, especially via smartphones and social media.

Afro-computation is an integral part of an 'ongoing Afro-techno-revolution' driven by mobile phones, which have transformed societies and cultures, in Africa and globally. Although Mbembe's account of how this has happened remains quite general, he is clear about the possibility of smartphones to facilitate scientific invention, cultural creativity, or technological innovation on the African continent (Mbembe 2016b). This type of technology has the potential to bypass technological or cultural 'gatekeepers' in the West, although in practice things might not be so simple. Afro-computation could offer a major technological, scientific, and cultural rebalancing towards Africa. However, much smartphone-related labour remains reliant on Western companies which have, in some cases, attempted to exploit local workers (Anwar 2022, 457–458).

Mbembe is not the only African philosopher to have engaged with digital technology. Social media and smartphones also play a key role in the thought of Congolese-Gabonese philosopher Joseph Tonda (1952–). Such media is central to Tonda's idea of 'dazzlement' or *éblouissment*. Smartphone users are, Tonda argues, continuously 'dazzled' or confronted by a surplus of images through their devices (Geschiere 2021, 71). These are drawn from everything from local media in the Gabonese capital of Libreville to the videos of American music stars like Lady Gaga. Tonda regards these images as powerful and having the power to 'colonize' the imagination. Like Mbembe, Tonda recognizes that much social media content is generated by users themselves, who routinely share 'selfies.' For residents of Brazzaville and Libreville such images prove so overwhelming that they complain of a digital barrage which 'kill[s] the eyes' (Geschiere 2021, 72). Simply navigating this image-oriented world causes emotional attrition, and individuals are forced to continuously fight just to distinguish the 'fake' from the genuine (Tonda 2015b). If Mbembe's critique of technology provokes anxiety, Tonda's vision of the colonizing power of digital images pushes these worries still further.

TECHNOLOGY II: ALGORITHMS, ABSTRACTION, AND LIFE UNDER TECHNOLOGY

Mbembe points out that digital technology addresses some of our deepest psychological needs. It offers the possibility of acting as 'our clinic,' offering self-enhancement and the potential of realizing previously untapped dimensions of our personalities.

But, Mbembe warns, this promise is false. It promises us reality, but then fails to deliver.

The COVID-19 lockdowns only made this seductive promise of a 'transfiguration' through technology more attractive. If actions 'in real life' ('IRL') led to the risk of exposure to contagion, technology seemed to promise a life 'cut away from [the] biological corruption' of physical interactions (Mbembe 2021b, S59). This promise only led to isolation and increasing dependence on technology. But despite these shortcomings, digital technology unavoidably mediates our social lives, language, and the way in which we think about our bodies (Mbembe 2020a, 37; Mbembe and Van der Haak, 2015d). Perhaps more insidiously, it has intruded on our patterns of thought and conditioned the ways in which we figure, symbolize, and remember the world and ourselves. Technology has come to demarcate our dreams.

Human and technological reason

How do forms of human and technological reason differ? Mbembe argues that the key distinction is abstraction. Because AI relies not on synapses and neurons, but on algorithms, it inevitably entails a labour of abstraction. It translates human life into numbers (Mbembe 2020a, 65). This abstraction is inherent in digitization: it entails the selecting, classification, and deployment of vast amounts of data. Within all these processes, mathematical calculation is also at work, substituting human thought processes, and formulating predictions and simulations of sentient behaviour. To appreciate how far this abstraction has become central to contemporary culture, we need only think of how governments dream of harnessing 'big data' in policy-making, using 'nudge' theories to influence public behaviour, or how social media companies harvest user analytics to rank influencers and musicians (Thaler and Sunstein 2009). To take this one step further, Mbembe argues that computers now play a key role not only in modelling social phenomena but also in creating such activities from scratch (Mbembe 2020a, 65–66). Technological reason fuses three distinct sub-forms: economic, biological, and algorithmic.

What are the social consequences of algorithmic reason? Even though the algorithmic work of abstraction and quantification might appear relatively benign, algorithms can behave nefariously, such as in routinely denying jobseekers the chance of an interview, or labelling city districts and individuals as allegedly more likely to commit crime based on dubious parameters. Our adulation of technology, Mbembe reminds us, has dangerous practical and social implications. He cites the example of juvenile crime, where 'targets are identified very early' in their lives, and 'it is enough to be a minor' to be labelled and stigmatized: 'so the door is closed and destiny is decided' (Mbembe 2020a, 45). Within this world, technology and private enterprise are symbiotic (Livingston and Ross 2022, 846; Ross 2022, 834). Electronic tags may be mandated as judicial penalties, but they impoverish the individual who is compelled to rent them, and pay the associated monthly and daily fees (Mbembe 2020a, 46). Some of these charges are payable not to the state, but to a private company that operates the tagging system. This penetration of technology into the penal system, Mbembe contends, amounts to a 'seizure' of the racialized body, from which the maximum profit is to be extracted. Technology provides new opportunities for control, but also for obtaining revenue (Mbembe 2020a, 47).

Pure language, and the mathematization of the world

Mbembe sees algorithmic reason as representing the cumulation of a longer-term project of the 'mathematization of the world' (Mbembe 2003a, 38). This attempt to translate the outside world into numbers, Mbembe argues, has tangible political implications. It has been heavily associated with a triumphalist account of the supposedly exclusive achievements of Western philosophy that is no longer tenable in the contemporary world. In any case, this desire to render the world in numerical terms carries the seduction of presenting a transparent or 'pure [mathematical] language' of the world.

Mbembe uses the term 'pure language' to designate a language shorn of all the messiness and contradictions of living languages. He draws it from philosopher Maurice Merleau-Ponty (1908–1961) and uses the term to describe a language superficially purged of all ambiguity, that offers a false certainty of clarity (Mbembe 2023, 38; Merleau-Ponty 1969, 7). This concept taps into a powerful fantasy whereby language combines with the idea of reason to offer 'pure information,' removed from any real-world impurities or errors. This idea of pure language is as culturally destructive as it is ultimately unattainable.

Mbembe argues that the false certainty of ideal language and information makes us vulnerable to the seductions of technology. What is more, he suggests that this susceptibility is particularly a consequence of Western philosophy's valuation of reason and technology. Such a triumphalist celebration of Western thought is out of step, Mbembe warns, with a world where Europe is increasingly losing power.

African cultures, multiplicity, and the resistance to pure language

African cultures potentially provide a remedy to these seductions. Mbembe suggests that the intellectual culture of several African peoples treated conceptual categories in a way that was multiple and fluid rather than fixed and static (Mbembe 2023, 40–41). He sees this as differing from Western adulation of digital culture and mathematics. Mbembe's argument here connects back to his claim that African objects challenge easy Western distinctions between the animate and inanimate, the material and immaterial, it also relates to his interest in African cultures of innovation.

Mbembe's sources here pose problems, as they partly include colonial-era ethnographies of peoples such as the Bambara or Dogon. These texts are heavily connected with the power relations of colonialism that Mbembe has critiqued elsewhere (Dieterlen 1952, 115; Griaule 1947, 443; Leiris 1948). Mbembe does not fully engage with this relationship, and particularly how it relates to his earlier critique of colonial discourse (see chapter 1). More generally, Mbembe is not always clear about how many African cultures he regards as supporting his point, or when, why, and to what extent they each specifically celebrated multiplicity.

AFROFUTURISM

The rise of technology has generated creative responses. In Afrofuturism, Mbembe sees a 'vibratory' power that has emerged from the 'radical imagination.' Afrofuturism is a literary genre that connects 'science, technology, and race' (Lavender 2019, 2). Mbembe understands Afrofuturism in general terms as 'combining [science fiction (SF), techno-culture, magical realism and non-European cosmopologies,' with the aim of interrogating the history and present condition of black people (Mbembe 2014, 125). Mbembe sees this genre as 'dominated by the motif of a quest for origins, traces and also of return' (Mbembe 2023, 9). Although works of fiction, Afrofuturist texts, Mbembe contends, have a practical application because they reveal 'a reserve of power' (Mbembe 2020a, 24). In terms of both content and form, these texts open the eyes of readers and audiences to 'an unlimited field of permutations and new structures' which could be implemented in the real world (Mbembe 2020a, 4).

Afrofuturism developed in relation to S.F. The former genre has been concerned with how notions of difference are produced and encountered, often in ways that challenge any straightforward understanding of what is 'normal' or mainstream (Roberts 2000, 28). This involves drawing attention to the ways in which S.F. themes such as 'abduction, displacement, and alienation' articulate black experience. More generally, Afrofuturism also engages in creative work that 'imagine[s] new black cultures and futures' (Lavender 2019, 1). The genre includes historical writing, as well as novels of writers such as Samuel R. Delany's (1942–) *The Einstein Intersection* (1968) and Octavia Butler's (1947–2006) *Xenogensis* trilogy, as well films like *Black Panther* (2018), and *Get Out* (2017) (Delany 1998; Roberts 2006, 98, 102; Lavender 2019, 1).

There are significant distinctions between Afrofuturist works written in North America and those originating from Africa

(Cleveland 2024). American-based Afrofuturism has had a controversial reception in Africa, and some writers on the continent have chosen instead to identify their work as a specific genre termed 'African Futurism.' This latter genre (sometimes also 'Africanfuturism') 'is specifically and more directly rooted in African culture, history, mythology and point-of-view...' (Mbembe 2014, 125). Writer Nnedi Okorafor complained, 'I was being called this word [an Afrofuturist] whether I agreed or not...' (Okorafor 2020; Talabi 2020).

Afrofuturism constitutes a key resource in Mbembe's thinking about technology. He sees it as rejecting any privileging of 'the human' as a distinct category. This emphasizing of the 'human' has been a key assumption, Mbembe argues, in strands of Western thought such as humanism (a philosophical tradition emphasizing human reason as autonomous). This tradition of humanism is associated, Mbembe contends, with the belief that humanity 'can constitute itself only by relegating some other subject or entity (living or inanimate) to the mechanical status of an object or an accident' (Mbembe 2014, 125). To define 'the human' always therefore entails an act of exclusion. Afrofuturism, by contrast, 'denounces the illusions of the "strictly human"': in its eyes, 'it is the idea of the human species which is put into question by the Black experience' (Mbembe 2014, 121, 125).

Due to European racism, black people were forced to share the status of 'object[s]' or 'thing[s],' and subject to a history of predation. All of this meant that the 'black man... would be the phantom that haunts Western humanist madness,' which was 'haunted by [his] ...ghost' (Mbembe 2014, 125). If humanism has thus become 'an obsolete category,' Afrofuturism instead offers an understanding of the contemporary condition as one of 'object-human' or 'human-object' assemblages.

Mbembe's reading of Afrofuturism challenges any privileging of the human. Afrofuturism forces us to confront the fact the 'human' always engages with other categories, including the 'the non-human, the "more than human," the "outside of the human," or the "other than human".' In this context, Afrofuturism, and its use of S.F., offers a way of imagining new and less exclusive ways of being human. The future is therefore a space of 'almost infinite plasticity' and transformation (Mbembe 2014, 125). This in turn has major implications for how human beings inhabit the earth and share it with other living creatures.

CRITIQUES OF MBEMBE'S THOUGHT ON TECHNOLOGY

Although his account of technology's dark reasoning power is compelling, Mbembe has faced criticism on a number of grounds. 'Afro-computation' has been criticized firstly in terms of its generality, for example, in arguing for a singular 'computation' across all Africans from Egypt to Botswana, and secondly for ignoring the social consequences of smartphone use in other areas of the world (Bahi 2021, 110). But, as anthropologist Peter Geschiere argues, it may be that because Africa was not entirely subsumed into capitalist economic relations that it offers a unique area for 'pluriversal' (indicating a plurality of forms of knowledge) thought (Geschiere 2021, 71–75). Scholars have also critiqued Mbembe's account of how AI and algorithms are rational. AI reflects algorithm-informed decision-making rather than moral reasoning, and therefore could be understood as representing 'agency without reason' (Robles-Anderson 2021, 38).

CONCLUSION

'Technolatry' and our compulsive 'animism of technology' is focused on seductive screens and images. Digital technology contributes to the attractive fiction of a unified and simple self or personal identity that can easily be commodified. Digitization brings with it a tendency to idealize what Mbembe terms as 'algorithmic reason' or the tendency to reduce human experience into chains of numbers and, ultimately, data.

Digital technologies offer the latest gloss on a longstanding fantasy that claims that humans have the ability to exercise mastery over the universe. This dream of control over the physical world easily extends to the exercise of domination over other people. Time and again, Mbembe argues, Western thought has used the same self-confidence it expresses in its relationship with machines in its attempts to justify colonialism and racism. The very dream of a 'pure' language and perfect data is itself the product, he reminds us, of a tradition of thought that cannot navigate the slippery, indeterminate, or ambiguous.

Against the seemingly irresistible damage caused by digital technology Mbembe sees positives. On the one hand, Afro-computation and the use of new technologies in African economies potentially give Africans a new leverage unavailable to them in more traditional sectors. On the other, the conceptual vision found in Afrofuturist literature and in some intellectual traditions on the African continent challenges distinctions between material and immaterial, human and non-human, self and the 'Other', that Mbembe sees as constraining Western philosophy.

JOSEPH TONDA (1952–)

Congolese-Gabonese philosopher Joseph Tonda shares key elements with Mbembe's thinking on the cultural and psychological impact of colonialism, as well as technology and social media. Tonda analyses urban life in Brazzaville and Libreville to explore the ways in which technology amplifies people's fears and anxieties in his *L'impérialisme postcolonial: critique de la société des éblouissements* (Postcolonial Imperialism: Critique of the Society of Dazzlement) (Tonda 2015b), while he has also written about Fanon's thought (Tonda 2016), including developing a concept of 'Afrodystopia' to account for repressive postcolonial politics, and his 2005 work *Le Souverain Moderne* (The Modern Sovereign) explores life in the postcolony (Tonda 2005).

MBEMBE AND COLONIAL FRENCH ETHNOGRAPHY IN WEST AFRICA

Mbembe bases his argument that African objects offer a compelling opportunity to rethink Western infatuation with technology on several sources, including colonial French ethnographic texts (Mbembe 2018c; 2023, 40–41). These are more than scholarly accounts of African societies and are closely implicated in their relationship with colonialism as well as with questions of power and knowledge.

MARCEL GRIAULE (1898–1956)

Marcel Griaule played a key role in exploring the philosophical, religious, and cosmological beliefs of the Dogon people of modern-day Mali. From the late 1940s, Griaule worked closely with the Dogon thinker Ogotemmêli, who provided Griaule's team of anthropologists with a detailed picture of Dogon belief systems, covering areas like language and cosmology. After Griaule's death, the products of his work with Ogotemmêli were published by collaborators, including *Le renard pâle* (The pale fox) by Germaine Dieterlen (Griaule and Dieterlen 1965) and *Ethnologie et langage: La parole chez les Dogon* (Ethnology and language: speech among the Dogon) (1965) by Griaule's daughter and professional anthropologist Geneviève Calame-Griaule (1987).

Having trained in Paris during the 1920s, Griaule led four ethnographic missions in Africa during the following decade, including the Dakar-Djibouti, Sahara-Soudan, Sahara-Cameroun, and Niger-Iro lake missions (Forde 1956, 217). These pioneered the idea that anthropological fieldwork was fundable by charitable and government agencies. Griaule relied heavily on France's colonial interests in Africa to secure funding, and his Dakar-Djibouti expedition was closely bound up with 'collecting' African objects, some 3,500 artefacts for Paris's Trocadéro museum. Local people resented some of Griaule's activities, such as the excavation of respected graves without consent and seizing funerary artefacts (Clifford 1988, 69; Jolly 2019).

Griaule's own writings include frank descriptions of colonial racism and abuse, including French researchers beating Africans who refused to cross the Nile (Clifford 1988, 76). Subsequently, his research has been challenged by African philosophers such as Hountondji (1996), who accuse him of presenting a single and static view of African belief systems and generalizing from one case. In addition, anthropologists have pointed out that Griaule relied on translators and tended to only work with male informants who shared his interests (Lettens 1971).

MICHEL LEIRIS (1901–1990)

French writer and 'secretary-archivist' to Griaule's 1931–1933 Dakar-Djibouti expedition, Michel Leiris does not form a part of Mbembe's arguments on technology but does appear elsewhere in his work (2017, 50). Leiris offers a different perspective to Griaule's confident attempt to construct an account of the entire belief systems of an African people. In the process, he challenges the very ability of European anthropologists to write about Africa, a question we have seen Mbembe address in Chapter 1. Leiris recorded just how much his expectations of Africa were bound up with his own feelings about his life in France, asserting that he was 'sick… of life in Paris,' and regarding the Dakar-Djibouti expedition as a 'poetic adventure' and opportunity to escape himself (Clifford 1988, 165). Leiris's lengthy account of the expedition, *Phantom Africa* (1934), was really a mesh of fragmentary detail that resisted imposing an overarching narrative. This book is often seen as foreshadowing later forms of self-aware or 'reflexive' ethnography, where scholar-travellers bring themselves into the story. Leiris incorporates a dizzying array of fragments regarding his experience of the Dakar-Dijbouti expedition, ranging from scholarly insights to reflections about his own dreams, doubts, and bodily problems (Hand 2002, 55–56).

8

THE PLANETARY AND THE COMMON

'In reality,' Mbembe observes, 'Africa has never been outside of the world' (Mbembe 2023, 10). He centers the history and thought of Africa as playing a critical role in mapping out the challenges faced by all of humanity in negotiating how to live on the Earth.

During this era of brutalism, the global or planetary represents the only scale on which inequality, extraction, and belonging can be understood. Non-humans are under pressure from ceaseless extraction and pollution enacted by humans, and the looming prospect of an apocalyptic 'combustion' of the Earth (Mbembe 2020a, 20). We will consider Mbembe's account of the 'common,' before turning to the emergence of a 'planetary era,' and finally consider the role of 'hospitality' and the 'passerby' within this.

Today, Mbembe observes, the relations of 'enmity' that he has charted in the colony and postcolony are aggravated by pollution and environmental degradation. Environmental change worsens existing inequalities. These problems are compounded when environmental devastation damages regions of the world which have already faced colonial violence.

A veritable 'combustion of the world' looms, indicating an excessive burning-up of the Earth's resources, whether natural, human, animal, or economic. It is a 'vertiginous exhaustion' of those natural resources, metals, and fossil fuels that 'support the material infrastructure of our existence' (Mbembe 2023, 8). This grand inferno threatens to consume the planet's very fabric (Mbembe 2020a, 24). Even before this combustion comes to pass, environmental exploitation is bringing about a new order in which extraction plays a devastating role. In this dying world, 'blind depredation' accompanies the mining of minerals in a combination that 'opens necessarily onto devastation' (Mbembe 2020a, 24, 44, 68). Mbembe does not shy away from the apocalyptic overtones of such a predicament, observing in quasi-Biblical tones that 'the hour of the great juncture has sounded' (Mbembe 2020a, 44).

Brutalism poses a mortal threat to all living beings. Yet, Mbembe also perceives a more optimistic dimension: he sees these new planetary processes as having the potential to unlock a fresh way for humans to relate to the non-human world, whether animal or material. As we saw in Chapter 5, Mbembe is interested in a utopian future that lies after decolonization, characterized by a 'New Era of the Earth.'

COMBUSTION, NECROCAPITALISM, AND THE THREAT TO THE EARTH

Imagine the Earth's surface wrapped in undersea cables, traversed by phone networks, and dotted by multiple screens and smartphones. Technology has so expanded across the planet's surface that it marks a veritable double of the Earth (Mbembe 2023, 37). But the planet, Mbembe reminds us, is under unprecedented threat, including from capital and technology. This is an era of the 'techno-cene,' he argues in a reworking of the term 'anthropocene' (the era during which the Earth has been shaped by humanity, often 1950) denoting the era of man's influence on Earth (Quenet 2017, 165).

Combustion

Mbembe uses the imagery of fire to communicate a planet stretched to the limit. But the current crisis of 'combustion' is neither inevitable nor natural. It is rooted in human history, and intimately related, Mbembe reminds us, to the experiences of slavery and colonialism. The looming ecological crisis reopens old habits of dividing and labelling human beings. Above all, biological engineering and modification risks accelerating a situation where 'only what can potentially generate value counts as life...' (Mbembe 2021b, 24). This is an era of 'combustion': burning, intense heat, accelerated, technology-driven interactions, and an unsustainable consumption of resources (Mbembe 2023, 12).

Necrocapitalism

Earth's 'combustion' is above all related to economic activity. Mbembe uses the term 'necrocapitalism' to describe how capitalist markets have become ever-hungry and begun to feast on all resources and beings, living and dead. They have 'morphed into complex extractive and digestive systems,' which turn people 'into waste' (Mbembe 2021b, 15). This process is not new, but, Mbembe warns, it is accelerating. The new speed of extraction is enabled by the way in which computers have transformed financial markets, enabling transactions to occur in nanoseconds.

These hungry markets of 'necrocapitalism' have a direct environmental impact: they are '*magnetic fields* as well as key determinants of the climate system on earth' (Mbembe 2021b, 15). The energy of these markets provokes ecological devastation as relentless mining and industry create 'countless uninhabitable zones,' poisoned by 'debris' and 'toxins.' In their wake, necrocapitalist markets leave behind 'waste heaps of humans...' (Mbembe 2021b, 16). Such activities have violated long-standing norms in how humans have interacted with the planet and caused a 'transgression of planetary boundaries.' This is most spectacular in the case of new materials and substances, such as nanoparticles and 'genetically engineered organisms...' (Mbembe 2021b, 16–17). Ultimately, a paradox exists between financial markets that increasingly trade over intangible, speculative values (leading Mbembe to see them as a 'hallucinatory phenomenon') and the all-too-real scars caused by continual extraction and the modification of life for profit by biotech and big pharmaceutical companies.

THE ERA OF THE EARTH: HOSPITALITY AND THE PLANETARY AGE

Against the barren backdrop of global climate change and the threat to life on the planet, Mbembe discerns the possibility for new forms of community, as well as fresh relations between humans and the animal and material worlds.

The *nomos* of the Earth and a universal hospitality

To move beyond the risk of planetary combustion, Mbembe argues that we must review how humans relate to their surroundings. We must build a sense of that which is held 'in common' between all humans. To do this, we must guard against the 'sacralisation' of frontiers and borders (Mbembe 2021b, 55). In place of barriers, a 'universal hospitality' should therefore be practised, according to which one must embrace the world collectively and unconditionally. The figure of the 'passerby' (Chapter 6) is imperative to this worldly hospitality (Mbembe 2021b, 56). The passerby's condition of being on the road means that the kind of politics necessary in this new era has to be a planetary democracy.

Mbembe is influenced here by German jurist Carl Schmitt (1888–1985), who saw the Earth as fundamentally shared. For Schmitt, each new era of human occupation of the Earth inevitably led to fresh spatial orders and divisions. To describe these orders, Schmitt used the Ancient Greek term *nomos* (law, custom), indicating the way that an individual or state could own the Earth. The Earth is shared and held in common. It cannot be appropriated by any species, nation, or individual (Mbembe 2020a, 59; Schmitt 2003, 85). For the Greeks, Schmitt argues, the Earth was for all, as expressed in the word *isonomia* (equality in the law). Those who inhabited the Earth were fundamentally equal and were fellow creatures among others, or *homoios* ('the same as' or 'one with') (Mbembe 2020a, 59). The use of the

Earth cannot be legitimately denied to any one group, and the law governing the Earth applies equally to all.

Nowhere is Schmidt's insight more apparent, Mbembe reflects, than in the potential of the Earth to equitably pay those who work it. In the face of economic and racial inequality, the Earth can represent 'the idea of an almost immanent justice' (Mbembe 2020a, 59). The Earth, and especially the soil itself, requires human labour to make it bear fruit. This enterprise is based around acts of division and appropriation (Mbembe 2020a, 60). This 'taking' of land by different human groups might seem a banal process, but it was, for Schmitt, of fundamental political significance. Cultivable land could be understood as the motor of world history; without food on the table, the concerns of high politics soon count for little. For Mbembe, this working or dividing of the Earth among many different people has the potential to give rise to the emergence of a new global order (Mbembe 2020a, 60; Schmitt 2003, 54).

The idea of shared possession of the Earth is central to Mbembe's account of hospitality. Sharing the Earth requires welcoming strangers or the 'passerby.' Mbembe develops his account of 'hospitality' to define these relations. 'Hospitality' has played a central role in the thought of philosophers such as Jacques Derrida (1930–2004), but Mbembe draws primarily on the German philosopher Immanuel Kant's (1724–1804) concept of hospitality as 'the right that a stranger has who arrives on the soil of another to not be treated as an enemy…' (Derrida 2001; Mbembe 2020a, 55). Kant's 'Perpetual Peace' (1795) argued for a future society in which a state of 'perpetual peace' pertained, ensuring that humans could live without war or standing armies (Kant 1957; Meckstroth 2018, 527). A final condition for the emergence of this 'perpetual peace' was a form of political identity shared between the citizens of these free states and articulated in terms of a universal hospitality (Habermas 1997; Shryock 2008, 411).

However, Mbembe argues, Kant's conceptualization of hospitality is not so much a 'right to hospitality,' open to any visitor indefinitely, but rather 'a visiting right.' This latter right might be used by any human being as a member of a society, because of their 'common possession of the Earth's surface': it facilitates coexistence. As a result, nobody has more of a right than another to find some place on the Earth (Mbembe 2020a, 55). Thus, as a member of society, any individual can invoke the right to common possession of the Earth.

Planetarity and symbiosis

Mbembe's notion of 'planetarity' is central to his account of the appearance of a new global order. The term has two dimensions: it presupposes the possibility of a 'global representation of the Earth' and the emergence of 'a spatial order embracing all humanity' (Mbembe 2020a, 61). In reflecting on the planetary, we are really engaging in a double task. We are not only focusing on the Earth itself but also the ways in which all peoples are linked in a cosmic consciousness that is 'not [only] worldly or global,' but 'truly astral' (Mbembe 2020a, 61).

Symbiosis is key to Mbembe's thinking on planetary relations. Earth's history is ultimately 'a history of bio-symbiosis' (Mbembe 2023, 16). It is imperative to preserve the 'symbiotic chain' of life on the planet, including everything from plants and animals, to microbes and the weather. The interaction of these elements not only connects all forms of life, but also is rooted in a geological history of long duration, stretching back to the formation of the Earth's crust (Mbembe 2023, 16).

The era of the Earth

This very general and cosmic significance of the 'planetary' is referred to by Mbembe as the coming of the 'era of the Earth.' This is a world emerging from decolonization. In it, the relations of enmity, including colonialism and racism, have come to an end. The 'passerby' receives hospitality and recognition from strangers. Mbembe sees three moments as key to living equitably on the Earth's surface: hospitality, the emergence of a 'democracy of living beings,' and the right of restitution and reparation.

Fanon, Glissant, and Gilroy are critical influences on Mbembe's thinking here. Fanon's utopian account of a future humanism (see Chapter 5) emerging from out of decolonization influences Mbembe in his account of an emergent future, mapping out social relations in this 'era of the Earth.' Gilroy serves as a further reference point. He has developed Fanon's account of a utopian future humanism in his own theorization of 'planetarity.' Gilroy argues that this latter concept has opened up the possibilities of community beyond the 'camp'-based mentalities of nationalism connecting this to Fanon's idea of the 'desalienation of humanity,' he argues that it entails liberation from racial division and white supremacy. 'According to Fanon,' Gilroy contends, 'the capacity to address the future… was a precondition for health and healing' (Gilroy 2000, 336).

The politics of a planetary age

A new 'planetary age' necessitates a 'democracy of living beings,' entailing 'a deepening [sense]…of' the 'in-common,' and 'a pact of care.' This pact necessitates relations of care: it includes both 'care for the planet,' and a 'blind care for all inhabitants of the world, human and other than human.' Humans must understand that they are neither the sole inhabitants of the Earth nor the only living beings that have rights. A planetary democracy must involve all living creatures together (Mbembe 2020a, 54).

A new planetary relation between humans and non-humans, for Mbembe, poses the possibility of a 'truly planetary justice' (Mbembe 2020a, 54). Key to this change is the practice of a 'universal hospitality,' but also a more general labour of repairing the surface of the Earth. This includes a duty to restitution and reparation as the initial step towards planetary justice (Mbembe 2020a, 54).

THE TERRESTRIAL COMMUNITY

Urgent new ethical questions emerge from our current era of increasing global connectedness. Not only is this an era where Europe has been newly displaced from its historical claim to dominance or 'Eurocentric certainties,' it is also an era of 'planetarisation,' in which the problems facing all life on Earth become unavoidable (Diagne 2022; Mbembe 2023, 5). Knowledge of the unsustainable climatic damage of industry and extractive capital, Mbembe argues, makes it impossible to imagine that life on our 'hot house' planet could continue in its present form. It is 'a house incapable of sustaining... life,' which will one day be 'cooked to death' (Mbembe 2023, 12). This planetary turn has been further accelerated by sciences such as 'astrobiology' and 'physical cosmology' which have taken scientific research beyond the confines of Earth and 'extra-terrestrialized' it. Now more than ever, it is possible that while Earth has been the cradle of humanity, it does not represent its final destination.

We must consider how to co-exist on the face of the Earth. Deteriorating climatic conditions force a 'test of extremes.' As the situation deteriorates, no wall, enclave, or border will be strong enough to protect us from those with whom we share our planet (Mbembe 2023, 8). A concept of debt rests at the heart of all communities. This burden necessarily remains insolvable and unending; it surpasses alliances to state or 'identity.'

AFRICA AND THE FUTURE OF THE EARTH

The inhabitants of Earth are no strangers to crisis. Africa has a particular role to play in helping humanity navigate environmental crisis. In modern (Western) reason, Mbembe contends, both African and Afrodiasporic people have been treated as signs of the 'becoming-cremated' *(devenir-crématoire)* of humanity. He argues that Africans have been treated in a manner similar to the minerals that humanity is so unsustainably consuming. Although Africans are central to the 'geological destiny of the Earth,' they have been treated as a 'primary material' that needed to be 'extract[ed]' and 'burned' so as to produce energy. A paradoxical relationship existed where people of Africa and its diaspora were both 'indispensable to human life,' and yet simultaneously 'were supposed not at all to belong [to it]' (Mbembe 2023, 10).

The challenges facing humanity in an era of climate degradation are closely related to long-standing concerns of African and diasporic thought, particularly Afropessimism and Afrofuturism (Mbembe 2023, 8). Within Afrofuturism, examined in Chapter 8, there has been a powerful 'desire for expatriation,' and a quest to reconnect with 'elementary forces and cosmic elements' (Mbembe 2023, 10).

CONCLUSION

Mbembe's notion of the planetary opens the way for new forms of politics, and a new relation between humans, non-humans, and the Earth. In particular, a 'universal hospitality' acknowledges the central role of the 'passerby' as common to the condition of all humans on the Earth's surface. Mbembe envisages a democracy of the living that enables the rights of human and non-human to be respected, without any claim to human sovereignty. But at the same time, he warns of the damage of inherent 'combustion of the Earth.' Mbembe argues that Africans have a long historical experience of being treated as a consumable material, while often facing the environmental damage caused by extractive industries.

AFTER MBEMBE

Mbembe's thought has moved from focusing on colonial and postcolonial Africa to an engagement with the African diaspora. Most recently it has engaged with questions of the survival of the planet and technology. In considering its emerging legacy, we focus on Mbembe's influence within Africa, before turning to focus on the way in which several themes in his thought have been adopted and used in different global contexts, including decolonization, necropolitics, and the postcolony.

Mbembe's thought has had significance far beyond the walls of the university, as evinced in his public contributions to #RhodesMustFall in South Africa, as well as debates over the decolonization of knowledge, and the identity of postcolonial France (Mbembe 2005b; 2005c; 2006a; 2007b; 2011c). More generally, his writing challenges an intellectual map that too often still relegates Africa to the margins. The continent, Mbembe reminds us, is ultimately at the heart of the entire world's future, both practically and intellectually.

Mbembe's work continues to subvert neat conceptual and academic boundaries. These include basic distinctions between academic and literary writing, as well as between different disciplines. Is Mbembe a philosopher, political scientist, cultural theorist, or historian (Mbembe 1992a, 123; Quayson 2001, 163)? He has specifically differentiated his thought from post- and decolonial thought, although this remains a common designation of his work. Ultimately, Mbembe engages with philosophy, anthropology, political science, theology, and, more recently, environmental, and technological science (Lloyd 2016, 241; Mbembe 2006d; Ngong 2020) and writes in a style that fosters new connections between these fields.

MBEMBE'S INFLUENCE WITHIN AFRICA

Mbembe's influence in Africa is uneven. In South Africa, he has been a major public intellectual, while in France-based media aimed at Africa, Mbembe is a prominent voice. However, in Francophone Africa, Mbembe's reception has been more mixed. Mbembe has played a key role in the *Ateliers* workshop in Dakar. His interventions on France's relationship with Africa and his analysis of July 26, 2023, coup in Niger have also attracted attention in the African media, including in Cameroonian news outlets (ActuCameroun 2023a, 2023b, 2023c; Juompan-Yakam 2023).

But some African scholars remain sceptical. In the Democratic Republic of Congo, for instance, one scholar reported relatively little interest in the Cameroonian thinker among Kinshasa-based intellectuals. Much the same could be said of intellectual culture in Cameroon; few thinkers in the country, with the exception of Célestin Monga (1960–) have engaged with Mbembe's work. A common critique among some scholars 'accuses Mbembe of defending colonialism and of "writing for the whites"' (Pype 2022, 51). Mbembe, they assert, writes not for Africa, but for Euro-American academics. Similar criticisms have been mounted against sociologist Joseph Tonda (see Chapter 7). Mbembe rarely cites Africa-based thinkers or research, with certain exceptions such as Hountondji, Ngugi wa Thiong'o, and Senghor. Key thinkers such as Nyamnjoh, Tonda, or Mahmood Mamdani receive relatively little coverage in Mbembe's work. This citation practice risks perpetuating the asymmetrical relationship with scholars in the global south and north, while obscuring the achievements of researchers based on the continent (Bahi 2021, 110–111).

DECOLONIZATION, KNOWLEDGE, AND THE RESTITUTION OF AFRICAN OBJECTS

Mbembe has voiced significant criticisms of student protest movements and more general calls for the decolonization of knowledge and universities. But, as we have seen, decolonization is a key strand in Mbembe's thought, including efforts to decolonize universities, and the question of the repatriation of African objects held in Western museums (Bernal 2021, 45; Mbembe 2024). A key example of Mbembe's practical engagement in the work of decolonizing knowledge is his role in organizing the *Ateliers* commencing in October 2016 in Dakar and Saint-Louis (Mbembe and Sarr 2017; Mbembe and Sarr 2022a; 2022b). Papers from the 2016 conference include engagements with European thinkers in African contexts, as well as the re-positioning of humanities scholarship from the geographical vantage point of Africa itself (Ndoye 2017, 369–378). The workshops also deliberately attempted to engage a wider public, hosting, in 2019, a first workshop for young researchers, artists, and curators (Gorz-Ngaté 2020, 703).

A number of Francophone intellectuals have entered into dialogue with Mbembe. Felwine Sarr, co-organizer of the *Ateliers* with Mbembe, has played a significant role in some areas close to Mbembe's own interests. In his book *Afrotopia*, Sarr identifies a 'double movement' in contemporary debates about Africa, in which 'a faith in a brilliant future' is counterbalanced by 'consternation' at 'a seemingly chaotic present.' He avers that 'from now on… the future will be African' (Sarr 2019, xi), a sentiment strikingly similar to Mbembe. Sarr has played a major practical role in the debate about returning artefacts in Western museums. Co-author of the *Report on the Restitution of African Cultural Heritage: Toward a New Relational Ethics* (a government-sponsored enquiry, widely known as the Sarr-Savoy Report) (2018), Sarr has advocated for the restitution of African art objects (Paquette 2020, 320; 'Restitution' 2018). Three types of '*captation*' or dominant acquisition of goods from Africa are outlined in the Report, including punitive expeditions and looting, increased European presence on the continent, and scientific and ethnographic research missions. The Quai Branly Museum, for instance, has no fewer than 600 objects handled by French scientist Jean Dybowksi (1856–1928) at the turn of the nineteenth and twentieth centuries (Paquette 2020, 305; Sarr and Savoy 2018, 47). At a more general level, former footballer and thinker Lilian Thuram (1972–) has engaged in dialogue with Mbembe, as part of his wider efforts to draw attention to racism in France (Dubois 2010, 281; Thuram 2021). On his retirement from professional sport, Thuram launched a foundation in 2008, dedicated to anti-racist education, and has more recently worked on a book examining 'white thought' and alleging that it subjugated non-white individuals (Ba 2020; Thuram 2021).

Conceptual decolonization is a key theme in Mbembe's work, which itself charts Europe's decline from being an intellectual, economic, and political hub of the world. Mbembe's interests here are paralleled in the work of philosopher Souleymane Bachir Diagne (1955–), who has underscored the importance of African languages in efforts to decolonize, highlighting the value of translation. Transitioning between languages, Diagne argues, enables one to see things from multiple perspectives, and mitigates against the promotion of any single worldview. The process of translation thus develops both self-knowledge and our awareness of the Other (Diagne 2017, 73).

NECROPOLITICS

Mbembe's neologism 'necropolitics' has entered mainstream media discourse. It captures growing awareness of the interrelationship between related forms of exclusion and discrimination, which connect to public demands for equity in healthcare provision, policing, and prisons, for example, in the #BlackLivesMatter movement. The term has been used by scholars seeking to make these forms of discrimination more visible, whether within academic or public spheres (Alphin and Debrix 2019; Ie 2019; Quinan and Thiele 2021; Ringer 2021; Truscello 2020). Critically, necropolitics has moved from Mbembe's original use of the term, focusing on colonial and contemporary wars in Africa, to the analysis of deteriorating public services in Western countries. The term's trajectory forms a clear example of Mbembe's ambition of centring African intellectual production within a broader global debate. Necropolitics has also been influential in hitherto unrelated areas, such as scholarship on sexuality, where scholars have argued for a 'queer necropolitics' which focuses on possibilities for resistance, while also recognizing the degree to which queer subjects can lobby against repressive social policies (Bassichi and Spade 2014; Haritaworn et al. 2014; Lamble 2014). Necropolitics has inspired readings of Western popular culture, such as the TV series *The Walking Dead* (2010–), which has been analysed to reveal dynamics of 'individual and group security' (Estévez 2021; O'Mahony et al. 2021, 89).

A further development of the term indicates the global reach of Mbembe's thought. This has seen 'necropolitics' adopted in the study of non-Western literature outside of Africa. Scholars of Arabic literature have deployed Mbembe's term to read Iraqi literature after the Second Gulf War (2003–2006), where they have discerned a 'neocolonial necropolitics' (O'Mahony, Motyl and Arghavan 2018, 128). Drawing on Iraqi fiction, such as Sinan Antoon's (1967–) *The Corpse Washer* (2016), Hassan Blasim's (1973–) short story 'The Corpse Exhibition,' and Ahmad Saadawi's (1973–) *Frankenstein in Baghdad*, Sai argues Mbembe's term can also be understood as an aesthetic strategy to navigate the violence immediately following war's end (Antoon 2016; Saadawi 2018; Sai 2019, 243). 'Necropolitics' has therefore become a term in circulation across global intellectual debate, from studies of the contemporary USA to readings of Iraqi fiction.

THE POSTCOLONY: CONVIVIALITY AND THE SOVEREIGN IN CAMEROON, GABON, AND THE CONGOS

Within Central Africa, Mbembe's account of the postcolony has also inspired engagement from philosophers (Adebanwi and Orock 2022, 42–48). Cameroonian philosopher Francis

Nyamnjoh has focused on Mbembe's notion of conviviality in the postcolony to argue that the very idea of 'incompleteness' itself represents a dominant ontological reality across the contemporary world (Nyamnjoh 2017a, 2020). Meanwhile, Mbembe's figure of the postcolonial 'potentate' or dictator finds parallels in Tonda's account of the 'modern sovereign' or 'the body of power.' Tonda sees this latter figure as exercising domination over the inhabitants of the postcolony 'from the inside' in a pattern dating back to colonialism (Tonda 2005, 18). This pernicious sovereign power emerges from a mixture of the state and missionary activities, and local beliefs about power. New forms of consumerism and entrepreneurial activity mix with occult values and religious discourses. All of this leads to a fetishization of consumption and power that typifies 'the modern sovereign.' Perhaps most insidiously, the colonial encounter, Tonda argues, ultimately led to the *déparentélisation* or dissolution of kinship structures which in turn produced spaces beyond the logic of existing family structures. Far from being a utopia, these new places are governed partly with the aid of repressive beliefs, such as witchcraft claims (Tonda 2005, 77).

CONCLUSION

Mbembe has emerged as the pre-eminent African thinker of the early twenty-first century. Within a body of thought that spans from African history to questions of digital technology and climate change, Mbembe repeatedly emphasizes the importance of Africa. He convincingly shows that the history and politics of postcolonial Africa ultimately presage wider global changes, such as neoliberal capitalism and environmental change. Mbembe identifies the present day as a moment of heightened enmity exacerbated by climate catastrophe and rapacious capital. His thought does not shy away from confronting organized violence and its brutal social consequences. He charts the long-term impact of European race and racism, particularly as they damaged Africa and its diaspora through the Atlantic slave trade and colonialism. 'Necropolitics' provides a chilling image of contemporary formal and informal warfare, replete with its torture chambers, indeterminable borders and checkpoints, and drone-operated death strikes. Digital technology offers Mbembe's most recent iteration of this vision.

Yet, Mbembe's thought, particularly in more recent work, is also hopeful and optimistic, particularly as regards the possibility of a future world order emerging from ongoing decolonization. This emergent conjuncture offers new ways of relating beyond historical forms of enmity, while also posing fresh ways for humans to relate to animals. Mbembe sees clues towards this new world in various cultural forms, including the imaginative universe of Afrofuturism, and the global connectivity of Afropolitanism. Even if humanity is ultimately destined to leave this overheating Earth, Mbembe reminds us that we first and foremost need to live together on its surface. However, the exact form that this might take remains to be determined.

CONTEMPORARY FRANCOPHONE AFRICAN THINKERS

Mbembe's thought must be contextualized against the writings of Francophone African philosophers, because these thinkers deal with parallel concerns, including Africa's relation to former colonial powers and languages.

FELWINE SARR (1972–)

Senegalese writer and philosopher Felwine Sarr has worked with Mbembe to organize the *Ateliers de la pensée* at Dakar since 2017 and played a key role in the movement for the restitution of African artefacts in French museums. Sarr has held positions at the Centre for Research in Civilisations, Religions, Arts, and Communication at Gaston Berger University in Saint-Louis, Senegal, before moving to Duke University, USA in 2020; his writings include *Dahij* (2009), *105 Rue Carnot* (2011), *Méditations africaines* (2012) (African Meditations), and *Afrotopia* (2016; translated 2019) (Karegeye 2016, 306; Sarr 2009; 2012; 2011).

SOULEYMANE BACHIR DIAGNE (1955–)

Like Mbembe, Senegalese philosopher Souleymane Bachir Diagne (1955) has brought African philosophy into dialogue with European thought. He has also connected it to Islamic philosophy and Sufism (Pilay and Fernandes 2016). Literature plays a role in Diagne's thought; at one point in *Open to Reason* he draws on the Arab Andalusian scholar Abu Bakr ibn Tufayl's (1105–1185) novel *Hayy ibn Yaqzan* ('Alive, Son of Aware'), a possible predecessor of Daniel Defoe's (c. 1660–1731) *Robinson Crusoe* (1719), to explore the philosophy of Avicenna (Ibn Sina's) (c. 980 –1037) (Diagne 2008; Diagne 2018; Diagne 2019). In comparative philosophy, Diagne's *Postcolonial Bergson* (2019; [2011]) examines responses to Bergson in the thought of Léopold Sedar Senghor (1906–2001) and Mohammed Iqbal (1877–1938), connecting European, Indian, Islamic, and African philosophy; *Open to Reason: Muslim Philosophers in Conversation with the Western Tradition* (2019; originally *Comment philosopher en Islam* (2008)) also focuses on the interface between divergent traditions of thought. Aside from his philosophical works, Diagne has also translated a hagiographical account of the West African Sufi Tijani Shaykh al-Hajj Abbass Sall (Diagne 2009). Diagne taught at Cheikh Anta Diop University in Dakar, before moving to the USA to professorships at Northwestern and then Columbia University.

FURTHER READING

Mbembe's writings are dispersed across books, academic journal articles, chapters, and journalism. This chapter collects some of Mbembe's major work, while also presenting his earlier Francophone scholarship. It is by no means exhaustive and does not cover Mbembe's large body of journalism. A 2004 bibliography of Mbembe's work exists at https://www.lib.uci.edu/library/publications/wellek/docs/Wellek2004AchilleMbembe.pdf.

BOOKS

Mbembe, A. (1984), *Le problème national kamerunais: Ruben Um Nyobè*, Paris: L'Harmattan.
Early collection of writings by Cameroonian resistance leader Nyobè, introduction discusses Mbembe's experience in attempting to study the independence war of the 1950s while still a student in Cameroon. Contains essay 'L'Etat-historien.'

Mbembe, A. (1986a), *Les jeunes et l'ordre politique en Afrique noire*, Paris: Karthala.

Mbembe, A. (1988), *Afriques indociles: christianisme, pouvoir et état en société postcoloniale*, Paris Karthala,
Includes one of Mbembe's most sustained engagements with Christianity, a key influence on his early thought while still based in Cameroon.

Mbembe, A. (1989b), *Écrits sous maquis: Ruben Um Nyobè*, Paris: L'Harmattan.
Presents writings by Um Nyobè, including selections from Nyobè's dream notebooks.

Mbembe, A., J.-F. Bayart, and C. Toulabor (1992), *Le politique par le bas en Afrique noire: contributions à une problématique de la démocratie*, Paris: Karthala.
Edited volume developing Mbembe's analysis of popular politics in postcolonial Africa, particularly in Cameroon. Collaboration with Mbembe's mentor and supervisor from his studies in Paris (Bayart), and Toulabor, a fellow student of Bayart and important influence on Mbembe's thinking while in Paris.

Mbembe, A. (1996b), *La naissance du maquis dans le Sud-Cameroun, (1920–1960): Histoire des usages de la raison en colonie*, Paris: Karthala.
Mbembe's doctoral thesis includes two parts, one examining colonial Cameroonian society, while also developing his account of colonial rationality, and a second section analysing the political and military career of Nyobè, including during the final months of his life fighting the French army in southwestern Cameroon.

Mbembe, A. (2001b [2000]), *On the Postcolony*, Berkeley: University of California Press Mbembe, A. (2000), *De la postcolonie: essai sur l'imagination politique dans l'afrique Contemporaine*. Paris: Karthala, 2000.
Mbembe's first widely read book-length intervention in the Anglophone world, examines the politics, culture, and social life of colonial and postcolonial Africa, with reference especially to Cameroon, as well as Togo, and the Republic of Congo. Develops Mbembe's ideas of 'commandement,' 'private indirect government,' the 'colony' and 'postcolony,' the

postcolonial potentate, the grotesque, and convivial power in the postcolony. There are some significant textual differences between the 2000 and 2001 editions, and the second edition 2020 contains a new introduction.

Mbembe, A. and S. Nuttall (eds.) (2008), *Johannesburg: The Elusive Metropolis*, Durham: Duke University Press.

Edited volume exploring Johannesburg's history and culture, includes an essay by Mbembe on his idea of 'superfluity,' and his account of the nineteenth- and early twentieth-century city as an African metropolis, which contextualises Mbembe's later thought on Afropolitanism.

Mbembe, A. (2017b [2013]), *Critique of Black Reason*, Durham: Duke University Press.

Explores the relationship between Africa and the Atlantic African diaspora in the Americas, particularly in terms of race and Mbembe's notion of the 'black man' or *le Nègre*. Mbembe discusses the legacies of slavery and the plantation, and relates this to the colony, while situating his idea of 'necropolitics' in terms of the history and cultural representations of the Atlantic slave trade, including in the novels of Amos Tutuola.

Mbembe, A. (2019b [2016d]), *Necropolitics*, Durham: Duke University Press.

Advances Mbembe's conception of 'necropolitics' originally elaborated in his *Public Culture* article, including a chapter heavily based on the English version of this article, and considers its relationship to warfare, and the politics of enmity. Elaborates Mbembe's engagement with Fanon developed in 'Night,' particularly in terms of the 'pharmakon' offered by the latter thinker for situating decolonization in the present day. Introduces Mbembe's thoughts on the environment and the 'great combustion.'

Mbembe, A. (2021a [2010]), *Out of the Dark Night: Essays on Decolonization*, New York: Columbia University Press.

Engaging recurrently with Fanon's thought, these essays examine multicultural France, decolonization and Fanon's thought, the restitution of art objects, and the role of Africa in the world, including an extended account of Mbembe's notion of the 'Afropolitan.' Note publication dates from over a decade before the appearance of the English translation.

Mbembe, A. and F. Sarr (2022a) [2017], *To write the Africa world*. Cambridge: Polity.

Papers from the second of Mbembe and Sarr's *Ateliers* in Dakar, particularly connecting to themes explored in Mbembe' work on Afropolitanism.

Mbembe, A. and F. Sarr (2022b) [2016], *The politics of time: imagining African becomings*. Cambridge: Polity.

Papers from the first Dakar *Ateliers* conference.

Mbembe, A. (2023), *La communauté terrestre*, Paris La Découverte.

Presents Mbembe's interventions on human relations with ecology, and the new global conjuncture ushered in by the displacement of Europe from its historically dominant role in the colonial era. An English language version (2022) exists, but this has significant differences from the French text, including at a structural level.

Mbembe, A. (2024) [2020a], *Brutalism*, Durham: Duke University Press.

Develops Mbembe's thought on the environment, connects human relations of hostility, racism, and enmity, with exploitative attitudes towards the environment and the non-human world. Examines computation and algorithmic reason, as well as screen-media and mobile devices. Proposes new links between Mbembe's thought and the technical and natural sciences, including neuroscience and computer programming. Includes a developed account example of Mbembe's engagement with calls for the restitution of African objects in Western museums, and his account of how these objects challenge the divide between animate/inanimate and human/nonhuman.

CHAPTERS AND ARTICLES

Mbembe, A. (1985) 'La palabre de l'indépendance: les ordres du discours nationaliste au Cameroun, 1948–1958,' *Revue Française de Science Politique*, 35 (3): 459–487.

Mbembe, A. (1986b), Pouvoir des morts et langages des vivants: les errances de la memoire nationaliste au Cameroun,' *Politique Africaine*, 22, 37–72.

Mbembe, A. (1986c), 'Postface,' In. R. Joseph (ed.), *Le mouvement nationaliste au Cameroun: Les origines sociales de l'UPC*, Paris: Karthala.

Mbembe, A. (1989a), 'Le spectre et l'État: des dimensions politiques de l'imaginaire historique dans le Cameroun postcolonial,' *Revue de la Bibliotheque Nationale*, 44, 2–13.

Mbembe, A. (1990a), 'Pouvoir, violence et accumulation,' *Politique Africaine*, 39, 7–24.

Mbembe, A. (1990b), 'Le Cameroun après la mort d'Ahmadou Ahidjo,' *Politique Africaine*, 37, 117–122.

Mbembe, A. (1992a) 'Prosaics of servitude and authoritarian civilities,' *Public Culture*, 5 (1), 123–145.

Mbembe, A. (1992c), 'Traditions de l'autoritarisme et problems de gouvernement en Afrique sub-saharienne,' *African Development/Afrique et Développement,* 17:1, 37 – 64.

Mbembe, A. (1993), 'Écrire l'Afrique à partir d'une faille,' *Politique Africaine*, 51, 69–97.

Provides a first-hand narrative of Mbembe's intellectual development in Cameroon, France, and his early career in the USA. Includes discussion of Mbembe's critical relationship with Roman Catholic thought in Cameroon, especially liberation theology, and the personal relations instrumental in Mbembe's doctoral years in Paris, as well as his move to American academia.

Mbembe, A. and J. Roitman (1995), 'Figures of the subject in times of crisis,' *Public Culture*, 7 (2), 323–352.
With detailed reference to Cameroon of the 1990s, explores the subjective strategies open to Africans seeking to navigate political corruption and state collapse.

Mbembe, A. (1997). 'The civil status and biographies of god in contemporary Africa,' *Afrika Zamani: revue annuelle d'histoire africaine*, 5–6, 7–12.

Mbembe, A. (1999a), 'On private indirect government,' *Politique africaine*, 73, 103–122.
Advances Mbembe's account of the postcolonial African state, and particularly the pervasive influence of authoritarianism across multiple levels of society, revealing how even seemingly obscure state functionaries are able to commandeer its power for their own interests.

Mbembe, A. (2002b), 'On the power of the false,' *Public Culture*, 14 (3), 629–641.
A response to critical engagement with Mbembe's article 'African Self-Writing.' Develops Mbembe's argument, exploring what he sees as the limiting power of 'nativism' and 'Afro-radicalism.' Examines the degree to which 'African discourses of the self' and philosophical language are 'possessed and haunted' both by the binary structure Mbembe identities in 'nativism' and 'Afro-radicalism,' and by earlier colonial and racist thought.

Mbembe, A. (2002c), 'African modes of self-writing,' *Public Culture*, 14 (1), 239–273.
Charts African modes of 'self-writing' or self-fashioning, particularly in terms of the influence of colonialism, including colonial anthropology, and claims of 'difference' in European Enlightenment thought and racism. Argues that two narratives of African identity emerged from these pressures: 'nativism' and 'Afro-radicalism.' Both are engaged critically by Mbembe, particularly in terms of their conceptual frameworks.

Mbembe, A. (2003b), 'Life, sovereignty, and terror in the fiction of Amos Tutuola,' *Research in African Literatures*, 34 (4), 1–26.
An important example of Mbembe's literary critical writing, and a direct engagement with Nigerian novelist Tutuola, who serves as a major reference point in works such as *Postcolony*.

Mbembe, A. and S. Nuttall (2004c), 'Writing the world from an African metropolis,' *Public Culture*, 16 (3), 347–372.
Forms part of a special issue concerned with the 'worldliness' of African life forms, relates to Mbembe's thought on Africa and the world, particularly in Afropolitanism.

Mbembe, A. 'The colony. Dirty little secret, cursed lot,' ['La colonie: son petit secret et sa part maudite'], *Politique africaine*, 102, 101–127.
Discussion of African memories of colonial power, including colonial monuments and their role postcolonial African states, with reference to D.R. Congo and South Africa.

Mbembe, A. (2005a), 'Variations on the beautiful in the Congolese world of sounds,' *Politique africaine*, 100 (4), 69–91.
Essay on Congolese musical aesthetics, revealing the degree to which music bridges the plural conceptual properties of text and music, while also being linked to rhythm and dance, including the ability to produce intoxication. Musical traditions such as rumba are situated in relation to the challenges of urban life in Kinshasa and Brazzaville during the 1990s.

Mbembe, A. (2005b), 'La république désoeuvrée: La France à l'ère post-coloniale,' *Le Débat*, 137:5, 159–175.
Examines the changing position of Europe in a world where it is no longer the dominant force, while also questioning the limits of France's Republican ideals, in particular its claims to universalism.

Mbembe, A. (2006e), 'Necropolitique,' *Raisons politiques: études de pensée politique.* 21:1, 29–60.
French translation of Mbembe's 2003 article on necropolitics.

Mbembe, A. (2008a), 'Passages to freedom: the politics of racial reconciliation in South Africa,' *Public Culture*, 20 (1), 5–18.
Article on post-apartheid South Africa.

Mbembe, A. (2011c), 'Provincializing France?' *Public Culture*, 23 (1), 85–119.
Essay on the reception of postcolonial theory in France, including commentary on Mbembe's own experiences in French universities, see related discussion in *Dark Night*.

Mbembe, A. (2012b), 'Metamorphic Thought: The *Works* of Frantz Fanon,' *African Studies*, 71 (1), 20–26.
Presents Mbembe's argument for the contemporary importance of Fanon's thought.

Mbembe, A. (2013d), 'Cinquante ans de décolonisation africaine,' *Naqd*, 30 (1), 137–144.
Essay on the relations between postcolonial Africa, Europe, the USA, and China, includes brief commentary on Afro-Chinese relations in relation to Mbembe's long-standing analyses of Occidental colonialism.

Mbembe, A. (2014), 'Afrofuturisme et devenir-nègre du monde,' *Politique Africaine*, 136, 121–133.
Article elaborating Mbembe's account of the importance of Afrofuturism and its relationship with the historical experiences of slavery and colonialism.

Nuttall, S. and A. Mbembe (2014), 'Mandela's mortality,' In. R. Barnard (ed.), *The Cambridge Companion to Nelson Mandela*. Cambridge: Cambridge University Press, 267–290.

Nuttall, S. and A. Mbembe (2015), 'Secrecy's softwares,' *Current Anthropology*, 56 (S12), S317–S324.
Discusses changing cultures of secrecy globally, with reference to the internet.

Mbembe, A. (2016f), 'Preface: Surmoi colonial et État sous tutelle,' In. T. Deltombe, M. Domergue, and J. Tatsitsa (eds.), *La Guerre Du Cameroun: L'invention De La Françafrique, 1948–1971*, Paris: La Découverte 7–15.

An account of the continuing importance of the Cameroonian resistance to French colonialism.

Mbembe, A. (2017c), 'Penser pour un nouveau siècle,' In. A. Mbembe and F. Sarr (eds.), *Écrire l'Afrique-Monde*, Dakar: Jimsaan, 7–17.
Outlines the role of Africa in global thought of the twenty-first century.

Mbembe, A. (2018a), 'La démondialisation,' *Esprit*, (450), 86–94.
Mbembe's account of global relations following the end of colonialism, 'new wars,' and borderization.

Mbembe, A. (2018b), 'Biko's testament of hope,' In. D. Accone, Z. Cindi, et al. (eds.), *We Write What We Like: Celebrating Steve Biko*, Johannesburg, Wits University Press, 135–150.

Mbembe, A. (2019a), 'Purger l'Afrique du désir d'Europe,' *Le Débat*, 205 (3), 100–107.
Explores the situation of global mobility that Mbembe sees as typifying the contemporary era.

Mbembe, A. (2020b [2005]), 'Afropolitanism,' In. I. Balseiro and Z. Rapola (eds.), *The Passport That Does Not Pass Ports: African Literature of Travel in the Twenty-First Century*, East Lansing: Michigan State University Press, 7–12, 10.
Influential essay exploring Africa's cultural links with the wider world, and the status of non-Africans within Africa itself.

Mbembe, A. (2021b), 'The universal right to breath,' *Critical Inquiry*, 47, S2, S58–62.
Contains Mbembe's reflections on COVID-19, and its links to his more general characterization of the contemporary world.

Mbembe, A. (2021c), 'Futures of life and futures of reason,' *Public Culture*, 33 (1), 11–33.
Develops Mbembe's thoughts on brutalism, digital technology, and the fate of the planet. Discusses themes treated in *Brutalisme* and *Communauté*.

SELECTED INTERVIEWS AND JOURNALISM

Mbembe, A. (2015a), 'Decolonizing institutions,' *Mail & Guardian*, August 6, https://mg.co.za/podcasts/2015-08-06-decolonising-institutions-achille-mbembe/

Mbembe, A. (2015d), 'The internet is Afropolitan,' originally published in The Chimurenga Chronic, May 2015, http://chimurengachronic.co.za.

Mbembe, A., L. Pignot, and J.-P. Saez (2021), 'Résister au « brutalisme » du monde contemporain à l'ère numérique,' *L'Observatoire*, N° 58 (2), 76–80.
Interview examining Mbembe's account of technology and brutalism.

KEY SECONDARY LITERATURE

The novels of writers like Labou Tansi, Tutuola, or Kourouma form a reference point throughout much of Mbembe's writing and, along with historical or anthropological works on Cameroon, the Democratic Republic of Congo and the Republic of Congo, or Togo, represent immediate reference points for those seeking to understand Mbembe's earlier thought in context. At the time of press, there is no monograph concerning Mbembe, or a sustained examination of Mbembe's thought. Below are some further literature suggestions, some of which examine Mbembe's work, and others are by individuals who have had a significant influence on Mbembe.

Bayart, J.F. (2009), *The State in Africa: Politics of the Belly*, Cambridge: Polity.
A key text by Mbembe's mentor during his graduate study in France. Useful to read in connection with *Postcolony*, owing to Bayart's discussion of the postcolonial state in Africa, including cultural and social perceptions of autocracies, often with reference to Cameroon.

Nuttall, S. (2006), *Beautiful/ Ugly: African and Diaspora Aesthetics*, Durham: Duke University Press.

Collection of essays on continental and diaspora aesthetics, can be read in terms of Mbembe's work on aesthetics, for example, in Congolese music, and also his later thought on Afropolitanism.

Syrotinski, M. (2012), '"Genealogical misfortunes": Achille Mbembe's (re-)writing of postcolonial Africa,' *Paragraph*, 35, 407–420.

Article focusing on Mbembe's intellectual self-positioning and its relationship with postcolonial theory. Discussion of Mbembe's 'Écrire l'Afrique à partir d'une faille.' Draws attention to the relation between Mbembe's thought and that of Derrida, and Jean-Luc Nancy.

WORKS CITED

Abane, B. (2011), 'Frantz Fanon and Abane Ramdane: brief encounter in the Algerian Revolution,' In. L. Gibson (ed.), *Frantz Fanon: Global Perspectives*, Basingstoke: Palgrave, 27–44.

Abbas, H. and S. Ekine (eds.) (2013), *Queer African Reader*, Nairobi: Pambazuka Press.

Abdel-Malek, A. (1963), 'Orientalism in crisis,' *Diogenes*, 11 (44), 103–140.

Achebe, B. (1980), 'Work and play in Tutuola's *The Palm Wine-Drinkard*,' In. B. Lindforths (ed.), *Critical Perspectives on Amos Tutuola*, Harlow: Heinemann, 256–266.

ActuCameroun (2023a), 'Niger: Calixte Beyala tacle sévèrement Achille Mbembe qui a dénoncé dans sa tribune le « néosouverainisme » comme une « version appauvrie et frelatée du panafricanisme »,' *Actu Cameroun.com*, August 13.

ActuCameroun (2023b), 'Niger – Achille Mbembe conseille à la France d'adopter « la juste distance »,' *Actu Cameroun.com*, September 3.

ActuCameroun (2023c), 'Achille Mbembe: « La France ne dispose plus des moyens de ses ambitions en Afrique »,' *Actu Cameroun.com*, October 1.

Adebanwi, W. and R. Orock (2022), 'Rethinking Achille Mbembe's "Provisional notes on the postcolony,"' *Africa*, 92, 42–48.

Adeleke, T. (2003), *Without Regard to Race: The Other Martin Robison Delany*, Jackson: University Press of Mississippi.

Adeleke, T. (2020), *Martin R. Delany's Civil War and Reconstruction: A Primary Source Reader*, Jackson: University Press of Mississippi.

Adesanmi, P. (2004), 'Of postcolonial entanglement and Dureé: reflections on the francophone African novel,' *Comparative Literature*, 56 (3), 227–242.

Adi, H. (2003), 'Cheikh Anta Diop (1923–1986),' In. H. Adi and M. Sherwood (eds.), *Pan-African History: Political Figures from Africa and the Diaspora Since 1787*, London: Routledge, 40–43.

Agamben, G. (1998), *Homo Sacer: Sovereign Power and Bare Life*, Stanford: Stanford University Press.

Akyeampong, E. (2000), '"Wo pe tam won pe ba" ("You like cloth but you don't want children") Urbanization, individualism and gender relations in colonial Ghana, c.1900–39,' In. D. Anderson and R. Rathbone (eds.), *Africa's Urban Past*, Oxford: James Currey, 222–234.

Al-Tahtawi, R. (2004), *An Imam in Paris: Account of a Stay in France by an Egyptian Cleric (1826–1831)*, London: Saqi.

Aldrich, R. (1996), *Greater France: A History of French Overseas Expansion*, Basingstoke: Macmillan.

Alphin, C. and F. Debrix (2019), *Necrogeopolitics: On Death and Death-Making in International Relations*, Abingdon: Routledge.

Anonymous (2021), 'Palestine between German Memory politics and (de-)colonial thought,' *Journal of Genocide Research*, 23 (3), 374–382, 377.

Antoon, S. (2016), *The Corpse Washer*, New Haven: Yale University Press.

Anwar, M. (2022), 'Locked in, logged out: pandemic and ride-hailing in South Africa and Kenya,' *Modern African Studies*, 60 (4), 457–478.

Appiah, K.A. (2006), *Cosmopolitanism: Ethics in a World of Strangers*, London: Allen Lane.

Arendt, H. (1966), *The Origins of Totalitarianism*, London: Allen & Unwin.

Argenti, N. (2007), *The Intestines of the State: Youth, Violence, and Belated Histories in the Cameroon Grassfields*, Chicago: University of Chicago Press.

Assmann, A. (2021), 'A spectre is haunting Germany: the Mbembe Debate and the new antisemitism,' *Journal of Genocide Research*, 23 (3), 400–411.

Atangana, M. (2010), *The End of French Rule in Cameroon*, Lanham: University Press of America.

Awondo, P., P. Geschiere, and G. Reid (2012), 'Homophobic Africa? Towards a more nuanced view,' *African Studies Review*, 55 (3), 145–168.

Ayalon, A. (1984), 'The Arab discovery of America in the nineteenth century,' *Middle Eastern Studies*, 20 (4), 5–17.

Ayeni, T. (2022), 'Netflix à l'heure africaine?,' *Jeune Afrique*, February 8, https://www.jeuneafrique.com/1309061/economie/netflix-a-lheure-africaine/.

Ba, M. (2020), 'Lilian Thuram: La pensée blanche imprègne également les Noirs>' *Jeune Afrique*, December 7, https://www.jeuneafrique.com/1085916/societe/lilian-thuram-la-pensee-blanche-impregne-egalement-les-noirs/.

Babilola, A. (1985), 'Yoruba literature,' In. B. Andrzejewski and S. Pilaszewicz, and W. Tyloch (eds.), *Literature in African Languages: Theoretical Issues and Sample Surveys*, Cambridge: Cambridge University Press, 157–189.

Bahi, A. (2021), 'Future Knowledges: une afrotopie futuriste sans chercheurs africains?' *African Studies Review*, 63 (4), 110–111.

Bakhtin, M. (1984), *Rabelais and His World*, Bloomington: Indiana University Press.

Balakrishnan, S. (2017), 'The Afropolitan idea: new perspectives on cosmopolitanism in African studies,' *History Compass*, 15 (2), 1–11.

Barber, K. (2012), *Print Culture and the First Yoruba Novel: I.B. Thomas's 'Life Story of Me, Segilola' and Other Texts*, Leiden: Brill.

Barrows, L. (2010), 'Edward Wilmot Blyden,' In. A. Irele and B. Jeyifo (eds.), *The Oxford Encyclopedia of African Thought*, New York: Oxford University Press.

Bassichis, M. and D. Spade (2014), 'Queer politics and anti-blackness,' In. J. A. Haritaworn Juntsman and S. Posocco (eds.), *Queer necropolitics*, Abingdon: Routledge, 191–210.

Bataille G, and J. Strauss (1990), 'Hegel, Death and Sacrifice,' *Yale French Studies*, 78, 9–28.

Bayart, J. (1993), *The State in Africa: The Politics of the Belly*, London: Longman.

Bayart, J. (2008), 'Hégémonie et coercition en Afrique subsaharienne. La "politique de la chicotte,"' *Politique africaine*, 100, 123–152.

Bayart, J.-F. (2022), 'Die Ungleichzeitigkeiten der Erinnerung,' In. M. Böckmann, M. Gockel, R. Kößler, and H. Melber (eds.), *Jenseits von Mbembe – Geschichte, Erinnerung, Solidarität*, Metropol Verlag: Berlin, 143–155.

Bénit-Gbaffou, C. (2016), 'Acualité de Fanon dans les mouvements étudiants sud-Africains contemporains: un entretien avec Achille Mbembe,' *Politique Africaine*, 143, 169–183.

Bergesen, A. (2008), *The Sayyid Qutb Reader*, New York: Routledge.

Bernal, V. (2021), 'Digitality and decolonization: a response to Achille Mbembe,' *African Studies Review*, 64 (1), 41–56.

Besteman, C., H. Cabot, and B. Kalir (2020). 'Post-Covid Fantasies: An Introduction,' In. C. Besteman, H. Cabot, and B. Kalir (eds.), *American Ethnologist* website, July 27, 2020, https://americanethnologist.org/features/pandemic-diaries/post-covid-fantasies/post-covid-fantasies-an-introduction.

Bevan, A. (2010), 'Alexander Crummell,' In. F. Irele and B. Jeyifo (eds.), *The Oxford Encyclopedia of African Thought*, Oxford: Oxford University Press.

Bhabha, H. (1994), *The Location of Culture*, London: Routledge.

Biko, S. (1988), *I Write What I Like*, London: Penguin.

Bishop, C. (2014), *Postcolonial Criticism and Representations of African Dictatorship: The Aesthetics of Tyranny*, London: Legenda.

Black, J. (2016), *War in Europe: 1450 to the Present*, London: Bloomsbury Academic.

Blyden, N. (2019), *African Americans & Africa: A New History*, New Haven: Yale University Press.

Böckmann, M., M. Gockel, R. Kößler, and H. Melber (2022), 'Einleitung,' In. M. Böckmann,. Gockel, R. Kößler, and H. Melber (eds.), *Jenseits von Mbembe – Geschichte, Erinnerung, Solidarität*, Metropol Verlag: Berlin, 9–24.

Boualaga, F. (1981), Christianisme sans fétiche, Paris: Présence Africaine.

Boualaga, F., A. Mbembe, and C. Monga (2006), 'Penser africain: raison, identité et liberté: Entretien avec Fabien Eboussi Boulaga,' *Esprit*, 12, 2006, 106–116.

Boulbina, S. (2019), *Kafka's Monkey and Other Phantoms of Africa*, Bloomington: Indiana University Press.

Boureau, A. (1998), *The Lord's First Night: The Myth of the Droit De Cuissage*, Chicago: University of Chicago Press.

Boyd, J. and B. Mack (1997), *The Collected Works of Nana Asma'u, Daughter of Usman dan Fodiyo (1793–1864)*, East Lansing: Michigan State University Press.

Braudel, F. (1981), *Civilization and Capitalism, 15th-18th Century. Vol. 1: The Structures of Everyday Life: The Limits of the Possible*, London: Collins.

Brown, V. (2010), *Reaper's Garden: Death and Power in the World of Atlantic Slavery*, Cambridge: Harvard University Press.

Butler, J. (1992), 'Mbembe's extravagant power,' *Public Culture*, 5 (1), 67–74.

Calame-Griaule, G. (1987), *Ethnologie et langage: la parole chez les Dogon*, Paris: Institut d'ethnologie.

Calvert, J. (2019), *Sayyid Qutb and the Origins of Radical Islamism*, New York: Oxford University Press.

Campos dos Santos, H., F. Maciel, K. Santos, C. Silva da Conceição, R. Silva de Oliveira, N. Ferreira da Silva, and N. Prado (2020), 'Necropolitics and the impact of COVID-19 on the Black community in Brazil: a literature review and a document analysis,' *Ciência & Saúde Coletiva*, 25 (Supplement 2), 4211–4224.

Capdepón, U. and A. Moses (2021), 'Introduction: forum: the Achille Mbembe controversy and the German debate about antisemitism, Israel, and the Holocaust,' *Journal of Genocide Research*, 23 (3), 371–373.

Chamayou, G. (2015), *Drone Theory*, London: Penguin.

Cherki, A. (2006), *Frantz Fanon: A Portrait*, Ithaca: Cornell University Press.

Chipkin, I. and M. Swilling (2018), 'Introduction,' In. I. Chipkin, and M. Swilling (eds.), *Shadow State: The Politics of State Capture*, Johannesburg: Wits University Press, 1–18.

Cisney, V. and N. Morar (2016), 'Introduction: why biopower? why now?' In. V. Cisney and N. Morar (eds.), *Biopower: Foucault and Beyond*, Chicago: Chicago University Press, 1–28.

Clark, P. and A. Ricard (2000), 'Sony Labou Tansi: from archive to corpus,' *Research in African Literatures*, 31 (3), 37–38.

Cleveland, K. (2024), *African Futurism: African Imaginings of Other Times, Spaces, and Worlds*, Athens: Ohio University Press.

Clifford, J. (1988), *The Predicament of Culture: Twentieth-Century Ethnography, Literature, and Art*, Cambridge: Harvard University Press.

Coetzee, C. (2016), 'Introduction,' *Journal of African Cultural Studies*, 28 (1), 101–103.

Coetzee, C. (2022), 'The myth of Oxford and Black counter-narratives,' *African Studies Review*, 65 (2), 288–307, 290.

Cole, T. (2012), *Open City*, London: Faber and Faber.

Conrad, J. (2018), *Heart of Darkness*, Cambridge: Cambridge University Press.

Cooper, F. (2004), *Africa since 1940: The Past of the Present*, Cambridge: Cambridge University Press.

Cooper, F. and A. Stoler (1997), 'Between Metropole and colony: rethinking a research agenda,' In. F. Cooper and A. Stoler (eds.), *Tensions of Empire*, Berkeley: California University Press, 1–58.

Copans, J. (1973), "Comment lire Marcel Griaule? A propos de l'interprétation de Dirk Lettens,' *Cahiers d'Études Africaines*, 13 (49), 154–157.

Coquery-Vidrovitch, C. (2018), 'The Dakar school of history,' *The Oxford Research Encyclopedia of African History*, https://doi.org/10.1093/acrefore/9780190277734.013.318.

Corcoran, P. (2007), *The Cambridge Introduction to Francophone Literature*, Cambridge: Cambridge University Press.

Coronil, F. (1992), 'Can postcoloniality be decolonized? imperial banality and postcolonial power,' *Public Culture*, 5 (1), 89–108.

Crenshaw, K. (2020), 'The unmattering of black lives,' *The New Republic*, May 21, https://newrepublic.com/article/157769/unmattering-black-lives.

Crétois, J. (2020), 'Achille Mbembe accuse d'antisemitisme: la polémique fait rage en Allemagne,' *Jeune Afrique*, May 6, https://www.jeuneafrique.com/941123/société/achille-mbembe-accuse-dantisemitisme-la-polemique-fait-rage-en-allemagne/.

Crowder, R. (1978), 'John Edward Bruce: pioneer black nationalist,' *Afro-Americans in New York Life and History*, 2 (July), 47–66.

Dabiri, E. (2014), 'Why I'm not an Afropolitan,' https://africasacountry.com/2014/01/why-im-not-an-afropolitan.

Dash, J. (1995), *Edouard Glissant*, Cambridge: Cambridge University Press.

Davies, O. (2007), *The Haunted: A Social History of Ghosts*, Basingstoke: Palgrave.

Dayo, B (2020). 'Netflix is launching in Nigeria, but not everyone is happy,' *Vice*, December 28, https://www.vice.com/en/article/k7agzn/netflix-naija-launch-nigeria.

De Boeck, F. (1998), 'Beyond the grave: history, memory, and death in postcolonial Congo/ Zaire,' In. R. Werbner (ed.), *Memory and the Postcolony: African Anthropology and the Critique of Power*, London: Zed, 21–57.

De Boeck, F. (2005), 'The apocalyptic interlude: revealing death in Kinshasa,' *African Studies Review*, 48 (2), 11–32.

De Boeck, F. and M.F. Plissart (2005), *Kinshasa: Tales of the Invisible City*, Ghent: Ludion.

Deacon, M. (2003), 'Trends in African philosophy,' In. P. Coetzee and A. Roux (eds.), *The African Philosophy Reader*, New York: Routledge, 115–191.

Delany, M. (2017), *Blake; or, the Huts of America: A Corrected Edition*, Cambridge: Harvard University Press.

Delaney, M. and R. Mbuh (2010), *Historical Dictionary of the Republic of Cameroon*, Lanham: Scarecrow Press.

Delany, S. (1998), *Einstein Intersection*, Middletown: Wesleyan University Press.

Delavignette, R. (2018 [1950]), *Freedom and Authority in French West Africa*, Abingdon: Routledge.

Delgado, R. (2017), *Critical Race Theory: An Introduction*, New York: New York University Press.

Deltombe, T. and M. Domergue (2011), *Kamerun!: une guerre cachée aux origins de la Françafrique, 1948–1971*, Paris: La Découverte.

Deltombe, T., M. Domergue, and J. Tatsitsa (2016), *La guerre du Cameroun: l'invention de la Françafrique, 1948–1971*, Paris: La Découverte.

Denijal, J. (2020), 'Colonial discourses are stifling free speech in Germany,' *Al Jazeera*, June 29, 2020, https://www.aljazeera.com/opinions/2020/6/19/colonial-discourses-are-stifling-free-speech-in-germany.

Derrida, J. (1981), *Dissemination*, London: Athlone Press.

Derrida, J. (2001), *On Cosmopolitanism and Forgiveness*, London: Routledge.

Desai, G. (1991), 'V. Y. Mudimbe: a portrait,' *Callaloo*, 14 (4), 931–943.

Deutsche, W. (2020), 'Why Achille Mbembe was accused of anti-Semitism,' *Deutsche Welle*, April 30, 2020, https://www.dw.com/en/why-achille-mbembe-was-accused-of-anti-semitism/a-53293797.

Diagne, S.B. (2008), *Comment philosopher en islam?* Paris: Panama.

Diagne, S.B. (2009), 'Shaykh al-Hajj Abbass Sall: in praise of the Tijaniya order,' In. J. Renard (ed.), *Tales of God's Friends:*

Islamic Hagiography in Translation, Berkeley: California University Press, 169–179.

Diagne, S.B. (2017), 'Penser de langue à langue,' In. A. Mabanckou (ed.), *Penser et écrire l'Afrique aujourd'hui*. Paris: Éditions du Seuil, 72–80.

Diagne, S.B. (2018), Open to Reason, New York: Columbia University Press.

Diagne, S.B. (2019), *Postcolonial Bergson*, New York: Fordham University Press.

Diagne, S.B. (2022), 'La fin de l'universalisme européen sera le commencement de l'universel,' *Philosophie magazine*, octobre 19.

Dieterlen, G. (1952), 'Classification des végétaux chez les Dogon,' *Journal de la Société des Africanistes*, 22, 115–158.

Dorestal, P. (2021), 'Reassessing Mbembe: postcolonial critique and the continuities of extreme violence,' *Journal of Genocide Research*, 23 (3), 383–391.

Dubois, L. (2004), *Avengers of the New World*, Durham: Duke University Press.

Dubois, L. (2010), *Soccer Empire: The World Cup and the Future of France*, Berkeley: University of California Press.

Dubois, L. and A. Mbembe (2014), 'Nous sommes tous Francophones,' *French Politics, Culture & Society*, 32 (2), 40–48.

Dyer, R. (2017), *White*, London: Routledge, 1997.

Eboko, F. (2018), 'Les <Ateliers de la pensée>, ou la nécessité d'un projet politique commune en Afrique,' *Jeune Afrique*, February 7, https://www.jeuneafrique.com/mag/526938/societe/les-ateliers-de-la-pensee-ou-la-necessite-dun-projet-politique-commun-en-afrique/.

Ede, A. (2016), 'The politics of Afropolitanism,' *Journal of African Cultural Studies*, 28 (1), 88–100.

Ede, A. (2019), 'Afropolitan genealogies,' *African Diaspora*, 11 (1–2), 35–52.

Ede, A. (2023), 'Area studies: from "global anglophone" to Afropolitan literature,' *Interventions*, https://doi.org/10.1080/1369801X.2022.2161058.

Edelman, E. (2014), '"Walking while transgendered": necropolitical regulations of trans feminine bodies of color in the U.S. nation's capital,' In. J. A. Juntsman Haritaworn and S. Posocco (eds.), *Queer Necropolitics*, Abingdon: Routledge, 172–190.

Edwards, J. and R. Graulund (2013), *Grotesque*, Abingdon: Routledge.

Estévez, A. (ed.) (2021), *Necropower in North America*, Basingstoke: Palgrave.

Eze, B. (2014), 'Rethinking African culture and identity: the Afropolitan model,' *Journal of African Cultural Studies*, 26 (2), 234–247.

Eze, C. (1997), *Race & Enlightenment: A Reader*, Oxford: Blackwell.

Eze, C. (2016), 'We Afropolitans,' *Journal of African Cultural Studies*, 28 (1), 114–119.

Fanon, F. (1967), *The Wretched of the Earth*, Harmondsworth: Penguin.

Fanon, F. (1967 [1964]), *Towards the African Revolution: Political Essays*, New York: Grove.

Fanon, F. (2008 [1952]), *Black Skin White Masks*, London: Pluto Press, 82–108.

Fanon, F. (2011), *Oeuvres*, Paris: La Découverte.

Fanon, F. (2021), *Black Skin, White Masks*, London: Penguin.

Fanon, F. and J. Azoulay (2018), 'Social therapy in a world of Muslim Men: methodological difficulties,' In. Fanon, F.,

J. Khalfa and R. Young (eds.), *Alienation and Freedom*, London: Bloomsbury, 353–372.

Fanon, F. and F. Sanchez (2018), 'Maghrebi Muslims and their attitudes to madness,' In. Fanon, F. J. Khalfa and R. Young (eds.), Alienation *and* Freedom, London: Bloomsbury, 421–422.

Fanon, F., Khalfa, J. and R. Young (2018), *Alienation and Freedom*, London: Bloomsbury, 3–5.

Farred, G. (2012), '"Keeping silent": the problem of citizenship for Lilian Thuram,' *Ethnic and Racial Studies*, 35 (6), 1040–1058.

Ferguson, J. (2015), *Give a Man a Fish: Reflections on the New Politics of Distribution*, Durham: Duke University Press, 1–6.

Firchow, P. (2000), *Envisioning Africa: Racism and Imperialism in Conrad's Heart of Darkness*, Kentucky: Kentucky University Press.

Forde, D. (1956), "Marcel Griaule," *Africa*, 26 (3), 217–218

Foucault, M. (1997), *Ethics: Subjectivity and Truth: The Essential Works of Michael Foucault, 1954–1984*, London: Penguin.

Foucault, M. (2019), *Discipline and Punish*, London: Penguin.

Foucault, M. (2020a), *Power*, London: Penguin.

Foucault, M. (2020b), *Society Must Be Defended: Lectures at the Collège de France, 1975–76*. London: Penguin.

Fox, R. (1998), 'Tribute: Tutuola and the commitment of tradition,' *Research in the African Literature*, 29 (3), 203–208.

Fraiture, P. (2017), *V.Y. Mudimbe: Undisciplined Africanism*, Liverpool: Liverpool University Press.

Fraiture, P. and D. Orrells (2016), Introduction, In. P. Fraiture and D. Orrells (eds.), *The Mudimbe Reader*, Charlottesville: University of Virginia Press, xi–xlv.

Funke, H. (2021), *Black Lives Matter in Deutschland: George Floyd und die Diffamierung von Achille Mbembe als*

Antisemit -eine Streitschrift über (post)koloniale Konflikte, VSA Verlag: Hamburg.

Garnier, X. (2015), *Sony Labou Tansi: une écriture de la decomposition impériale*, Paris: Karthala.

Gates, H., E. Akyeampong, and S. Niven (2012), 'Delany, Martin (1812–1885),' In. H. Gates, Akyeampong, E. and S. Niven (eds.), *Dictionary of African Biography*, New York: Oxford University Press.

Gehrmann, S. (2016), 'Cosmopolitanism with African roots: Afropolitanism's ambivalent mobilities,' *Journal of African Cultural Studies*, 28 (1), 61–72.

Genova, J. (2004), 'Constructing Identity in Post-War France: citizenship, nationality, and the Lamine Guèye Law, 1946–1953,' *The International History Review*, 26 (1), 56–79.

Gershoni, I. and J. Jankowski (1995), *Defining the Egyptian Nation, 1930–1945*, Cambridge: Cambridge University Press.

Geschiere, P. (2009), *The Perils of Belonging: Autochthony, Citizenship, and Exclusion in Africa and Europe*, Chicago: University of Chicago Press.

Geschiere, P. (2013), *Witchcraft and Intimacy*, Chicago: University of Chicago Press.

Geschiere, P. (2017), 'A "vortex of identities": freemasonry, witchcraft, and postcolonial homophobia,' *African Studies Review*, 60 (2), 7–35.

Geschiere, P. (2021), 'Dazzled by new media: Mbembe, Tonda, and the mystic virtual,' *African Studies Review*, 64 (1), 71–85.

Gibson, N. (2016), 'Fanon et les mouvements étudiants sud-africains en 2015,' *Politique Africaine*, 143, 35–57.

Gilroy, P. (1993), *The Black Atlantic: Modernity and Double Consciousness*, London: Verso.

Gilroy, P. (2000), *Against Race*, Cambridge: Harvard University Press.

Gilroy, P. (2001), 'Joined-up politics and postcolonial melancholia,' *Theory, Culture, and Society*, 18 (2–3), 151–67.

Goldberg, D. and P. Essed (2002), 'Introduction,' In. D. Goldberg and P. Essel, *Race Critical Theories: Text and Context*, Oxford: Blackwell, 1–14.

Gomez, M. (2005), *Black Crescent: The Experience and Legacy of African Muslims in the Americas*, Cambridge: Cambridge University Press.

Gonzalez, J. (2019), *Maroon Nation: A History of Revolutionary Haiti*, New Haven: Yale University Press.

Gorsz-Ngaté, M. (2020), 'Knowledge and power: perspectives on the production and decolonization of African/ist knowledge,' *African Studies Review*, 63 (4), 689–718.

Gray, L. (2006), 'Lagos Stori Plenti,' *New Internationalist*, September 1, 26.

Griaule, M. (1947), 'Mythe de l'organisation du monde chez les Dogons du Soudan,' *Psyche*, 6, 443–453.

Griaule, M. and G. Dieterlen (1965), *Le renard pâle*, Paris: Institut d'ethnologie.

Gruesser, J. (2001), 'Bruce, John E. (1856–1924),' In. W. Andrews, F. Foster, and T. Harris (eds.), *The Concise Oxford Companion to African American Literature*, New York: Oxford University Press.

Grunawalt, J. (2021), 'The Villain Unmasked: COVID-19 and the Necropolitics of the Anti-Mask Movement,' *Disabled Studies Quarterly*, 41 (3), https://dx.doi.org/10.18061/dsq.v41i3.8343

Guyer, J. (1996), 'Traditions of invention in equatorial Africa,' *African Studies Review*, 39 (3), 1–28.

Habermas, J. (1997), "Kant's idea of perpetual peace. at two hundred years' historical remove,' In. J. Bohman and M. Lutz-Bachmann (eds.), *Perpetual Peace: Essays on Kant's Cosmopolitan Ideal*, Cambridge: MIT Press, 113–154.

Hammond, M. (2018), 'Qasida,' In. M. Hammond (ed.), A *Dictionary of Arabic Literary Terms and Devices*, Oxford: Oxford University Press.

Hand, S. (2002), *Michel Leiris: Writing the Self*, Cambridge: Cambridge University Press.

Hanspal, J. (2023), 'Le divorce entre Sama et Facebook relance la controverse sur la modération en Afrique,' *Jeune Afrique*, January 28, https://www.jeuneafrique.com/1412554/economie-entreprises/le-divorce-entre-sama-et-facebook-relance-la-controverse-sur-la-moderation-en-afrique/

Harbi, M. (2013), 'Avant-propos sur Achille Mbembe et le principe autoritaire,' *Naqd*, 30 (1), 15.

Haritaworn, J. and A. Kuntsman (eds.) (2014), *Queer Necropolitics*, Abingdon: Routledge.

Hawkins, P. (2002), 'Ouologuem, Yambo,' In. M. Majumdar (ed.), *Francophone Studies: The Essential Glossary*, London: Arnold, 195.

Hirsch, D. (2018), Contemporary Left Antisemitism, Abingdon: Routledge.

Hegel, G. (1975), *Lectures on the Philosophy of World History: Introduction: Reason in History*, Cambridge: Cambridge University Press.

Hitchott, N. and D. Thomas (2014), 'Francophone Afropeans,' In. N. Hitchott and D. Thomas (eds.), *Francophone Afropean Literatures*, Liverpool: Liverpool University Press, 1–16.

Hountondji, P. (1996), *African Philosophy: Myth and Reality*, Bloomington: Indiana University Press.

Howe, S. (1998), *Afrocentrism: Mythical Past and Imagined Homes*, London: Verso.

Hunwick, J. (2003–2004), '"I wish to be seen in our land called Afrika": Umar b. Sayyid's appeal to be released from slavery,' *Journal of Arabic and Islamic Studies*, 5, 63–77.

Hutson, A. (2019), 'Nana Asma'u,' In. The Oxford Research Encyclopedia of African *History*, https://doi.org/10.1093/acrefore/9780190277734.013.468.

Jagannathan, S. (2021), 'The necropolitics of neoliberal state response to the Covid-19 pandemic in India,' *Organization*, 29 (3), 1–23, https://doi.org/10.1177/13505084211020195.

Jansen, J.J.G. (2012), 'Sayyid Ḳuṭb,' In. P. Bearman, Th. Bianquis, C.E. Bosworth, E. van Donzel and W.P. Heinrichs (eds.), *Encyclopaedia of Islam*, Leiden: Brill, Second Edition, https://doi.org/10.1163/1573-3912_islam_COM_1012.

Jeune, A. (2018), 'Restitution du patrimoine africain: le combat de Felwine Sarr,' *Jeune Afrique*, November 26, https://www.jeuneafrique.com/mag/671042/culture/restitution-du-patrimoine-africain-le-combat-de-felwine-sarr/.

Jewisewicki, B. (2002), 'The subject in Africa: in Foucault's footsteps,' *Public Culture*, 14 (3), 593–598.

Jolly, E. (2019), 'Ethnologie de sauvegarde et politique coloniale: les engagements de Marcel Griaule,' *Journal des Africanistes*, 89 (1), 6–31.

Jones, R. (2019), *At the Crossroads: Nigerian Travel Writing and Literary Culture in Yoruba and English*, Woodbridge: Boydell & Brewer.

Juompan-Yakam, C. (2021a), 'Achille Mbembe: "Pourquoi j'ai accepté de travailler avec Emmanuel Macron,"' *Jeune Afrique*, March 21, https://www.jeuneafrique.com/1140087/politique/achille-mbembe-entre-lafrique-et-la-france-le-moment-est-propice-pour-provoquer-lhistoire/.

Juompan-Yakam, C. (2021b), 'Achille Mbembe: Macron, Thuram et la pensée décoloniale,' *Jeune Afrique*, August 8, https://www.jeuneafrique.com/1202857/culture/achille-mbembe-macron-thuram-et-la-pensee-decoloniale/.

Juompan-Yakam, C. (2023), 'Achille Mbembe: <La critique de la Françafrique est devenue le masque d'une indigence

intellectuelle>,' *Jeune Afrique*, August 9, https://www.jeuneafrique.com/1140087/politique/achille-mbembe-entr...rique-et-la-france-le-moment-est-propice-pour-provoquer-lhistoire/.

Juompan-Yakam, C, (2024a), 'L'historien Achille Mbembe reçoit le prix Holberg 2024,' Jeune Afrique, https://www.jeuneafrique.com/1547167/culture/historien-achille-mbembe-recoit-le-prix-holberg-2024/

Juompan-Yakam, C. (2024b), 'Achille Mbembe: <En France, la parole raciste a cessé d'être considérée comme scandaleuse>,' Jeune Afrique, https://www.jeuneafrique.com/1584954/politique/achille-mbembe-en-france-la-parole-raciste-a-cesse-detre-consideree-comme-scandaleuse/

Julien, E. (2006), 'The extroverted African novel,' In. F. Moretti (ed.), *The Novel, Volume 1: History, Geography, and Culture*, Princeton: Princeton University Press, 667–703.

July, R. (1967), *The Origins of Modern African Thought: its Development in West Africa During the Nineteenth and Twentieth Centuries*, New York: Praeger.

Kahyana, D. (2018), 'Shifting marginalities in Ham Mukasa and Sir Apolo Kagwa's "Uganda's Katikiro in England,"' *Journal of African Cultural Studies*, 30 (1), 36–48.

Kant, I. (1957 [1795]), 'Perpetual Peace,' New York: Macmillan.

Karegeye, J. (2016), 'Entretien avec Felwine Sarr,' *Contemporary French and Francophone Studies*, 20 (2), 306–313.

Karlström, M. (2003), 'On the aesthetics and dialogics of power in the postcolony,' *Africa*, 73 (1), 57–76.

Khalfa, J. (2018), 'Fanon: revolutionary psychiatrist,' In. Fanon, F., J. Khalfa and R. Young (eds.), *Frantz Fanon: Alienation and Freedom*, London: Bloomsbury Academic, 167–202.

Klein, H. (2010), *The Atlantic Slave Trade*, Cambridge: Cambridge University Press.

Kumar, L. (2017), 'Mbembe, Achille,' In L. Kumar (ed.), *Encyclopedia of World Biography*, Farmington Hills: Gale, 37, 240–242.

Labou Tansi, S. (1988a), *Les yeux du volcan: roman*, Paris: Seuil.

Labou Tansi, S. (1988b), *The Anti-People: A Novel*, London: Boyar.

Labou Tansi, S (1995), *The Seven Solitudes of Lorsa Lopez*, Oxford: Heinemann.

Labou Tansi, S. (1997), *L'autre monde: écrits inédits*. Paris: Revue Noire.

Labou Tansi, S. (2011), *Life and a Half*, Bloomington: Indiana University Press.

Labou Tansi, S. (2015), *The Shameful State*, Bloomington: Indiana University Press.

Laburthe-Tolra, P. (1985), *Initiations et sociétés secretes au Cameroun: les mystères de la nuit*, Paris: Karthala.

Lamble, S. (2014), 'Queer investments in punitiveness: sexual citizenship, social movements and the expanding carceral state,' In. J. A. Juntsman Haritaworn and S. Posocco (eds.), *Queer Necropolitics*, Abingdon: Routledge, 151–171.

Launay, R. and B. Soares (1999), 'The formation of an "Islamic sphere" in French Colonial West Africa,' *Economy and Society*, 28 (4), 497–519.

Lavender, I. (2019), *Afrofuturism Rising: The Literary Prehistory of a Movement*, Columbia: Ohio State University Press.

Le Marcis, F. (2019), 'Life in a space of necropolitics: toward an economy of value in prisons,' *Ethnos*, 84 (1), 74–95.

Lee, C. (2015), *Frantz Fanon: Towards a Revolutionary Humanism*, Athens: Ohio University Press.

Lee, C. (2021), *Kwame Anthony Appiah*, New York: Routledge.

Leiris, M. (1948), *La langue secrete des Dogons de Sanga*, Paris: Institut d'ethnologie.

Leiris, M. (2019), *Phantom Africa*, London: Seagull Books.

Lettens, Dirk (1971), *Mystagogie et mystification: évaluation de l'oeuvre de Marcel Griaule*. Bujumbura, Presses Lavigerie.

Livingston, J., and A. Ross (2022), 'Cars, debt, and carcerality,' *South Atlantic Quarterly*, 121 (4), 846–853.

Lloyd, V (2016), 'Achille Mbembe as black theologian,' *Modern Believing*, 57 (3), 241–251.

Lynn, T. (2016), '"Redemption Song": Slavery's Disruption in Amos Tutuola's My Life in the Bush of Ghosts,' *English Studies in Africa*, 59, 53–64.

MacDonald, K. (2007), 'Cheikh anta diop and ancient Egypt in Africa,' In. A. Reid and D. O'Connor (eds.), *Ancient Egypt in Africa*, London: UCL Press, 93–105.

Mann, G. (2009), 'What was the "Indigénat"? The "Empire of Law" in French West Africa,' *Journal of African History*, 50 (3), 331–353.

Manning, P. (1999), *Francophone Sub-Saharan Africa 1880–1995*, Cambridge: Cambridge University Press.

Manzini, Z. (2016), 'Violence is a Necessary Process of Decolonisation,' *Mail & Guardian*, March 2, https://thoughtleader.co.za/mandelarhodesscholars/violence-is-a-necessary-process-of-decolonisation/

Mbaku, J. (2000), *Culture and Customs of Cameroon*, Westport: Greenwood Press.

Mbembe, A. (1982–1983), 'Les pratiques politiques et les protestations populaires au Cameroun, de 1930 à 1960,' *Afrique noire*, 7, 116–131.

Mbembe, A. (1984), *Le problème national kamerunais: Ruben Um Nyobè*, Paris: L'Harmattan.

Mbembe, A. (1985), 'La palabre de l'indépendance: les orders du discours nationaliste au Cameroun (1948–1958),' *Revue française de science politique*, 35 (3), 459–486.

Mbembe, A. (1986a), *Les jeunes et l'ordre politique en Afrique noire* Paris: Karthala.

Mbembe, A. (1986b), 'Pouvoir des morts et langage des vivants les errances de la memoire nationaliste au Cameroun,' *Politique africaine*, 22, 37–72.

Mbembe, A. (1986c), 'Postface,' In. R. Joseph (ed.), *Le mouvement nationaliste au Cameroun: les origines sociales de l'UPC*, Paris: Karthala, 363–374.

Mbembe, A. (1988), *Afriques indociles: christianisme, pouvoir, et état en société postcoloniale*, Paris: Karthala.

Mbembe, A. (1989a), 'Le spectre et l'État: des dimensions politiques de l'imaginaire historique dans le Cameroun postcolonial,' *Revue de la Bibliotheque Nationale*, 44, 2–13.

Mbembe, A. (1989b), *Écrits sous maquis: Ruben Um Nyobè*, Paris: L'Harmattan.

Mbembe, A. (1990a), 'Pouvoir, violence et accumulation,' *Politique Africaine*, 39, 7–24.

Mbembe, A. (1990b), 'Le Cameroun après la mort d'Ahmadou Ahidjo,' *Politique Africaine*, 37, 117–122.

Mbembe, A. (1991a), 'Domaines de la nuit et autorité onirique dans les maquis du sud-cameroun (1955–1958),' *Journal of African History*, 31, 89–121.

Mbembe, A. (1991b), 'Violence Et Pouvoir,' *Politique Africaine*, 39, 7–24.

Mbembe, A. (1991c), 'Power and obscenity in the post-colonial period – the case of Cameroon,' In. J. Manor (ed.), *Rethinking World Politics*, London: Longman, 166–182.

Mbembe, A. (1992a), 'Prosaics of servitude and authoritarian civilities,' *Public Culture*, 5 (1), 123–145.

Mbembe, A. (1992b), 'Provisional notes on the postcolony,' *Africa: Journal of the International African Institute*, 62, 1, 3–37.

Mbembe, A. (1992c), 'Traditions de l'autoritarisme et problèmes de gouvernement en Afrique sub-saharienne,' *Africa Development*, 17 (1), 37–64.

Mbembe, A. (1992d), 'The banality of power and the aesthetics of vulgarity in the postcolony,' *Public Culture*, 4 (2), 1–30.

Mbembe, A. (1993), 'Écrire l'Afrique à partir d'une faille,' *Politique africaine*, 51, 69–97.

Mbembe, A. (1996a), 'La "chose" et ses doubles dans la caricature camerounaise,' *Cahiers d'études africaines*, 36 (141/142), 143–170.

Mbembe, A. (1996b), *La naissance du maquis dans le Sud-Cameroun (1920-1960): histoire des usages de la raison en colonie*, Paris: Karthala.

Mbembe, A. (1997), 'The civil status and biographies of god in contemporary Africa,' *Afrika Zamani: revue annuelle d'histoire africaine*, 5–6, 1–12.

Mbembe, A. (1999a). 'On private indirect government,' *Politique africaine*, 73, 103–122.

Mbembe, A. (1999b), 'The idea of "social sciences,"' *African Sociological Review*, 3 (2), 129–141.

Mbembe, A. (2001a), 'The subject of the world,' In. G. Oostinde (ed.), *Facing Up to the Past: Perspectives on the Commemoration of Slavery from Africa, the Americas and Europe*, Kingston: Ian Randle Publishers, 21–28.

Mbembe, A. (2001b), *On the Postcolony*, Berkeley: University of California Press.

Mbembe, A. (2002a), 'The power of the archive and its limits. Refiguring the archive,' In. C. Hamilton (ed.), *Refiguring the Archive*, Dordrecht; London: Kluwer Academic, 19–26.

Mbembe, A. (2002b), 'On the power of the false,' *Public Culture*, 14 (3), 629–641.

Mbembe, A. (2002c), 'African modes of self-writing,' *Public Culture*, 14 (1), 239–273.

Mbembe, A. (2003a), 'Necropolitics,' *Public Culture*, 15 (1), 11–40.

Mbembe, A. (2003b), 'Life, sovereignty, and terror in the fiction of Amos Tutuola,' *Research in African Literatures*, 34 (4), 1–26.

Mbembe, A. (2004a), 'Essai sur le politique en tant que forme de la dépense,' *Cahiers d'études africaines*, 44 (173–174), 151–192.

Mbembe, A. (2004b), 'Aesthetics of superfluity,' *Public Culture*, 16 (3), 373–405.

Mbembe, A. (2005a), 'Variations on the beautiful in the Congolese world of sounds,' *Politique africaine*, 100 (4), 69–91.

Mbembe, A. (2005b), 'La république désoeuvrée: La France à l'ère post-coloniale,' *Le Débat*, 137(5), 159–175.

Mbembe, A. (2005c), 'La République et sa Bête: à propos des émeutes dans les banlieues de France,' *Africultures*, n° 65 (4), 176–181.

Mbembe, A. (2005d), 'Faces of freedom: Jewish and black experiences,' *Interventions*, 7 (3), 293–298.

Mbembe, A. (2006a), 'The colony. dirty little secret, cursed lot, La colonie: son petit secret et sa part maudite,' *Politique africaine*, 102, 101–127.

Mbembe, A. (2006b), 'On the postcolony: a brief response to critics,' *African Identities*, 4 (2), 143–178.

Mbembe, A. (2006c), 'On politics as a form of expenditure,' In. J. Comaroff and J. Comaroff (eds.), *Law and Disorder in the Postcolony*, Chicago: University of Chicago Press, 299–336.

Mbembe, A. (2006d), 'Afropolitanisme,' *Africultures*, 66, https://www.africultures.com/php/index.php?nav=article&no=4290.

Mbembe, A. (2006e), 'Necropolitique,' *Raisons politiques: études de pensée politique*. 21 (1), 29–60

Mbembe, A. (2007a), 'De la scène coloniale chez Frantz Fanon,' *Rue Descartes*, 58, 37–55.

Mbembe, A. (2007b), 'L'Afrique de Nicolas Sarkozy,' *Mouvements*, 52 (4), 65–73.

Mbembe, A. (2007c), 'Penser Pour Un Nouveau Siècle,' In. A. Mbembe and F. Sarr (eds.), crire *l'Afrique-Monde*, Dakar: Jimsaan, 7–17

Mbembe, A. (2008a), 'Passages to freedom: the politics of racial reconciliation in South Africa,' *Public Culture*, 20 (1), 5–18.

Mbembe, A. (2010), *Sortir de la grande nuit*, Paris: La Découverte.

Mbembe, A. (2011a), 'La pensée métamorphique: à propos des oeuvres de Frantz Fanon,' In. F. Fanon (ed.), *Oeuvres*, Paris: La Découverte, 9–21.

Mbembe, A. (2011b), 'Fanon's nightmare our reality,' *Mail & Guardian*, December 23, 2011, https://mg.co.za/article/2011-12-23-fanons-nightmare-our-reality/.

Mbembe, A. (2011c), 'Provincializing France?' *Public Culture*, 23 (1), 85–119.

Mbembe, A. (2012a), 'Préface,' In. Fanon-Mendès-France (ed.), *Frantz Fanon par les textes de l'époque*, Paris: Les Petit Matins, 1–29.

Mbembe, A. (2012b), 'Metamorphic Thought: the *Works* of Frantz Fanon,' *African Studies*, 71 (1), 20–26.

Mbembe, A. (2013a), 'Le Noir n'existe pas plus que le Blanc,' *Africultures*, 92–93 (2), 24–30.

Mbembe, A. (2013b), 'L'esclave, figure de l'anti-musée?' *Africultures*, 91 (1), 38–42.

Mbembe, A. (2013c), 'Le principe autoritaire,' *Naqd*, 30 (1), 17–39.

Mbembe, A. (2013d), 'Cinquante ans de décolonisation africaine,' *Naqd*, 30 (1), 137–144.

Mbembe, A. (2014), 'Afrofuturisme et devenir-nègre du monde,' *Politique Africaine*, 136, 121–133.

Mbembe, A. (2015a), 'Decolonizing Institutions,' *Mail & Guardian*, August 6, https://mg.co.za/podcasts/2015-08-06-decolonising-institutions-achille-mbembe/.

Mbembe, A. (2015b), 'Achille Mbembe on the State of South African political life,' *Africa Is a Country*, September 19, africasacountry.com/2015/09/achille-mbembe-on-the-state-of-south-african-politics/.

Mbembe, A. (2015c), 'Exorcise our white ghosts,' *City press*, September 22, city-press.news24.com/Voices/Exorcise-our-white-ghosts-20150918.

Mbembe, A. (2015d), 'The internet is Afropolitan,' originally published in The Chimurenga Chronic, May 2015, http://chimurengachronic.co.za.

Mbembe A. (2015e), 'Foreward,' In. S. Jacobs, J. Soske, and A. Mbembe (eds.), *Apartheid Israel: The Politics of an Analogy*, Chicago: Haymarket Books, vii–viii.

Mbembe, A. (2016a), 'Mantashe and student protestors agree on university shutdowns but this is the last thing Africa needs,' *Mail and Guardian*, November 22, https://mg.co.za/article/2016-09-22-mantashe-and-student-protesters-agree-on-university-shutdowns-but-this-is-the-last-thing-africa-needs-1/.

Mbembe, A. (2016b), 'Future knowledges,' Abiola Lecture, presented at the African Studies Association Annual Meeting in Washington DC, December 1-3, https://www.youtube.com/watch?v=J6p8pUU_VH0

Mbembe, A. (2016c), 'Achille Mbembe writes about Xenophobic South Africa,' *Africa Is a Country*, April 15, africasacountry.com/2015/04/achille-mbembe-writes-about-xenophobic-south-africa/.

Mbembe, A. (2016d), *Politiques de l'inimité*, Paris: La Découverte.

Mbembe, A. (2016e), 'The society of enmity,' *Radical Philosophy*, 200, 23–36.

Mbembe, A. (2016f), 'Preface: surmoi colonial et État sous tutelle,' In. T. Deltombe, M. Domergue, and J. Tatsitsa (eds.), *La Guerre Du Cameroun: L'invention De La Françafrique, 1948–1971*, Paris: La Découverte, 7–15.

Mbembe, A. (2017a), 'Penser le Monde à partir de l'Afrique: questions pour aujourd'hui et demain,' In. A. Mbembe and F. Sarr (eds.), *Écrire l'Afrique-Monde*, Dakar: Jimsaan, 353–368.

Mbembe, A. (2017b), *Critique of Black Reason*, Durham: Duke University Press.

Mbembe, A. (2017c), Nanoracism and the force of emptiness,' In. B. Nicolas, B. Pascal, and T. Dominic (eds.), *The Colonial Legacy in France: Fracture, Rupture, and Apartheid*, Bloomington, Indiana University Press, 363–367.

Mbembe, A. (2018a), 'La démondialisation,' *Esprit*, 450, 86–94.

Mbembe, A. (2018b), 'Biko's testament of hope,' In. D. Accone, Z. Cindi, et al. (eds.), *We Write What We Like: Celebrating Steve Biko*, Johannesburg: Wits University Press, 135–150.

Mbembe, A. (2018c), 'The idea of a borderless world,' *Africa Is a Country*, November 11, https://africasacountry.com/2018/11/the-idea-of-a-borderless-world.

Mbembe, A. (2019a), 'Purger l'Afrique du désir d'Europe,' *Le Débat*, 205 (3), 100–107.

Mbembe, A. (2019b), *Necropolitics*, Durham: Duke University Press.

Mbembe, A. (2020a), *Brutalisme*, Paris: La Découverte.

Mbembe, A. (2020b [2005]), 'Afropolitanism,' In. I. Balseiro, and Z. Rapola (eds.), *The Passport That Does Not Pass Ports: African Literature of Travel in the Twenty-First Century*, East Lansing: Michigan State University Press, 7–12.

Mbembe, A. (2021a), *Out of the Dark Night: Essays on Decolonization*, New York: Columbia University Press.

Mbembe, A. (2021b), 'The universal right to breath,' *Critical Inquiry*, 47, S2, S58–62.

Mbembe, A. (2021c), 'Futures of life and futures of reason,' *Public Culture*, 33 (1), 11–33.

Mbembe, A. (2021d), 'Ré-enchanter l'Afrique,' *Multitudes*, 81 (4), 132–141.

Mbembe, A. (2022), 'Pour contrer le projet raciste de Marine Le Pen, s'abstenir ne suffira pas,' *Jeune Afrique*, April 20, https://www.jeuneafrique.com/1340444/politique/pour-contrer-le-projet-raciste-de-marine-le-pen-sabstenir-ne-suffira-pas/.

Mbembe, A. (2023), *La communauté terrestre*, Paris: La Discouverté.

Mbembe, A. (2024) [2020], *Brutalism*, Durham: Duke University Press.

Mbembe, A. and S. Balakrishnan (2016), 'Pan-African legacies, Afropolitan futures,' *Transition*, 120, 28–37.

Mbembe, A. and F. Bayart (1992), *Le politique par le bas en afrique noire: contributions à une problématique de la démocratie*, Paris: Karthala.

Mbembe, A. and S. Nuttall (2004), 'Writing the world from an African metropolis,' *Public Culture*, 16 (3), 347–372.

Mbembe, A. and S. Nuttall (2008), *Johannesburg: The Elusive Metropolis*, Durham: Duke University Press.

Mbembe, A., L. Pignot and J.-P. Saez (2021), 'Résister au «brutalisme » du monde contemporain à l'ère numérique,' *L'Observatoire*, n° 58 (2), 76–80.

Mbembe, A. and J. Roitman (1995), 'Figures of the subject in times of crisis,' *Public Culture*, 7 (2), 323–352.

Mbembe, A. and B. Van der Haak (2015), 'The Internet is Afropolitan,' originally published in The Chimurenga Chronic, https://chimurengachronic.co.za (May 2015).

Mbembe, A., B. van der Haak, and F.-R. Dubois (2017), 'Afrocomputation,' *Multitudes*, 69 (4), 198–204.

Mbembe, A. and F. Sarr (2017), 'Penser pour un nouveau siècle,' In. A. Mbembe and F. Sarr (eds.), *Écrire l'Afrique-Monde*, Dakar: Jimsaan, 7–17.

Mbembe, A. and F. Sarr (2022a), *To write the Africa world*. Cambridge: Polity.

Mbembe, A. and F. Sarr (2022b), *The politics of time: imagining African becomings*. Cambridge: Polity.

Mccarney, J. (2000), *Hegel on History*, London: Routledge.

McDougall, J. (2017), *A History of Algeria*, Cambridge: Cambridge University Press.

McDougall, J. (2021), "ʿAbd al-Qādir, Amīr,' In. K. Fleet, G. Krämer, D. Matringe, J. Nawas, and E. Rowson (eds.), *Encyclopaedia of Islam*. Consulted online on July 2, 2021, https://doi.org/10.1163/1573-3912_ei3_COM_24657.

Meckstroth, C. (2018), 'Hospitality, or Kant's critique of cosmopolitanism and human rights,' *Political Theory*, 46 (4), 537–559.

Merchant, M. and S. Order (2021), 'Necropolitics in a post-apocalyptic zombie diaspora: the case of A.M.C.'s The Walking Dead,' *Journal of Postcolonial Writing*, 57 (1), 89–103.

Merleau-Ponty, M. (1969), *La Prose du monde*, Paris: Gallimard.

Miller, C. (2008), *The French Atlantic Triangle: Literature and Culture of the Slave Trade*, Durham: Duke University Press.

Miller, F. (1975), *The Search for a Nationality: Black Emigration and Colonization, 1787–1863*, Urbana: University of Illinois Press.

Monnier, L. (2002), '"Immediate History': remembering the golden age of research in political science at the University of Kinshasa,' In. E. Mudimbe-Boyi (ed.), *Remembering Africa*, Portsmouth: Heinemann, 283–301.

Mudimbe, V. (1988), *The Invention of Africa: Gnosis, Philosophy, and the Order of Knowledge*, Bloomington: Indiana University Press, 1–23.

Mudimbe, V. (1992), 'Save the African continent,' *Public Culture*, 5 (1), 61–62.

Mukasa, H. (1998), *Uganda's Katakiro in England*, Manchester: Manchester University Press.

Mulemi, B. (2010), 'Animism,' In. F. Irele and B. Jeyifo (eds.), *The Oxford Encyclopedia of African Thought*, New York: Oxford University Press.

Murand, N. (2008), 'Psychiatrie institutionnelle à Blida,' *Tumultes*, 23 (31), 31–45.

Murphy, L. (2012), *Metaphor and the Slave Trade in West African Literature*, Athens: Ohio University Press.

Murray, A. (2010), *Agamben*, Abingdon: Routledge.

Mystakidis, S. (2022), 'Metaverse,' *Encyclopedia*, 2, 486–487, https://doi.org/10.3390/encyclopedia2010031.

Nayar, P. (2013), *Frantz Fanon*, New York: Routledge.

Ndiaye, S. (2000), 'Dictatorship and the emptiness of the rhetoric of totalitarian discourse in Sony Labou Tansi's "La Vie et demie,"'*Research in African Literatures*, 34 (2), 112–126.

Ndlovu-Gatsheni, S. (n.d.), 'Africa Decolonial Research Network (ADERN),' https://din.today/en/sabelo-j-ndlovu-gatsheni-we-needed-to-shift-the-geography-of-knowledge-as-well-as-the-biography-of-knowledge/.

Ndlovu-Gatsheni, S. (2018), *Epistemic Freedom in Africa: Deprovincialization and Decolonization*, New York: Routledge.

Ndoye, B. (2017) 'Réenchanter le monde: Husserl en postcolonie,' In. Mbembe, A and F. Sarr (eds.), Écrire l'Afrique-Monde, Dakar: Jimsaan, 353–368.

Newell, S. and K. Pype (2021), 'Decolonizing the virtual: future knowledges and the extrahuman in Africa,' *African Studies Review*, 64 (1), 5–22.

Ngong, D. (2020), 'Recent developments in African political theology,' *Religion Compass*, 14, e12372, https://doi.org/10.1111/rec3.12372.

Ngongkum, E. (2018), 'The dictator-novel in Cameroonian literature: Mongo Beti's 'Perpetua and the habit of unhappiness' and John Nkemngong Nkengasong's "across the Mongolo,"' *Research in African Literatures*, 49 (3), 1–17.

Nizamis, K. (2000), 'Pharmakon,' In. V. Taylor and C. Winquist (eds.), *Encyclopedia of Postmodernism*, London: Routledge, 279–281.

Njami, S. (2005), *Africa Remix: Contemporary Art of a Continent*, London: Hayward Gallery.

Nkwi, W. (2019), 'Ruben Um Nyobe: Camerounian maquis, radical, and liberator, ca. 1948–1958,' In. De Bruijin (ed.) *Biographies of Radicalization: Hidden Messages of Social Change*, Berlin: Walter de Gruyter, 65–83.

Nugent, P. (2004), *Africa since Independence: A Comparative History*, Basingstoke: Palgrave Macmillan.

Nuttall, S. (2006), *Beautiful/ Ugly: African and Diaspora Aesthetics*, Durham: Duke University Press.

Nuttall, S. and A. Mbembe (2007), 'Afropolis: from Johannesburg,' *PMLA*, 122 (1), 281–288.

Nuttall, S. and A. Mbembe (2014), 'Mandela's mortality,' In. R. Barnard (ed.), *The Cambridge Companion to Nelson Mandela*, Cambridge, Cambridge University Press, 267–290.

Nuttall, S. and A. Mbembe (2015), 'Secrecy's softwares,' *Current Anthropology*, 56 (S12), S317–S324.

Nyamnjoh, F. (2011), 'Cameroonian bushfalling: negotiation of identity and belonging in fiction and ethnography,' *American Ethnologist*, 38 (4), 701–713.

Nyamnjoh, F. (2015), *#Rhodes Must Fall: Nibbling at Resilient Colonialism in South Africa*, Bamenda: Langaa Research & Publishing.

Nyamnjoh, F. (2017a), 'Incompleteness: frontier Africa and the currency of conviviality,' *Journal of Asian and African Studies*, 52 (3): 253–257.

Nyamnjoh, F. (2017b), *Drinking from the Cosmic Gourd: how Amos Tutuola Can Change Out Minds*, Mankon: Langaa Research & Publishing.

Nyamnjoh, F. (2020a), 'A post-COVID-19 fantasy on incompleteness and conviviality,' In. "Post-Covid Fantasies," Besteman, C., H. Cabot, and B. Kalir (eds.), American Ethnologist website, 27th July 2020, https://americanethnologist.org/features/pandemic-diaries/post-covid-fantasies/a-post-covid-19-fanatasy-on-incompleteness-and-conviviality.

Nyamnjoh, F. (2020b), *Decolonising the Academy: A Case for Convivial Scholarship*, Basel: Basler Afrika Bibliographien.

Nyeck, S. (2019), 'Introduction,' In. S. Nyeck (ed.), *Routledge Handbook of Queer African Studies*, Abingdon: Routledge, 1–11.

Nzabatsinda, A. (2009), In. 'Sony Labou Tansi,' S. Gikandi (ed.), *The Routledge Encyclopedia of African Literature*, London: Routledge.

O'Mahony, L., K. Motyl, and M. Arghavan (2018), 'Writing against neocolonial necropolitics: literary responses by Iraqi / Arab writers to the US 'War on Terror,' *European Journal of English Studies*, 22 (2), 128–141.

Ochonu, M. (2022), *Emirs in London: Subaltern Travel and Nigeria's Modernity*, Bloomington: Indiana University Press.

Okorafor, N. (2020), 'Africanfuturism defined,' In. W. Talabi (ed.), *Africanfuturism: An Anthology*, Brittle Paper, www.brittlepaper.com, no page range.

Okwunodu Ogbechie, S. (2008), '"Afropolitanism": Africa without Africans (II),' https://aachronym.blogspot.com/2008/04/afropolitanism-more-africa-without.html.

Orkin, M. and A. Joubin (2019), *Race*, Abingdon: Routledge.

Orock, R. (2022), 'Chinua Achebe's postcolony: a literary anthropology of postcolonial decadence,' *Africa*, 92, 71–92.

Osman, G. and C. Forbes (2004), 'Representing the West in the Arabic language: the slave narrative of Omar ibn Said,' *Journal of Islamic Studies*, 15 (3), 331–343.

Ostle, R. (1998), 'Shawqi, Ahmad (1868–1932),' In. J. Mesiami and P. Starkey (eds.), *Encyclopedia of Arabic Literature*, London: Routledge.

Osuri, G. (2009), 'Necropolitical complicities: (re) constructing a normative somatechnics of Iraq,' *Social Semiotics*, 19 (1), 31–45.

Ouédrago, J. (2003a), 'Yambo Ouologuem,' In. S. Gikandi (ed.), *The Routledge Encyclopedia of African Literature*, London: Routledge.

Ouédrago, J. (2003b), 'Kourouma, Ahmadou,' In. S. Gikandi (ed.), *The Routledge Encyclopedia of African Literature*, London: Routledge.

Ouologuem, Y. (1971), *Bound to Violence*, Oxford: Heinemann.

Ouologuem, Y. (2003), *Lettre à la France nègre*, Paris: Le serpent à plumes.

Ouologuem, Y. (2015), Les mille et une bibles du sexe, La Roque d'Anthéron: Vents d'ailleurs.

Paquette J. (2020), 'France and the restitution of cultural goods: the Sarr-Savoy report and its reception,' *Cultural Trends*, 29 (4), 302–316.

Parker, J. (2020), *In My Time of Dying: A History of Death and the Dead in West Africa*, Princeton: Princeton University Press.

Parry, B. (1983), *Conrad's Imperialism: Ideological Boundaries and Visionary Fronters*, London: Macmillan.

Patterson, O. (1982), *Slavery and Social Death: A Comparative Study*, Cambridge: Harvard University Press.

Petit, P. and G. Mutambwa (2005), '"La crise": lexicon and ethos of the second economy in Lubumbashi,' *Africa*, 75 (4), 467–487.

Pierrot, G. (2022), 'Nègre (Noir, Black, Renoi, Nègro),' *Small Axe*, 26 (2), 100–107.

Pillay, S. and C. Fernandes (2016), 'Transmission, obligation and movement: an interview with Souleymane Bachir Diagne,' *Social Dynamics*, 42 (3), 542–554.

Pype, K. (2016), '(Not) talking like a Motorola: politics of masking and unmasking in Kinshasa's mobile phone culture,' *Journal of the Royal Anthropological Institute*, 22 (3), 633–652.

Pype, K. (2022), '"Provisional notes on the postcolony" in Congo studies: an overview of themes and debates,' *Africa*, 92, 49–70.

Quayson, A. (2001), 'Breaches in the commonplace,' *African Studies Review*, 44 (2), 151–165.

Quenet, G. (2017), 'The anthropocene and the time of historians,' *Annales H.S.S. (English Edition)*, 72 (2), 165–197.

Quinan, C. and K. Thiele (eds.) (2021), *Biopolitics, Necropolitics, Cosmopolitics: Feminist and Queer Interventions*, Abingdon: Routledge.

Qutb, S. (2006), *Milestones*, Lahore: Islamic Book Service.

Qutb, S. (2016 [1946]), *A Child from the Village*, New York: Syracuse University Press.

Roberts, R. (2006), 'Introduction: African intermediaries and the "bargain" of collaboration,' In. B. Lawrence, E. Osborn, and R. Roberts (eds.), Intermediaries, *Interpreters, and Clerks: African Employees in the Making of Colonial Africa*, Madison: University of Wisconsin Press, 3–34.

Reid Out (2021), 'The reid out,' Transcript of March 3, 2021 Broadcast, March 4, 2021, https://www.msnbc.com/transcripts/transcript-reidout-3-3-2021-n1260939.

Riesz, J. and A. Allen (2000), 'From L'état sauvage to L'état honteux,' *Research in African Literatures*, 31 (3), 100–128.

Renfrew, A. (2015), *Bakhtin*, Abingdon: Routledge.

Reno, W. (2011), *Warfare in Independent Africa*, Cambridge: Cambridge University Press.

Riley Snorton, C. and J. Haritaworn (2013), 'Trans Necropolitics: a transnational reflection on violence, death, and the trans of color afterlife,' In. S. Stryker, and A. Aizura (eds.), *The Transgender Studies Reader 2*, New York: Routledge, 66–76.

Ringer, C. (2021), *Necropolitics: The Religious Crisis of Mass Incarceration in America*, Lanham: Lexington.

Roberts, A. (2000), *Science Fiction*, Abingdon: Routledge.

Robertson, H. and J. Travaglia (2020), 'The necropolitics of COVID-19: will the COVID-19 pandemic reshape national healthcare systems,' Impact of Social Sciences, London School of Economics Blogs, https://blogs.lse.ac.uk/impactofsocialsciences/2020/05/18/the-necropolitics-of-covid-19-will-the-covid-19-pandemic-reshape-national-healthcare-systems/.

Robles-Anderson, E. (2021), '"Wave fronts of calculation": a response to Achille Mbembe,' *Public Culture*, 33 (1), 35–40.

Roca, R. (2015), 'Fetishism,' In. J. Wright (ed.), *International Encyclopedia of the Social & Behavioral Sciences*, 9, 105–110.

Ross, A. (2022), 'Introduction: punishment by debt,' *South Atlantic Quarterly*, 121 (4), 834–837.

Rothberg, M. (2020), 'Comparing comparisons: from the "historikerstreit" to the Mbembe affair,' *Geschichte der Gegenwart*, September 2020, https://geschichtedergegenwart.ch/comparing-comparisons-from-the-historikerstreit-to-the-mbembe-affair/.

Saadawi, A. (2018), *Frankenstein in Baghdad*, London: Oneworld.

Sai, F. (2019), 'Flesh and blood: necropolitics of literature,' In. S. Guth and T. Pepe (eds.), *Arabic Literature in a Posthuman World: Proceedings of the 12th Conference of the European Association for Modern Arabic Literature*, Wiesbaden: Otto Harrassowitz, 243–247.

Said, O. (2014), 'Omar ibn Said (1770–1864),' In. G. Jarrett (ed.), *The Wiley Blackwell Anthology of African American Literature: Volume 1, 1746–1920*, Chichester: Wiley-Blackwell, 143–146.

Sandset, T. (2021), 'The necropolitics of COVID-19: race, class and slow death in an ongoing pandemic,' *Global Public Health*, 16 (8–9), 1411–1423.

Santana, S. (2013), 'Exorcizing Afropolitanism: Binyavanga Wainaina Explains Why "I am a Pan-Africanist, not an Afropolitan" at ASAUK 2012,' February 8. https://africainwords.com/2013/02/08/exorcizing-afropolitanism-binyavanga-wainaina-explains-why-i-am-a-pan-africanist-not-an-afropolitan-at-asauk-2012/

Santana, S. (2016), 'Exorcizing the future: Afropolitanism's spectral origins,' *Journal of African Cultural Studies*, 28 (1), 120–126, 120–121.

Sarr, F. (2009), *Dahij*, Paris: Gallimard.

Sarr, F. (2011), *105 rue Carnot: récits*, Montréal: Mémoire d'encrier.

Sarr, F. (2012), *Méditations africaines*, Montréal: Mémoire d'encrier.

Sarr, F. (2017), 'Écrire les humanités à partir de l'Afrique,' In. A. Mbembe and F. Sarr (eds.), *Écrire l'Afrique-Monde*, Dakar: Jimsaan, 369–378.

Sarr, F. (2019), *Afrotopia*, Minneapolis: University of Minnesota Press.

Sarr, F. and B. Savoy (2018), *Rapport sur la restitution du patrimoine africain. Vers une nouvelle éthique relationnelle*, Paris: Ministère de la culture.

Schmitt, C. (2003), *The Nomos of the Earth in the International Law of the Jus Publicum Europaeum*, New York: Telos Press.

Schmitt, C. (2005), *Political Theology: Four Chapters on the Concept of Sovereignty*, Chicago: University of Chicago Press.

Scott, R. (2005), *Degrees of Freedom: Louisiana and Cuba After Slavery*, Cambridge: Harvard University Press.

Selasi, T. (2013), 'Ghana must go,' London: Viking.

Selasi, T. (2020 [2005]), 'Bye bye Babar,' In. I. Balseiro, and Z. Rapola (eds.), *The Passport That Does Not Pass Ports: African Literature of Travel in the Twenty-First Century*, East Lansing: Michigan State University Press, 3–6.

Shryock, A. (2008), 'Thinking about hospitality, with Derrida, Kant, and the Balga Bedouin,' *Anthropos*, 103 (2), 405–421.

Smart, B. (2002), *Michael Foucault*, London: Routledge.

Smith, D. (2007), *A Culture of Corruption: Everyday Deception and Popular Discontent in Nigeria*, Princeton: Princeton University Press, 5–7.

Somerville, E. (2007), 'Robert Wedderburn,' In. D. Dabydeen, J. Gilmore and C. Jones (eds.), *The Oxford Companion to Black British History*, Oxford: Oxford University Press.

Soske, J. (2015), *Apartheid Israel: The Politics of an Analogy*, Chicago: Haymarket Books.

Spivak, G. (2013), 'From ghostwriting,' In. M. Blanco and E. Peeren (eds.), *The Spectralities Reader: Ghosts and Haunting in Contemporary Cultural Theory*, London: Bloomsbury, 317–334.

Stapleton, T. (2018), *Africa: War and Conflict in the Twentieth Century*, Abingdon: Routledge.

Starkey, P. (1998), 'Ibrahim, (Muhammad) Hafiz, (1872 (?)-1932),' In. J. Mesiami and P. Starkey (eds.), *Encyclopedia of Arabic Literature*, London: Routledge, 386.

Stern, R. and R. Stern (2013), *The Routledge Guidebook to Hegel's Phenomenology of Spirit*, Abingdon: Routledge.

Syrotinski, M. (2007), *Deconstruction and the Postcolonial: At the Limits of Theory*, Liverpool: Liverpool University Press.

Syrotinski, M. (2012). '"Genealogical misfortunes": Achille Mbembe's (re-)writing of postcolonial Africa,' *Paragraph*, 35, 407–420.

Sznaider, N. (2021), 'The summer of discontent: Achille Mbembe in Germany,' *Journal of Genocide Research*, 23 (3), 412–419.

Talabi, W. (2020), Africanfuturism: An Anthology, Brittle Paper, www.brittlepaper.com.

Tarquini, V. (2020), 'Quelles perspectives pour l'Afrique-Monde? Une étude relationnelle,' *Trans: revue de literature générale et compare*, 25, https://doi.org/10.4000/trans.3464.

Taylor, C. (2011), 'Race and racism in Foucault's Collège de France Lectures,' *Philosophy Compass*, 6 (11), 746–756.

Terretta, M. (2005), '"God of independence, god of peace": village politics and nationalism in the Maquis of Cameroon, 1957–71, *Journal of African History*, 46, 75–101.

Terretta, M. (2010), 'Cameroonian nationalists go global: from forest *Maquis* to a Pan-African Accra,' *Journal of African History*, 51, 189–212.

Terretta, M. (2013), *Nation of Outlaws, State of Violence: Nationalism, Grassfields Tradition, and State Building in Cameroon*, Athens: Ohio University Press.

Thaler, R. and C. Sunstein. *Nudge: Improving Decisions about Health, Wealth and Happiness*, London: Penguin, 2009.

Thiong'o, N. (1986), *Decolonising the Mind: The Politics of Language in African Literature*, Woodbridge: James Currey.

Thuram, L. (2021), *White Thinking: How Racial Bias Is Constructed and How to Move Beyond It*, London: Hero.

Tibawi, A. (1964), 'English-speaking orientalists,' *Islamic Quarterly*, 8 (1), 24–45, 8 (3), 73–88.

Timol, U. (2023), 'Chat GPT ou le miroir de nos illusions,' *Jeune Afrique*, March 16.

Titley, B. (1997), *Dark Age: The Political Odyssey of Emperor Bokassa*, Montreal: McGill-Queen's University Press.

Tonda, J. (2005), *Le souverain moderne*, Paris: Karthala.

Tonda, J. (2015a), *L'impérialisme postcolonial: critique de la société des éblouissements*, Paris: Karthala.

Tonda, J. (2015b), 'La politique avunculaire de la chicotte,' In. F. Bayart (ed.), *À bas les fonctionnaires apathiques et ventripotents! Pour un fonctionnaire intellectuellement fécond et physiquement disponible, en avant!*, Paris: Karthala, 195–209.

Tonda, J. (2016), 'Fanon au Gabon: sexe onirique et Afrodystopie,' *Politique Africaine*, 3, 143, 113–136.

Toulabor, C. (1981), 'Jeu de mots, jeux de vialin: Lexique de la derision politique au Togo,' *Politique Africaine*, 3, 55–71.

Toulabor, C. (1986), *Togo sous Eyadema*, Paris: Karthala.

Toulabor, C. (1994), 'Political Satire Past and Present in Togo,' *Critique of Anthropology*, 14 (1), 59–75.

Trouillot, M.-R. (1992), 'The vulgarity of power,' *Public Culture*, 5 (1), 75–81.

Truscello, M. (2020), *Infrastructural Brutalism: Art and the Necropolitics of Infrastructure*, Cambridge: MIT Press.

Tucker, B. (2013), 'The other Afripolitans,' https://africasacountry.com/2013/03/introducing-malitia-malimob.

Tutton, M. (2012), 'Young, urban and culturally savvy, meet the Afropolitans,' CNN, February 17, https://edition.cnn.com/2012/02/17/world/africa/who-are-afropolitans/index.html.

Tutuola, A. (2014a [1954]), *My Life in the Bush of Ghosts*, London: Faber and Faber.

Tutuola, A. (2014b [1952]), *The Palm-Wine Drunkard and His Dead Palm-Wine Tapster in the Deads' Town*, London: Faber and Faber.

Tveit, M. (2013), 'The Afropolitan must go,' https://africasacountry.com/2013/11/the-afropolitan-must-go.

Vergès, F. (2013), 'Mémoires fragmentées, histoires croisées. esclavage colonial et processus de décolonisation,' *Naqd*, 30 (1), 117–136.

Verghese, N. (2021), 'What is necropolitics? the political calculation of life and death,' *Teen Vogue*, March 10, https://www.teenvogue.com/story/what-is-necropolitics.

Vergos, N. (2021), 'Augmented Reality,' *The Gale Encyclopedia of Science*, Vol. 1, A-B, Gale: Famington Hills, 428–430.

Videau, A. (1997), 'Clando: film camerounais de Jean-Marie Téno,' *Hommes & Migrations*, 120, 144.

wa Thiong'o, N. (1986), *Decolonising the Mind: The Politics of Language in African Literature*, Woodbridge: Boydell & Brewer.

Wainaina, B. (2005), 'How to write about Africa,' *Granta*, 92. https://granta.com/how-to-write-about-africa/

Wainaina, B. (2012), 'How not to write about Africa in 2012 – a Beginner's Guide,' *The Guardian*, June 3.

West-Pavlov, R. (2013), *Temporalities*, Abingdon: Routledge.

Whidden, J. (2017), *Egypt: British Colony, Imperial Capital*, Manchester: Manchester University Press, 8–15.

Weitzman, M. (2023), 'Holocaust Denial and Distortion,' In. Weitzman, R., R. Williams, and J. Wald (ed.), *The Routledge History of Antisemitism*. London: Routledge, 373–382.

Williams, P. (2013), *Paul Gilroy*, Abingdon: Routledge.

Wilson, L. (2012), *Steve Biko*, Athens: Ohio University Press.

Wise, C. (1999), *Yambo Ouologuem: Postcolonial Writer, Islamic Militant*, Boulder: Lynne Rienner.

Wolfrey, J. (2008), *Transgression: Identity, Space, Time*, Basingstoke: Palgrave.

Yékú, J. (2020), 'Anti-Afropolitan ethics and the performative politics of online scambaiting,' *Social Dynamics*, 46 (2), 240–258.

INDEX

#BlackLivesMatter 3, 146
#RhodesMustFall 84, 92
419 scams 111

African American literature 24–26, 28–30, 126–128
African American thought 24, 28–30
African Futurism 127
African languages 39, 40, 86–87, 111–113; decolonization and 86–87; literature in 39, 40, 112–113; proverbs in 111
African literature 25–27, 39–40, 51, 54–57, 71–73, 99–102; Afropolitanism and 114; necropolitics and 2, 71–73; newspapers and 39–40; postcolonial dictator novels 71–73, 101; pre-colonial works and 25–26, 112–113; women's writing and 112–113
African philosophy: decolonization and 85–87; the environment and 133–141; the future of philosophy 116, 145–146; Islam and 150; materiality and 121; the representation of Africa and 22–25; technology and 119–121
African Reception of Mbembe 144
Afrocentrism 30–31, 99, 177
Afrocomputation 121
Afrofuturism 126–128
Afropolitanism 93–115; Afrofuturism and 126–128; competing conceptions of 94–96; critiques of 106–110; digital culture and 110–112; elite 105–107; historical contexts 96–99; literature and 114; popular 99, 104–105; resistance to 106
Agamben, Giorgio 67
Ahmadou Ahidjo 49
Akede Eko (newspaper) 39–40
Akinitan, Awobo 41
Al-Qadir, Abd 37
Al-Shinqiti, Ahmad b Muhammad 112
Algeria 37, 56, 76–78
'Algiers School' of Psychiatry 77
algorithms 117, 122–124, 128
Ali, Duse Mohammed 30
Amin, Idi 50
animals 134, 136, 139

anthropology *see* ethnography
antisemitism allegations 3, 4
Antoon, Sinan 147
Arabic language 26–27, 29
Armies, Colonial 70
Armies, Post-colonial 66, 71
artificial intelligence (A.I) 114
Asma'u, Nana 112–114

Bamba, Amadou 37
Bassa People (Cameroon) 61
Bataille, Georges 66
Bayart, Jean-François 51
Biko, Steve 85
biopolitics 63–68, 70–71; Agamben and 67; Foucault and 64–66
Biya, Paul 44
Black Atlantic 23–24
Blake, Or the Huts of America (novel) 30
Blyden, Edward Wilmot 25, 29
Bokassa, Jean-Bedel 50
borders 88, 96, 117, 136–137, 149; and hospitality 136–137
Boulaga, Fabien Éboussi 7
brutalism 10, 115–117, 123–124, 154, 160; and architecture 116; race and 116–117, 123–124
Butler, Octavia 126

Cairo 26, 88–90
Cameroon 6–7, 43–75, *passim*; 108–109, 144–146; authoritarianism and 44, 49, 54, 60, 155; as an exemplar of the postcolony 54; independence war in 2, 60–62; Mbembe's journalism in Cameroonian media 7; reception of Mbembe in 108, 144
Central African Republic 50
checkpoints 46
Christianity 6, 7, 28, 29, 39

Clando (film) 44
Code de L'indigénat 40
colonial discourse 17–22; critiques of 22; Hegel and 19; hyperbole and 21; impact on colonized peoples 21; time and 20
colonial mobility and travel 112
colonised peoples and violence 77–80
colony 33–41; agency 38–39; commandement and 35–38; Francophone Africa 34–36, 40; historical background 34–36; necropolitics and 69–70; psychiatry and 75–77; public rationality 38; violence and 77–80; war 70
combustion of the Earth 135
Congo, Democratic Republic of, (Congo-Kinshasa) 31, 51, 55
Congo, Republic of, (Congo-Brazzaville) 43, 54–56, 157
content moderation (social media) 109
conviviality 46
COVID-19, 59
Crummell, Alexander 25, 28

Dan Fodio, Uthman 114
dead people 71, 73
death 59–74; death-worlds 68; living death and 67; necrocapitalism and 135; of the planet 133; and public services 146; in West African history 72
Delany, Martin 25, 30
Delany, Samuel R 126
Derrida, Jacques 137
Diagne, Souleymane Bachir 146, 150
diaspora 22–30, 94, 107, 111, 140
Diop, Cheikh Anta 30–31

Djinn 22, 77
Dominican Order 5
Douala 44, 46
dream divination 61, 62
dreams 60–63
droit de cuissage 51
droit de glaive (right of the sword) 65
drones and unmanned aerial vehicles 64, 71, 149

Enlightenment, the 14, 157
Equiano, Olaudah 23
era of the Earth 134, 136–139
ethnography 14–15, 17–22, 129–131; colonial discourse and 17–22; colonial French ethnographic missions 14–15; of digital media 117–118; *Phantom Africa* and 131; reflexive ethnography and 131
Europe 4–5, 13–22, 28, 31, 36, 48, 51, 95, 109, 112, 139; critique of representations of Africa and Africans in 13–22, 31; knowledge and 13–15; reception of Mbembe's thought in 4–5; slavery and 15–17

Fanon, Frantz 75–93, *passim*
fetish 48
financial sector 108
Floyd, George 3
Foucault, Michel 7, 33–34, 36, 39, 47, 64–67, 71; biopolitics and 63–66; power and 33–34
France 2, 5–7, 36–37, 60, 77, 81, 91, 129–131, 143, 146, 154, 155, 158; colonialism and 36–37; the far-right in 91; Mbembe's career in 5–7; postcolonial theory and universities in 158; racism in 146

French language 8–9, 86–87, 144, 151; as an African language 86–87; Mbembe's journalism and African publications in 144; Mbembe's use of 8–9; multiculturalism and 151
frontiers *see* borders

gender 9, 15, 43, 48, 105–106, 114, 131
Germany 3–4
Geschiere, Paul 103, 106, 122, 128, 165
ghosts 71–73
gig economy 116
Glissant, Edouard 88
global warming 135–140, 148
Griaule, Marcel 130
grotesque 47
Guyer, Jane 116

hajj 27
haunting 71–73, 157
Hegel, Friedrich 19–20, 111; account of African history 19; relationship to African philosophy 111
history 1–10, 13–39, 43–59, 75–100; Africa's past and European understandings of 19–20, 31; Afropolitanism and 96–97; of Algeria 37, 77; of colonialism 34–39, 60–63; Hegel and Africa 19; historiography and 61; Mbembe and 1–10, 60–63; of the postcolony 44–55
Holocaust relativization 3
homophobia 106

Ibn Said, Omar 25–27
Ibn Tufayl, Abu Bakr 150
Igbo philosophy 111
immigration 65, 98, 133–136, 138–139

Iqbal, Mohammed 150
Iraqi fiction 147
Islam 25–27, 29, 77–78, 92, 112–114, 150; Arabic language and 27; disalienation and 92; enslaved people and 25; Fanon and 77, 78; Islamism and 91; Philosophy and 150; Women's writing and 122
Israel 3, 4

jargon 49
Jeunesse étudiante *chrétienne* 7
jihad 27
Johannesburg 85, 98, 109

Kabylia Mountains (Algeria) 77
Kant, Immanuel 137
Kinshasa 144, 157
Kourouma, Ahmadou 56

Labou Tansi, Sony 51, 55
Lagos (Nigeria) 1, 5, 30, 39–41
Lagos Studies Association 5
Le Tout-Monde 88
Leiris, Michel 130
life-writing 25–27
Life Story of Me Segilola (novel) 39–40
living dead, the 59, 67–68

Macaulay, Herbert 40
Mali 26, 56
Malinké language 56
marabouts 77
Mbembe, Achille 1–163; Afropolitanism and 93–114; Ateliers de la pensée 3; Cameroon and 7–8, 144; comments on 2023 coup in Niger and 144; COVID and 3; decolonization and 84–87; disciplinarity and 143; doctoral studies and 7–8, 152; environment and 133–142; Fanon 75–78, 84–85; Holberg Prize of 2024 and 5; Holocaust and 3–4; journalism by 144, 151; life and career 5–8; necropolitics and 1–3, 59–74; Palestine and 4; reception in Africa 144; South African universities and 84–85; technology and 115–131; translation and 8–9
mercenaries 66, 71
Merleau-Ponty, Maurice 125
migration *see* immigration
Mobutu Sese Seko 51
Mudimbe, Valentin 31
music 100, 122, 123, 157

Nasser, Gamal Abdel 91
National Liberation Front (FLN, Algeria) 78
nationalism 40, 61, 68, 89, 90
necropolitics 59–74; Arabic literary studies and 147; biopolitics, and 63, 67–68; Brutalism and 116–117; changing meanings of 144–147; colonialism and 69–70; contemporary warfare and 70–71; COVID and 3; ghosts and 71–73; ideas about the dead in Cameroon 60–61; media appropriation of 3; necrocapitalism and 135–136; night and 62–63; queer necropolitics 147; racism and 64–66; slavery and 68–69, 71–73
Négritude 95, 101
Negro Society for Historical Research 30
Niger 144
nocturnal sphere 61–63
nomos of the Earth 136
Nyamnjoh, Francis 73, 92
Nyobè, Ruben Um 60–62

Ogotemmêli 130
oneiric power 61, 62
oneiromancy 62
Ouologuem, Yambo 54

Palestine 3
pharmakon 76
planetarity *see* the era of the Earth
postcolonial theory and Mbembe 144
postcolony 43–57; autocracy and 50–52; commandement and 45–46; conviviality and 46–47; critiques of 52–54; daily life in 44–49; Francophone novelists and 55–56; humour in 47–49; the obscene and 47–48; the potentate 50–51
precarious labour 99, 103, 110, 116
print culture 40–41
prisons 68, 146
private indirect government 153
Private Military and Security Companies (PMSCs) 70

Qasida (poetic form) 112
Qur'an 26–27, 91–92, 112–113
Qutb, Sayyid 88–90

racism 3, 29, 65, 68, 74, 76, 80–82, 85, 88, 98, 124, 126–127, 130, 138, 146, 148; antisemitic racism 3–4; European accounts of Africa and 18; Foucault' account of 64–65; Holocaust relativisation and 4; racist language 14; relationship of enmity and 65; South Africa and 4; whiteness and 17
Ramdane, Abane 78
reconstruction era (USA) 25

restoration of African objects 121, 145
Roman Catholicism 5, 39, 156

Sahel 96, 97
Sall, Shaykh al-Hajj Abbass 150
Sanaga-Maritime region (Cameroon) 61
Sarr, Felwine 145, 149
Sarr-Savoy Report 145
Sassou-Nguesso, Denis 54
Schmitt, Carl 136
Schomburg, Arthur 30
science fiction 126
screens 128, 134
Senegal 3, 5, 6, 26, 31, 37, 149
Senghor, Léopold Sedar 144, 150
sexuality 50, 147
slavery 15–16, 22–27, 28–30, 68–69, 71–73, 97
smartphones 111, 117, 119, 121, 122, 128, 134
social death 69
social media 108–110, 112, 115, 119–123, 129
Sokoto Caliphate 114
South Africa 4–6, 9, 84–86, 92, 96–98, 143, 144, 158
spectrality *see* ghosts
speed 116, 117, 135
Sufism 97
The sweet shall succeed the bitter, or the orphan (novel) 41

terror 22, 72
Thomas, Isaac Babalola 39
Thuram, Lilian 146
Timbuktu 26
Togo 43
Tonda, Joseph 122, 129, 144
Tonton-macoute 46
torture 78, 79
Toulabor, Comi 8
Towa, Marcien 7

travel 14, 20, 21, 26, 29, 77, 103, 109, 112
Tunisia 77–78
Tutuola, Amos 71–73

Um Nyobè, Ruben 2, 7, 60–63
UNESCO General History of Africa 31
Union of Cameroonian Peoples (UPC) 61

visas 107

The Walking Dead (TV series) 147
war machines 70–71
warfare 60–63, 69–70
warlords 70
Wedderburn, Robert 23
witchcraft 21, 60, 148

Yoruba colonial novels 40

Zairianisation 51
zombies 22, 55
zombification *see* zombies

For Product Safety Concerns and Information please contact our EU representative GPSR@taylorandfrancis.com
Taylor & Francis Verlag GmbH, Kaufingerstraße 24, 80331 München, Germany

www.ingramcontent.com/pod-product-compliance
Lightning Source LLC
Chambersburg PA
CBHW071818230426
43670CB00013B/2494